GUEST WORKERS OR COLONIZED LABOR?

GUEST WORKERS OR COLONIZED LABOR?
MEXICAN LABOR MIGRATION TO THE UNITED STATES

Gilbert G. Gonzalez

Paradigm Publishers

Boulder • London

Chapters 2 and 7 are reprinted by permission of Sage Publications Ltd. from articles of the same title by Gilbert G. Gonzalez in *Sage Race Relations Abstracts*, Vol. 30, no. 1 (2005) and Vol. 29, no. 3 (2004) respectively.

Published in the United States by Paradigm Publishers, 5589 Arapahoe Avenue, Boulder, CO 80303.

Paradigm Publishers is the trade name of Birkenkamp & Company, LLC, Dean Birkenkamp, President and Publisher.

Library of Congress Cataloging-in-Publication Data

Gonzalez, Gilbert G., 1941–
    Guest workers or colonized labor? : Mexican labor migration to the United States / Gilbert G. Gonzalez. — Second edition.
        pages cm
    Includes bibliographical references and index.
    ISBN 978-1-61205-447-6 (hardcover : alk. paper) —
    ISBN 978-1-61205-448-3 (pbk. : alk. paper)
    1. Foreign workers, Mexican—United States.   2. Mexico—Foreign economic relations—United States.   3. United States—Foreign economic relations—Mexico.   I. Title.
    HD8081.M6G6648 2013
    331.6'272073—dc23
                                                                2013015835

Printed and bound in the United States of America on acid-free paper that meets the standards of the American National Standard for Permanence of Paper for Printed Library Materials.

Designed and Typeset in New Baskerville by Straight Creek Bookmakers.

17 16 15 14 13
1 2 3 4 5

Contents

Acknowledgments

As in each of my works I owe special thanks for the assistance and support of a number of people. This book emanated from a previous work that I authored with Raul Fernandez, in which we developed a theoretical approach to explaining Mexican migration—an approach that is applied in this work. However, my interest in the topic, braceros, I owe to Henry Anderson, whose invaluable works on the bracero program, including The Bracero Program in California, spurred me to investigate braceros as a variation of Mexican migration. Henry graciously supplied important papers, documents, and other materials from his personal archive that I included where appropriate in this study.

Alicia Anaya worked as my undergraduate research assistant and assisted me in interviewing braceros in northern California as well as transcribing the interviews. A grandchild of a bracero and a one-time migrant laborer herself, Ms. Anaya participated in important ways and contributed significantly over the course of this study. Academic staff support is most essential as well, and, indeed, administrative assistants Barbara Abell, Renee Martin, and Stella Ginez never failed to answer my continual requests for assistance, small or large. I owe a great deal to their commitment and skills, which made my work so much easier than would otherwise have been the case.

In addition, I want to thank the many students in my courses who expressed much interest in the topic of braceros, the "guest workers" of the mid-twentieth century. I have been continually surprised by the number of students and administrators at the University of California, Irvine (UCI) with a family history in which a bracero formed a part, a factor that has only increased my own interest in the bracero program.

My colleagues from the UCI Chicano Latino Studies Program and the Labor Studies Program were crucial to this study; their suggestions and comments on drafts of chapters or of articles that led to chapters were important to the development of my ideas. I am especially indebted to my colleagues Rosaura Tafoya, Lisa Garcia Bedolla, Roberto Gonzales, Rodolfo Torres, Vivian Price, and Linda Trinh Vo. I also wish to note the interest and support I've received over the years from Anna Gonzales and Sunny Lee at the UCI Cross Cultural Center; many thanks are extended to them. Helen Chenut, Doug Haynes, Vinayak Chaturvedi, and Amelia Lyons of the UCI History Department offered their timely and important suggestions for further reading, which are integral to this book. I thank them, too, for their valuable responses to my queries.

Funding is critical to the success of research, and this work is no exception. The University of California Institute for Labor and Employment, the UCI Labor Studies Program, the Latinos in a Global Society Program, and the Office of Research and Graduate Studies all provided the financial support necessary to complete this study.

My family's constant encouragement and abiding interest in my research has made my work a much more valuable undertaking than I alone could ever have made it. I can only offer simple but sincere thanks to Frances, Antonio, Alicia, Xochitl, Ramon, Ninaz, and Aric for their abiding support.

Although I was fortunate to receive the support and assistance of a good number of people, there should be no doubt that I am ultimately responsible for the content of this work.

Introduction

COMPREHENSIVE IMMIGRATION REFORM, a fiery political issue in Washington, D.C., for the past two decades, is perpetually beyond enactment, or so it appears. Some topics, like a path to legalization for undocumented migrants or the Dream Act, propel storms of controversy. But on the other hand, the matter of temporary contract workers has been included in many reform proposals and does not generate fractious debates. According to the Congressional Research Service, since 2006 most comprehensive reform proposals have favored "[l]arge-scale low skilled temporary worker programs."[1] If there is any unity of thought within immigration reform negotiations, a proposed temporary worker program brings it forward. However, that aspect of reform agendas is often left out of the media and immigrant rights organizations' discourses.

A central question addressed in all the reform proposals remains: How will the United States most effectively utilize Mexican and Central American labor power, whether undocumented migrants or imported temporary migrant labor? Meanwhile, the laborers and the national governments of countries from which the labor is to come are absent from the deliberations, viewing them from the sidelines. They have no part in the shaping of the final policies. The matter of temporary contract workers as an important ingredient in comprehensive immigration reform proposals now circulating in Washington, D.C., remains to be critically addressed.

The central topic of this book, the bracero program, has undergone numerous critical studies demonstrating systemic corruption in the way it functions. This book critically addresses the general understanding that the labor importation program is little more than a policy between two neighboring nations. However, as I hope to illustrate, it is much more than that.

Pathways to writing books often take unusual turns, and that is certainly the case with this book. My focus on Chicano History again served as the foundation, but other factors shaped the outcome. I go back to my experiences in conducting research on a century of Mexican migration with Raul Fernandez, in which we concluded that we cannot explain Mexican migration apart from the social conditions created by U.S. economic corporations operating within Mexico since the late nineteenth century. Large-scale U.S. enterprises encompassing railroads, mining, and oil invested $1 billion in Mexico by 1910, which uprooted 300,000 peasants from traditional self-subsistence villages, leading to a huge demographic shift northward. Vast numbers of the Mexican population migrated from the central valley to towns and cities, and there became a surplus labor pool recruited to work on the new industrial operations brought in from the United States, many of which were near the border. Eventually they were recruited north across the border by the very same corporations operating on both sides of it.

The second phase of migration, the bracero program, a temporary contract labor system, was established in 1942. The program, a state-managed migration, institutionalized working in the United States, and upon the end of the program in 1964, the men continued to migrate as undocumented. Soon the cry of "illegal aliens" began to tear across the nation. Later, NAFTA uprooted nearly 2 million peasants, sending them on the same migratory path northward to construct the third phase of Mexican migration. That migration, whether legal, undocumented, or as temporary contract labor, has served the economic development of the United States very well. Indeed, as Ernesto Galarza pointed out, Mexico serves as a huge pool of cheap, accessible, and, when necessary, disposable labor for U.S. enterprises. One can add that migration is a consequence of U.S.-designed policies, and there is no better example of this than the bracero program, a temporary contract labor program popularly known as a guest worker program.

And what does that have to do with writing this book? What I have addressed above relates directly to the political turmoil roiling across the nation, created by the dramatic increase of Mexican migration in the latter part of the twentieth century. An anti-immigrant political movement alleging large-scale damage that "illegal aliens" purportedly bring upon the nation exploded while Raul Fernandez and I engaged in the research project in the mid-1990s. The matter of Mexican and

Central American migration emerged as a topic of great concern from both sides of the political aisle, often leading to rancorous exchanges. The contentious discourse motivated organizations across the political spectrum to enter into the political discourse, and I was invited to give a talk on migration at a meeting of the Orange County Peace and Freedom Party, which I gladly accepted. On a bright Sunday afternoon, I was introduced to the fifty or so in the audience and presented my talk based on my work with Raul Fernandez, detailed above.[2] I spoke on the central role of the United States in creating a century of Mexican migration. I finished my talk, followed by a very active question and answer session, and the meeting ended.

Well, I thought the meeting had ended. As I walked to the parking lot and was about to enter my car, a person who was in the audience came up to me, thanked me for the talk, and provided information that I had never heard before, nor ever contemplated. He explained that the economic expansion of U.S. enterprises into Mexico in the late nineteenth century and the consequent uprooting of peasants transforming them into a huge labor pool, a central theme in my talk, was very similar to what had happened in his native India under British imperialism. I was immediately intrigued by his comment; I had never heard of anything remotely similar. I asked if he could provide some readings or sources of information where I could study the interconnections between U.S.-Mexico relations and those of the British in India during colonialism. He could not offer sources, but I thanked him for his comments, which moved deeply into my thoughts. However, I had no real conceptualization of any connection between British imperialism and U.S. economic expansionism and the subsequent domination over Mexico. I needed to plow the ground, which I did when I stepped onto campus a few days later.

I called my colleagues in various departments and informed them what had prompted me to ask them of what I sought. Critical in my estimation were the colonial policies pursued by the British in India and their social consequences. My colleagues were taken in by the objective I had in mind (for they, too, had never contemplated the possible connection), and immediately I was provided with a number of works and names of individuals whom I might wish to speak with, including academics in India. As I continued to gather sources, the case of French imperialism in Algeria was brought forward by a graduate student. As I reviewed the materials suggested, I was immediately struck by the stark similarities between the social consequences: the mass uprooting of peasants created during the late nineteenth century by U.S. economic expansionism into Mexico and the mass uprooting of peasants under the British colonial rule in India and French rule in Algeria. Moreover, the implementation of policies to utilize temporary contract labor occurred in all three of the cases.[3]

I then began to realize that the bracero program was much more than a temporary contract labor program between two neighboring countries; it was also a means of securing labor by an empire, a means utilized by the British in India, the French in Algeria, and the United States in Mexico. The glaring gap in the literature came into view, and the motive to study temporary contract labor programs embedded in imperialist labor policies came into focus. The window now opened to a topic that had not been addressed and that became the second chapter in this book.

Comprehensive Immigration Reform

A "guest worker" program remains a staple in U.S. political discourse. Not long after entering the White House, President Bush initiated a discussion on immigration reform including a guest worker program under the banner of resolving the problem posed by several million undocumented. Bush proposed "a new guest worker status that would legitimize many who entered the country unlawfully."[4] Regardless of the fact that the temporary worker proposal came from a neoconservative and had the full support of Mexico's President Fox, future discussion in the Republican Party moved from questioning any path to legalization for the undocumented to outright opposition and an eventual split in party ranks. The ultra-conservative Republicans defined a temporary worker agreement for the undocumented migrant as a form of amnesty and an invitation for more migrants to cross the border illegally, and opposed it. As Frank Sharry, head of the pro-immigrant rights group National Immigration Forum, described the atmosphere: "We're at the beginning of a long, complicated, contentious debate."[5] He accurately foretold the future, which went even further downhill after 9/11. The negotiations with Mexico came to a complete halt, although the temporary worker measure never left the president's political agenda. Reform was redefined to be hundreds of miles of border walls and a huge increase in border control personnel.

Not surprisingly, border enforcement funding rose to new heights over the next decade. The federal government allocated $17.9 billion in fiscal year 2012 to fund the two key immigration enforcement agencies, U.S. Customs and Border Enforcement and U.S. Visitor and Immigration Status Indicator Technology, which amounted to approximately fifteen times the level of funding than when the Immigration Reform and Control Act (IRCA) was passed in 1986. Funding for border enforcement increased significantly as well, from $6.3 billion in 2005 to $11.7 billion in 2012. The number of Border Patrol officers rose substantially. In 2004 10,819 officers patrolled the border; by 2012 the number skyrocketed to 23,643. There is no better example of the vast increase in border vigilance than the patrols in Cochise County, Arizona. In the late 1990s fifty agents patrolled the border; by 2005 400 Border Patrol agents were assigned to secure thirty miles of border.[6]

Into the first decade of the twenty-first century, immigration never remained far from the central political agendas of each party; indeed, the dialogue rose to new heights. Bush continued to push immigration reform, but new aspects were incorporated into the term "guest workers." Employers like custom Texas homebuilder Steve Sorrells worried that if undocumented workers were to be deported en masse, "it would be devastating."[7] Populist conservatives were pitted against business interests like the U.S. Chamber of Commerce. Not surprisingly, Bush proposed in 2004 that undocumented migrants be incorporated into a newer version of a temporary contract workers program. Under the Bush program, undocumented were to "be authorized as guest workers for three years, then required to return home. The plan offered illegal immigrants ... the possibility of becoming legal by registering as temporary workers."[8] That proposal went nowhere. A year later the plan proposed by Senators Edward Kennedy and John McCain offered "a path to citizenship for undocumented after fees and other penalties" and "put more emphasis on importing workers," that is, a guest worker program. In 2006 Senator Arlen Spector (R-PA) followed with a bill to implement a six-year temporary worker program for undocumented migrants and to enforce border security.[9] Senator John Cornyn (R-TX) introduced a bill that would require all undocumented to return to their home country, where they would then be allowed to apply to become a temporary worker.[10] None gathered sufficient support for passing.

In 2006 Senator Dianne Feinstein (D-CA) and her colleagues proposed an AgJOBS bill that would contain two parts: the first for agricultural labor and the second for importing temporary contract labor, or, as the sponsors called it, "a realistic and effective guest worker program."[11] With amendments added in 2007, the proposed immigration law put forward by a bipartisan senate group led by Senators Kennedy and Feinstein was designed to make it possible for undocumented agricultural workers to gain legal status. The provisions stated that all farm workers who had worked for 150 days during the twenty-four month period up to December 2006 and were free of crime or felony histories could pay a $100 fine and apply. To gain legal status they were obligated to work 100 days each year for a five-year period or 150 days per year for a three-year period, plus pay a $400 fine.[12] Given that AgJOBS was a modification of the H2-A temporary contract farm worker program, agribusiness interests supported the measure, which was not surprising, due to the fact that the undocumented farm workers would continue to labor in the fields for three or five years and most would probably continue to work there long after earning legal status.

The May 2007 report issued by Senator Feinstein's office addressed the determinates of reform and noted that in the discussions over AgJOBS,

> Senator Feinstein was joined at a news conference by dozens of growers and nurserymen. These growers were among more than 100 members of the Agricultural Coalition for Immigration Reform (ACIR) who have traveled to Washington, DC, this week to call on Congress to pass responsible immigration reform.[13]

Later that year, Senator Feinstein noted that "agriculture faces a major crisis. The only way farmers and growers can harvest their crops is with undocumented workers.... The situation must be addressed."[14] Such policies went nowhere. Republican Party leadership opposition in these cases proved too strong to overcome and collapsed the measure. The opposition argued that AgJOBS and like measures amounted to amnesty and "would only result in more illegal immigration."[15] The Bush administration followed with increased border patrols and policies to "verify immigrant worker status ... bolstering partnerships between Federal immigration agents and local police departments" and emphasizing raids on factories and farms to ferret out the undocumented.[16]

Proposed measures such as the Dream Act to legalize young undocumented high school graduates or those willing to join the military services were put forward, but immediate opposition denied their passage. As in the past, the Act was labeled amnesty, a word that from conservative quarters has come to mean rewarding violators of the nation's immigration laws. Immigration reform proposals followed two general approaches. The Tea Party's agenda for immigration reform meant rounding up the undocumented and sending them back, no amnesty, and keeping the undocumented migrants out by strengthening border patrols. The Democratic liberal agenda included border patrol, AgJOBS, a path to legalization for the undocumented, and a temporary contract worker program. The former won the day. No serious attempts to reform immigration laws followed until 2013.

Over the first decade of the twenty-first century, a chorus of critics from a variety of organizations put forward a plethora of policies to rid the nation of undocumented, popularly labeled "illegal aliens." Originally, over 300 anti-immigrant organizations from across the nation voiced their concerns and campaigned for ridding the nation of the undocumented. Eventually, the majority coalesced into the Tea Party, a grassroots sector of the Republican Party.[17] Tea Party narratives incorporated into the Republican Party defined undocumented immigrants as welfare burdens, sources of criminality and drug trade, a culturally inassimilable people, outright criminals, and much more. As these labels made their way across the national media networks, policies were put forward to rid the country of undocumented, including a bill sponsored by Senator Sensenbrenner (R-WI) to construct 700 miles of border walls built of two "layers of reinforced fencing," along with "new lighting, cameras and underground sensor."[18] Enforcement included making it a crime to assist an undocumented migrant by offering to transport him or her to work or for churches to offer sanctuary. Anti-immigrant politics grew stronger and new policies emerged from twelve states, beginning with Arizona's draconian law that made being undocumented a state crime. Other policies were put forward that included a vastly increased national budget aimed to strengthen border control; excluding the undocumented from elementary, secondary, and higher public education; closing day worker centers; paramilitarized border patrols; proposals to deny citizenship to children born to undocumented; police requiring motorists stopped for traffic violations to prove citizenship; and many more. The Migration Policy Institute reported that a philosophy known as "enforcement first" has become the de facto nation's singular response to illegal immigration, and changes to the immigration system have focused almost entirely on building enforcement programs and improving performance.[19]

Comprehensive Immigration Reform into the Obama Era

Indeed, the matter of comprehensive immigration reform handed down from the Bush administration has been tethered onto the Obama administration and mired in the political gridlock, which Obama described as a "slash and burn, take no prisoners" dysfunctional approach to negotiation in Washington. A comprehensive immigration reform remained on his desk, but transforming it into law was another thing. As President Obama prepared for the inauguration for his second term in office, immigration remained a key element, alongside gun reform, the debt ceiling, retreat from Afghanistan, Medicare, and the "sequester," all arousing taut exchanges as the issues remained unresolved. The matter of immigration, particularly undocumented migration from Latin America, remained a major national question that evaded any substantial resolution. Policies enmeshed in political diatribes continued erupting over resolving the problem as defined from multiple quarters. However, what is rarely mentioned is that the Obama administration's versions of a comprehensive immigration reform included a new temporary contract worker program. The policy known as "guest workers" lodged within immigration reform is disguised by the word *reform*. There is nothing reformist about a temporary contract labor program; if anything such legislation continues past practices such as the bracero program. Nevertheless, Obama not only favored a guest worker program within immigration reform, but his first term of office continued the Bush policy of ridding the nation of the undocumented within the nation's borders. The two worked toward similar if not identical goals.

The Obama administration actively engaged in deportation drives to return 1.5 million to their homelands, and in 2012 alone Homeland Security deported 409,849 immigrants, less than half of whom had criminal records, many of them parents leaving their children behind and breaking up families. By the end of Obama's first term, at least 5,000 children had been orphaned due to deportation drives and several hundred thousand young men and women raised in the United States had been deported to the nations where they were born. The Bush administrations never came close to the level of deportations achieved by Obama, who proudly reminded the audience of his record on border control in his second inaugural address:

> Real reform means strong border security, and we can build on the progress my administration has already made—putting more boots on the Southern border than at any time in our history and reducing illegal crossings to their lowest levels.[20]

While deportations rose to unsurpassed levels, the administration made sure that its position on a guest worker program would be clear. In May 2011, the White House issued a report titled "Building a 21st Century Immigration System," which laid out the administrations reform plans, including a temporary worker program and AgJOBS. The report made clear that the United States must reform "employment visa programs ... so they will contribute to the vitality of our economy. We must design a better system that provides legal channels for U.S. employers to hire needed foreign workers." A few sentences down, the report conveyed that "we need to reform our current agriculture labor program by passing and implementing the AgJOBS Act, which would provide farms a legal way to hire the workers they rely on and a path for those workers to earn legal status." The proposal asks that changes be made to the H2-A (agricultural workers) and H2-B (non-agricultural low-skilled workers) program "that carefully balances the needs of businesses and worker rights," and for a "new, small, and targeted temporary worker program for high skilled workers when American employees are not available."[21] In 2011 over 100,000 H2 workers were brought to the United States. Clearly, temporary worker programs are very much a part of national policy and the Obama comprehensive immigration reform plans.

With the 2012 elections a few months away and in preparation to harvest the Latino vote, Obama put forward two policies that appeared to be versions of amnesty in the minds of the anti-immigrant organizations, of which the Tea Party is the central figure. The administration independently put forward a deferred action policy for undocumented immigrants who were brought to the United States as young children, are under thirty years of age, and are either in high school or graduated from high school. If after a background check the applicant is found to have no criminal record, he or she would be granted a two-year deferment and possible two-year extension to work or study, without a guarantee of citizenship. That policy was shortly followed by a decision to allow the undocumented with family in the United States to request a visa and remain in the United States while his or her request is reviewed and approved, before returning to the country of origin to obtain the visa. According to State Department officials, a shorter stay (said to be two weeks rather than the ten years in Mexico City) would be granted to the visa holder.

The 2012 presidential campaign brought the two approaches into heightened relief, particularly when the Republican candidates raised the measure in their debates. At the Iowa debate Newt Gingrich responded to Diane Sawyer's question regarding policies and the undocumented with:

> I think most of the workers who are here who have no ties to us should go home immediately. I think we should make deportation dramatically easier. This is, I think frankly we oughta make English the official language of government. And we oughta have an effective guest worker program with very severe penalties for those employers who hire people illegally.[22]

Mitt Romney repeated the need for a hardened policy that would drive the undocumented back to their countries of origin as the solution to undocumented migration. As president he promised to

> secure the border. Once we do that, we can start talking about the 11 million or whatever number that may be that are in the country illegally. My own view is those 11—11 million people should register the fact that they're here in the country. They should be given some transition period of time to allow them to—settle their affairs and then return home and get in the—in line at the back of the line with everybody else that wants to come here.[23]

With the loss of the 2012 election, and the recognition that the Latino vote substantially enlarged the liberal side of the aisle, the Republican Party establishment took on a milder, more compromising approach to immigration reform and even joined in proposing policies to adjust the undocumented into legal status. Within the policy negotiations, a guest worker policy along with border security remains central in the reform agenda.

Into Obama's second term in office, immigration reform appears a more bipartisan objective, which portends that a temporary contract worker program for accessing labor from Latin America is on the horizon. Although Obama's initial reform design, "Fact Sheet: Fixing our Broken Immigration System so Everyone Plays by the Rules," issued in January 2013 did not specifically call for a temporary worker program as did the May 2011 White House paper, such a program was widely expected in Obama's ultimate plans.[24] It was generally accepted in the news media that the White House 2011 immigration plan provided an "immigration blueprint" for any proposal expected from the Obama White House.[25] One news report asserted that for the final reform proposal "Obama will flesh out his 2011 immigration blueprint."[26] The news corps anticipated nothing new from the White House.

Not to be outdone, two bipartisan groups, from the Senate and the House, met separately to author their own proposals for comprehensive immigration reform. While the deliberations progressed, a newspaper headline spoke of the nationalistic approach taken to determine the final version of comprehensive immigration reform: "Mexico on the Sidelines in D.C. Debate."[27] The governments whose citizens were to be dealt with under immigration reform as well as the citizens themselves were absent from the discussions. Three proposals are in the works in Washington and a full discussion of legislation to determine the fate of immigrants is expected to reach a final resolution in August 2013.

The Bipartisan Senate Comprehensive Immigration Reform Proposal

With these proposals, immigration reform once again entered the national limelight. Eight senators from both sides of the aisle put forward their blueprint after eight meetings and agreed on including what until then was understood to be "amnesty," such as the Dream Act, plus several other measures including a guest worker program. One news journalist described the Proposal as one which "roughly tracks what Obama has said publicly he would like to see."[28] Interestingly, the proposal restated what had been proposed in the Senate in 2007 and soundly rejected by at least one member of the committee,

Senator Marco Rubio.[29] Under the shadow of the lost election, the principles were brought back to life with support from around the table mirrored in a statement made by President George W. Bush's right hand man, Karl Rove, who termed the Senate Proposal a "huge step forward."[30] The failure to capture the White House, as well as a desire to develop ties with Latino voters, led the Republican Party to promote a compromising approach and appear to part ways with its Tea Party regulars. In keeping with previous reform proposals, a guest work program along with the AgJOBS was locked in.

Under the section titled "Admitting New Workers and Protecting Worker's Rights," the proposal lays out a plan to channel potential undocumented migrants into a temporary contract labor program:

> The overwhelming majority of the 327,000 illegal migrants apprehended by CBP [Customs and Border Protection] in FY2011 were seeking employment in the United States. We recognize that to prevent future waves of illegal immigration a humane and effective system needs to be created for these immigrant workers to enter the country and find employment.[31]

Channeling the undocumented into a temporary worker program is precisely what Public Law 78 of 1951, which initiated the second phase of the bracero program, intended to accomplish. Assisted by the mass deportation drive known as Operation Wetback, PL 78 funneled the potential undocumented.

The Senate committee's proposal is expected "to provide businesses with the ability to hire lower-skilled workers in a timely fashion when Americans are unavailable or unwilling to fill those jobs."[32] The proposal identifies the obligations that fall upon the shoulders of employers, such as hiring imported workers only if no domestic workers are available and observing strong labor protections. Such terms were found in the legislation establishing the bracero program, but they were seldom upheld and there is no guarantee that future temporary worker will be protected. Moreover, agribusiness is legally entitled to child labor and the 400,000 children who work in agriculture are no more protected than adults.[33] Research conducted by the Southern Poverty Law Center determined that systematic violations of the protections afforded current H2-A temporary workers are widespread, that "protections exist on paper," and concluded that far from being treated like "guests," these workers are systematically exploited and abused.... Guestworkers do not enjoy the most fundamental protection of a competitive labor market.[34]

The International Labor Recruitment Working Group, an immigrant rights organization, reported that temporary contract laborers, and there are thousands in agriculture, commonly experience "fraud, discrimination, severe economic coercion, retaliation, blacklisting, and in some cases, forced labor."[35] One thing is certain: if enacted, the reform ensures that low-wage imported labor will be available for agribusiness when employers determine that the need arises and returned when no longer needed, a definition of disposable labor. The legal protections in the bracero's contract were seldom enforced and those that protect temporary workers in today's U.S. economy are largely ignored and at best ineffective. What can we expect from promises to protect temporary workers in a new program?

While all the above discussions continued taking place, the AFL-CIO and National Chamber of Commerce were invited to privately meet and navigate an agreed-upon approach for the Senate version of a guest worker program. The GOP and Democratic Party leaders were most concerned with the negotiations proceeding between the National Chamber of Commerce and the AFL-CIO. The most contentious question raised by the AFL-CIO is how to identify a labor shortage. The Chamber asks that the employer make that decision while the labor organization asks that an independent commission working with objective data make the decision. The question is not whether there should be a temporary contract worker program; the question for the labor group is how to prevent an artificially constructed surplus of labor and the consequent downhill wage slide.[36] After weeks of negotiations an accord was reached. The Chamber accepted an independent government review committee to determine labor shortages and the AFL-CIO agreed to a low-skilled temporary labor program to supply the labor.[37] The independent government body is to determine the prevailing wages in particular regions and occupations. In the first year, 20,000 workers will be admitted and within five years up to 200,000. Nevertheless, conflict remains over wages: labor asks that guest workers be paid wages that set the bar and that do not lower wages for domestic workers. Growers, on the other hand, insist that high wages will deter their use of guest workers and force them to hire undocumented and reject the notion of high wages for H2 labor. In addition, under AgJOBS the workers are given the right to apply for temporary legal status, a "blue card," if they work 150 days per year for two years. If they continue to work for 150 days per year for three of the next five years they become eligible for permanent residency and citizenship. Again, permanent status is not guaranteed, only the right to apply. However, a more permanent labor supply is guaranteed.

Whether the worker is a separate category of labor, plus cheap, accessible, and disposable, is not a question that the AFL-CIO addressed. The chief economist at the Salt Lake Chamber of Commerce, Natalie Gochnour, lauded the agreement and summed up the purpose of temporary contract labor for business: "Fixing the immigration system will create a more attractive labor supply, will lower the cost of business and we will have more customers."[38] The agreement met the general objectives of the Chamber. House Majority Leader Eric Cantor (R-VA) approvingly called the deal "a positive step on immigration reform."[39] The "devil's bargain" moves haltingly toward final agreement. Conflict over guest workers in 2007 led to the failure to secure reform, and current CIR blueprints include a pathway to legalization and a eventual visa for the undocumented. However, the House and Senate Committees continue to debate and negotiate.

At the Senate immigration committee hearings, the tone was less than friendly at times. The matter of securing the border and "amnesty" via a pathway to citizenship infuriated some Republicans. Warnings were aired that the final guest worker item could generate conflict even though it was generally agreed upon in the blueprint. One such issue was raised by Senator Al Franken (D-MN), who maintains that Minnesota dairy farmers have difficulty acquiring workers on a year-round basis and that a guest worker program should be available for hiring year-round workers, rather than just a seasonal program.[40] Franken was joined by Joe Wright, president of the 300-member Southeast Milk Cooperative, who claimed that "we cannot milk cows without Hispanic labor, period."[41] A year-round program that might invite permanent migrants alarmed conservatives; dairy owners like Wright, however, argue that "conservative Republicans are just plain wrong." Fortunately for dairy businesses, the deal reached by the AFL-CIO and the Chamber includes year-long guest worker contracts. The political tension in the Republican Party over temporary workers originates from the Tea Party but not from the employers of imported labor.

The House and Senate Committees continued negotiating and eventually an 844-page Senate CIR was presented, containing a guest worker program, increased border security, and a path to citizenship. Senate Judiciary Committee hearings began in mid-April 2013.

The Obama Comprehensive Immigration Reform Proposal

A day after the Senate committee issued its report, the White House released "Fact Sheet: Fixing our Broken Immigration System so Everyone Plays by the Rules," which outlined four measures: effective border control; tighter restrictions blocking companies from hiring undocumented; earned legalization and citizenship for the undocumented; and a streamlined legal immigration system for workers, families, and employers. Obama made it clear that his reform plan would not differ from previous proposals. He underscored in his talk on immigration reform given in Las Vegas a few weeks before his inauguration that "the ideas I'm proposing have traditionally been supported by both Democrats like Ted Kennedy and Republicans like President George W. Bush. You don't get that matchup very often."[42] The White House immigration paper issued in 2011 included the four measures, so the Fact Sheet did not indicate any significant modifications. However, it does not specifically call for a temporary worker program as did the White House 2011 plan; the Fact Sheet section titled "Cut Red Tape for Employers" recommends expanding the H1-B program to bring in professional and highly skilled employees and immediately grant them green cards. However, the Fact Sheet resuscitates the AgJOBS bill, which was included in the Senate Proposal and the 2011 White House immigration reform paper. Undocumented agricultural workers are offered a path to eventual citizenship under a process removed from that of the remainder of the undocumented population. The Proposal justifies the measure because

> agricultural workers who commit to the long term stability of our nation's agricultural industries will be treated differently than the rest of the undocumented.... They play a role in ensuring that Americans have safe and secure agricultural products to sell and consume.[43]

It is doubtful that farm workers who earn poverty wages personally "commit to the long term stability" of agricultural corporations, but their labor supplies the market with affordable products for public consumption and high profits for agribusiness. One expects that the approach taken by Senator Feinstein in 2007 will be applied under the Obama Proposal; that is, the farm workers must first pass an initial examination, pay a fine, and then be required to perform farm work for a certain number of days per year for several years running before gaining a path to legalization. Although the Proposal does not lay out the traditional temporary worker program that many expected given the 2011 White House immigration reform recommendations that included a guest worker program, we can assume that the Obama administration, which has long supported temporary worker programs, will support the Senate Proposal's inclusion of a temporary worker program.[44]

In his second inaugural address Obama devoted only two minutes to immigration reform; he praised the work of the Senate and Congress committees for coming together to shape comprehensive immigration reform and he steered clear of criticism. In asserting his leadership, the Obama administration issued a draft of its own immigration reform proposal several weeks after issuing the Fact Sheet. According to reports, the draft reiterates measures included in the immigration reform proposal issued by Senators Kennedy and McClain in 2007, which offered a temporary worker program and was voted down.[45] Of particular importance to the final proposal put forward will be the power of national organizations such as the Essential Immigrant Worker Coalition and the National Chamber of Commerce in including a guest worker program and ultimately shaping the final product.

The Bipartisan Congressional Comprehensive Immigration Reform Proposal

Eight House members joined the effort to craft an immigration reform proposal and aimed to provide a final piece of legislation rather than a blueprint, which the Senate and Obama provided.[46] Even though it was said that the Committee had met for several years off and on in attempting to come to some agreement, the political shifting created by the 2012 election allowed the eight to begin behind-the-scenes negotiations on a regular basis. Democrat Luis Gutiérrez commented that "since Nov. 6 there's [*sic*] a lot of new dance partners, and that's good."[47] Even though there may be new dance partners, the political conditions in the House have never been positive toward immigration reform other than strong border enforcement. Nevertheless, the House committee continues meeting and intends to craft a complete legislative package by summer 2013. What is most fascinating is that the committee includes members from the furthest wings of each party. Republican Raul Labrador has opposed any form of legalizing the undocumented and enjoys Tea Party support, while Democrat Gutiérrez authored a 2009 immigration reform legislation that among other things provides a path to citizenship for the undocumented. The House committee has not received the media attention that the Senate has, but members from the two committees have been meeting regularly in the hopes of finalizing a bill that works well together. Despite the history of wide differences and heated conflicts, Speaker of the House John Boehner confidently spoke of a basic agreement emerging from the committee, a committee he described as "the right group of members."[48]

The House committee is in general agreement with the Senate blueprint, and both groups have been meeting regularly to ensure that their final bills are basically of one voice; it is the details that will obligate compromises. Again, the matter of temporary workers is expected to be contained in the House reform. Republican Mario Diaz-Balart confirmed that from his wing of the committee, "The goal is to fix what's broken, and it's pretty clear what's broken.... Do we recognize the need for agricultural workers? Yes."[49] Democrat Gutiérrez authored a 2009 bill that contained, in addition to a path to citizenship for undocumented, the Dream Act, AgJOBS, and a temporary worker program. His bill titled "Comprehensive Immigration Reform for America's Security and Prosperity" described the labor importation aspects which mirrored the Senate's proposal:

> The bill would create an independent commission that would make recommendation towards the future flow of workers based on the needs of the marketplace. The bill would also establish a work match system that allows employers who have historically relied on illegal workers to find workers through an internet-based system.[50]

Eric Cantor, the second leading House Republican and one who opposed the Dream Act but switched to favor it after the election, underscored the need for a new guest worker program in a talk before a research group in Washington, D.C., in February 2013:

I'm pleased these discussions make border security, employment verification and creating a workable guest worker program an immediate priority. It's the right thing to do for our families, for our security, and for our economy.[51]

Cantor and his Committee's colleagues in Washington, D.C., reiterated the main goals of the Essential Immigrant Worker Coalition, an organization comprised of fifty national organizations including the United States Chamber of Commerce. The EWIC's Principles of Immigration Reform makes clear its position on a temporary worker program:

Reform should create an immigration system that allows for sufficient immigrants and temporary workers to meet the economic needs of the country.[52]

After the Committees had met and the Senate had issued its draft and the House was busy meeting, Obama made available a reform draft incorporating a path to citizenship beginning after an eight-year waiting period and requiring that the undocumented wait at the end of the line for a visa. The plan incurred the wrath of the Republicans, particularly Marco Rubio, who accused Obama of issuing a "half-baked and seriously flawed" proposal and of attempting to shape the work of the bipartisan Committees.[53] Rubio, the emerging Latino voice in the Republican Party, and his cohort raised the old demands that before any path to legalization the border must be secured. However, Republicans realize that winning Latino voters will not be secured with such posturing. This was born out of a meeting with President Obama attended by Republican Senators Graham and McCain about immigration reform, held after the draft was issued. Graham reported that

it's one of the best meetings I've ever had with the President.... We'll have presidential leadership in a very productive way on immigration reform, and with that we've got a very good chance of doing it this year.[54]

The post-2012 election conversion of former Florida Governor Jeb Bush to support a path to citizenship for the undocumented and the way he awkwardly distanced himself from his previous vehement opposition to citizenship in his recently published book titled *Immigration Wars* affirmed the shifting political landscape. However, in 2011

Jeb Bush supported, in his words, "a very aggressive guest worker program that ebbs and flows with demand," a central objective in comprehensive immigration reform in 2013.[55]

The Senate draft turned into an 844-page bill and moved into the Judiciary Committee while the House deliberates CIR. New concerns began to be raised in the wake of the Boston bombing on April 15, 2013. The two parties, which had appeared to be moving toward a unified reform, were again cast into divisive dialogue. At this writing, conservative senators are attempting to break the bill into sections for deliberation, but reform-oriented Republicans and Democrats stand with a CIR. Meanwhile, House Republicans are dividing immigration reform into sections, expecting to draft a bill on each instead of deliberating over a comprehensive bipartisan bill. Such an objective means a grueling negotiation and may prevent any passage within a year, if at all. However, a guest worker program is the very first measure proposed for House discussion, considered of vital importance and capable of securing broad support across party lines.

Conclusion

Ultimately a temporary worker program within immigration reform is decided by employers assisted by the AFL and by politicians, but not by the people who are to live the experiences of a temporary worker. In the case of undocumented agricultural workers, the fact that well over half of all farm workers live in dire poverty and that to get a legal status via AgJOBS one must work as a temporary worker for several years does not enter into the discourse. Seldom is it mentioned that low-wage work tends to retain workers within its grasp, and farm work is low-wage work.[56] And never is it mentioned that economic policies designed in the United States, such as NAFTA, drove peasants in Mexico off their lands and northward across the border. The century-old theory used to construct current immigration reform, the push-pull model, contends that migrants cross borders to escape conditions independently created within their nations and removes any responsibility from the U.S. free trade policy designed in Washington. NAFTA uprooted nearly 2 million Mexican peasants and sent them northward to escape an economic disaster, and there they are labeled "illegal aliens." Meanwhile, those who remained behind are projected as the future temporary contract labor force by political leaders fashioning an immigration policy for the benefit of the wealthiest corporations on earth. Senator Graham summed up the key objective: "I think the problem for immigration reform will be about the future flow, access to future labor.... The reason you have about 11 million illegal workers is that lots of employers can't find labor, so we have got to address that."[57]

Comprehensive immigration reform ensures that corporate interests, who define the "economic needs" of the country, are satisfied, while the needs of the undocumented farm workers employed via AgJOBS and those of imported workers are placed on the far back burner, if they are present at all. The utilization of temporary contract workers remains on the political table, with or without terrorist bombings. The rampant violations of the contract protections and rights afforded braceros continue into the twenty-first century. And just as importantly, the proposed temporary labor programs follow a history of international labor programs that employ the dispossessed peasant labor of poor countries for the economic benefit of the wealthy nations, like those of the British imperialists in India and the French colonials in Algeria.

Notes

1. Marc R. Rosenblum, William Kandel, Clare Ribando Seelke, and Ruth Ellen Wasem, "Mexican Migration to the United States: Policy and Trends," *Congressional Research Service Report for Congress,* June 7, 2012, p. 32.

2. Gilbert G. Gonzalez and Raul Fernandez, *A Century of Chicano History: Empire, Nations and Migration,* New York: Routledge, 2003.

3. Rather than the misused term "guest worker" as the definition for imported labor, I will use *temporary contract worker.* Temporary contract workers are not guests under any definition of the term; they are an easily accessed, controlled, disposable form of labor imported when the need appears.

4. Edwn Chen, "Bush Hints at Broader Amnesty," *Los Angeles Times,* August 27, 2001; see also Dena Bunis, "Bush Says He'll Push for Worker Amnesty," *Orange County Register,* September 5, 2001.

5. Edwin Chen, "Bush Hints at Broader Amnesty,"

6. Cindy Carcamo, "Residents in Arizona Town Feel 'Invaded' by Border Patrol," *Los Angeles Times,* January 12, 2013; see also Doris Meisner, Donald Kerwin, Muzaffar Chishti, and Claire Bergeron, "Immigration Enforcement in the United States: The Rise of a Formidable Machinery," *Migration Policy Institute,* 2013, p. 19.

7. Warren Vieth, "Immigration Plan Troubles President's Texas Neighbors," *New York Times,* January 1, 2006.

8. "Immigration and Emigration," *New York Times,* January 20, 2013.

9. Mary Curtius, "Immigration Proposal Attacked from All Sides," *Los Angeles Times,* February 25, 2006.

10. Ibid.

11. "Senators Feinstein, Craig, Kennedy, Martinez, Boxer, Voinovich Introduce AgJOBS Bill to Address Agricultural Worker Shortages," United States Senator Dianne Feinstein, January 10, 2007, http://www.feinstein.senate.gov.

12. "Summary of AgJOBS: The Agricultural Job Opportunities, Benefits and Security Act of 2007," *Immigration Policy Center,* http://www.immigrationpolicy.org.

13. "Senator Feinstein Calls for Inclusion of AgJOBS Legislation in Comprehensive Immigration Reform Package," United States Senator Dianne Feinstein, May 15, 2007. http://www.feinstein.senate.gov.

14. "Statement of Senator Dianne Feinstein On the Need to Pass Agriculture Workers Legislation," United States Senator Dianne Feinstein, July 3, 2007. http://feistein.senate.gov. A year later Feinstein stated that AgJOBS "is not amnesty. It is an agricultural worker bill, which will give protected status.... Agriculture needs a consistent workforce. Without it, they can't plant, they can't prune, they can't pick, and they can't pack," in "Senate Appropriations Committee Approves Feinstein and Craig Emergency Legislation to Relieve Labor Shortage in Agriculture," United States Senator Dianne Feinstein, May 15, 2008. http://feinstein.senate.gov.

15. Peter Walsten, "Immigration Rift in GOP Up for Vote," *Los Angeles Times,* January 20, 2006.

16. "Immigration and Emigration."

17. Devon Burghart and Leonard Zeskind, "Beyond Fair: The Decline of the Established Anti-Immigrant Organizations and the Rise of Tea Party Nativism," *Institute for Research and Education Human Rights,* 2012, p. 2.

18. Hector Tobar, "Border Plan Seen as Conceit," *New York Times,* February 26, 2012.

19. Doris Meisner, Donald M. Kerwin, Muzaffar Chishti, and Claire Bergeron, "Immigration Enforcement in the United States: The Rise of a Formidable Machinery," *Migration Policy Institute,* 2013, p. 1.

20. "President Barack Obama's 2013 State of the Union Address—as Delivered." February 12, 2012. http://www.whitehouse.gov/state-of-the-union-2013.

21. "Building a 21st Century Immigration System," The White House, May 2011, pp. 25–26.

22. "Full Transcript: ABC News Iowa Republican Debate with Diane Sawyer and George Stephanopoulos," December 11, 2012.

23. Ibid.

24. See, for example, Julia Preston, "Obama Will Seek Citizenship Path in One Fast Push," *New York Times,* January 12, 2013. Preston writes: "The President's plan would ... create some form of guest worker program to bring in low-wage immigrants in the future." See also Julie Pace, "Obama to Launch Push for Immigration Overhaul at Las Vegas Event," *Orange County Register,* January 29, 2013. The journalist noted that "administration officials said the president would bolster his 2011 immigration blueprint with some fresh details." In that blueprint, the White House included a guest worker program in the "details."

25. Julie Pace, "Obama to Launch Push for Immigration Overhaul at Las Vegas Event."

26. Steven T. Dennis, "Obama Won't Offer Immigration Bill—Yet," *Roll Call,* January 28, 2013.

27. Richard Fausset, "Mexico on Sidelines in D.C. Debate," *Los Angeles Times,* January 30, 2013.

28. Kathleen Hennessey, "Obama Cautious on Immigration," *Los Angeles Times,* January 27, 2013.

29. Senator Rubio supported Arizona's SB 1070, which attempted to use state power to deport the undocumented using, among other things, racial profiling. Rubio also campaigned with Mitt Romney, who favored harsh measures to promote "self-deportation," and he opposed the original Dream Act.

30. Bill Keller, "Selling Amnesty," *New York Times,* February 3, 2013.

31. Senators Schumer, McCain, Graham, Menendez, Rubio, Bennet, and Flake, "Bipartisan Framework for Comprehensive Immigration Reform," January, 2013. The Framework appeared in Michael D. Shear, "Bipartisan Plan Faces Resistance in G.O.P.," *New York Times,* January 28, 2013.

32. "Bipartisan Framework for Comprehensive Immigration Reform"; The Essential Immigrant Worker Coalition stands for the very same principles regulating a guest worker program within immigration reform. See Essential Immigrant Worker Coalition, "Principles and Policies," EWIC Principles for Immigration Reform, http://www.ewic.org.

33. "In Our Own Backyard: The Hidden Problem of Child Farmworkers in America," American Federation of Teachers, http:www.ourownbackyard.org.

34. "Close to Slavery: Guestworker Programs in the United States," *Southern Poverty Law Center,* 2013 edition.

35. "Fair Labor Recruitment," International Labor Recruitment Working Group, http://fairlaborrecruitment.wordpress.com; see also "Immigration Reform and Worker's Rights," editorial, *New York Times,* February 20, 2013.

36. Benjy Sarlin, "Labor and Business Groups Deny Immigration Talks Are Collapsing," *Talking Points Memo,* February 14, 2013; see also Anna Palmer, "Labor-Chamber Immigration Talks Stall," *Politico,* February 13, 2013.

37. Ashley Parker, "Visas Are Urged for Lower-Skilled Work," *New York Times,* February 21, 2013; Brian Bennet, "Key Deal Is Reached on Immigration," *Los Angeles Times,* February 21, 2013.

38. Brian Bennet, "Key Deal Is Reached on Immigration."

39. Ibid.

40. Alan Gomez, "Doubts Set Testy Tone at Senate Immigration Hearing," *USA Today,* February 13, 2013.

41. Alana Samuels, "Business Owners Getting Vocal on Immigration," *Los Angeles Times,* February 23, 2013.

42. "Full Transcript of President Obama's Remarks on Immigration Reform," *New York Times,* January 29, 2013, p. 3.

43. "Bipartisan Framework for Comprehensive Immigration Reform," p. 3.

44. See Julia Preston, "Obama Will Seek Citizenship Path in One Fast Push," *New York Times,* January 12, 2013; Jordan Fabian, "What Will Obama's Immigration Proposal Look Like?," *Univision News,* January 3, 2013; "Obama to Push Immigration Overhaul

in Early 2013: Report," *Reuters,* January 13, 2013, reprinted in *HuffPost Home,* January 18, 2013; Michael D. Shear and Mark Landler, "On Immigration, Obama Assumes Upper Hand," *New York Times,* January 30, 2013. Shear and Landler noted that the Senate Proposal "includes a guest worker program for low income workers, something Mr. Obama and his allies have been concerned about in the past"; Kathleen Hennessey, "Obama Cautious on Immigration." Hennessey writes: "Obama is expected to draw from his May 2011 immigration blueprint and may declare some elements nonnegotiable"; Ashley Parker, "Obama and Senators to Push for an Immigration Overhaul," *New York Times,* January 25, 2013. Parker echoed several other journalists when he noted that "Mr. Obama's approach will largely echo his 2011 immigration 'blueprint.'"

45. Alan Gomez, "White House Immigration Bill Offers Path to Residency," *USA Today,* February 17, 2013.

46. The eight are: Xavier Becerra (D-CA), Zoe Lofgren (D-CA), Luis Gutiérrez (D-IL), John Yarmuth (D-KY), John Carter (R-TX), Sam Johnson (R-TX), Mario Diaz-Balart (R-FL), and Raul Labrador (R-ID).

47. Ashley Parker, "House Group Works to Present Its Own Immigration Plan," *New York Times,* February 2, 2013.

48. Russell Berman, "Boehner Says Bipartisan Group 'Basically' Has Deal on Immigration Reform," *The Hill,* January 26, 2013.

49. Ashley Parker, "House Group Works to Present Its Own Immigration Plan."

50. "Rep. Gutierrez Introduces Mass Amnesty Bill, December 15, 2009, http://numbersusa.com.

51. Ibid.

52. Essential Immigrant Worker Coalition, "Principles and Policies," EWIC Principles for Immigration Reform. http://www.ewic.org.

53. Michael D. Shear and Julia Preston, "Obama's Plan Sees 8-Year Wait for Illegal Immigrants," *New York Times,* February 17, 2013.

54. Steven T. Dennis, "McCain, Graham Positive After Immigration Meeting With Obama," *Roll Call,* February 26, 2013.

55. Cameron Joseph, "Jeb Bush Shows Rust with Stumble," *The Hill,* February 3, 2013; Mary Anastasia O'Grady, "Jeb to GOP: How to Appeal to Hispanics," *Wall Street Journal,* January 15, 2011.

56. John Schmitt, "Low Wage Lessons," Center for Economic and Policy Research, January 2012, p. 9.

57. Alexander Bolton, "Pressure Builds Up on Senate Group to Unveil Immigration Plan Details," *The Hill,* February 3, 2013.

Chapter 1

Constructing Transnational Labor Migration

A LONG-STANDING CONVENTION EMPLOYED BY American academics specializing in Mexican migration, as well as by legislators concerned with migration policy affecting Mexico, maintains that U.S.-Mexico relations are normal relations, an expression of reciprocity, interdependence, and equality. The convention further holds that a hundred years of Mexican migration comprise one more migrant stream coming to America to struggle for and experience the mythological "American Dream." However, this commonly held perspective of U.S.-Mexico relations has not always been borne by Americans, particularly large-scale investors and corporate heads, who in the late nineteenth century deemed Mexico a colonial prize to be exploited for its natural resources as well as for its cheap and easily accessed labor.

Well into the twentieth century a widespread imperial mindset regarding Mexico mirrored an ongoing economic expansionism, or what amounted to a neocolonial strategy to systematically exploit Mexico's resources and labor. That international relationship, which assumed a central place in U.S. State Department policy going back to the late nineteenth century, bears the imprints of imperialist domination. The major social consequences of this U.S. imperialist domination—the mass uprooting of people from the countryside and the migration of that labor to the heart of the U.S. economy—will be the subject of the chapters that follow.

U.S. Imperialism and Mexican Migration

The U.S. imperialist agenda and, specifically, the labor policies contained within that agenda provide the context for this study. The analysis covers the long-standing American tradition by large-scale enterprises of employing temporarily imported Mexican workers, known today as "guest workers." Particular attention is accorded here to the bracero contract labor agreements lasting from 1942 until 1964, designed and initiated by U.S. agribusiness interests and signed onto by the Mexican government. By examining the bracero program (with attention to the 1917–1921 labor importation program and the current H2-A "guest worker" program), we can better understand the historic antecedents for the currently discussed guest worker agreements proposed by President George W. Bush (as well as those of then–Democratic presidential candidate John Kerry) and thereby more effectively evaluate current guest worker proposals.

The vast majority of commentary on the Bracero Agreements analyzes the program as if it were unique, no more than an agreement between two sovereign nations; indeed, none comes to mind that defines the program as a labor policy fitting an imperialist scheme.[1] In this book, however, the bracero program is understood to comprise a series of state measures designed to organize Mexican migration—measures that, in the period under discussion, conformed to an imperialist schema. Ample evidence demonstrates conclusively that, in many respects, bracero labor utilization paralleled traditional forms of colonial labor exploitation such as that practiced by the British and French colonial regimes in India and Algeria, respectively. In each case, workers were transported across borders as *indentured labor;* in other words, they were systematically placed under employer control (as well as state control), segregated, and denied the rights to organize, to bargain for wages individually or collectively, to protest, and to freely change residence or employer. Moreover, little if any oversight enforced rights and privileges legally accorded to the laborers.

Over the course of the bracero program, nearly a half-million workers were imported to the United States to work in agriculture and during the war on railroads, for wages—and in housing and working conditions—considerably less than the depressingly low standard for the period. Braceros who demonstrated "rebellious" tendencies or poor work performance faced a quick departure to Mexico and were placed on a blacklist. In their colonies the British and French commonly applied these practices as well.

More important, the bracero program operated within the context of an economic relationship between Mexico, which is an underdeveloped nation, and the economically powerful United States.

Three fundamental themes related to this relationship underscore the present study. First, the economic relations between Mexico and the United States since the late nineteenth century have exhibited the classic hallmarks of neocolonialism.[2] Beginning in the 1880s, large-scale U.S. enterprises under the control of men of the Robber Baron era—such as J. D. Rockefeller, Jay Gould, William Randolph Hearst, and David Guggenheim, among others—sought to control significant sectors of the Mexican economy and accomplished that goal well before the 1910 Mexican Revolution. In the postrevolutionary period, U.S. capital not only maintained its dominance in several critical areas of Mexico's economy, including oil, mining, and agriculture; it strengthened its position.[3] U.S. capitalist interests expressed their power in ways other than through direct investment by entering into Mexico's banking and financing institutions. In the mid-1930s, for example, the Mexican government under Lazaro Cardenas established Nacional Financiera, Mexico's central financing body, and U.S. banking institutions occupied the leading position, holding a one-third stake in the institution's capital assets in the mid-1940s. It is therefore understandable that future economic programs ostensibly aimed at Mexico's economic development would follow the path established by the first wave of American investors during the late nineteenth century.

Another example is the construction of main highways in the northwest in the 1940s (largely funded by U.S. banks), which followed the blueprint of the U.S.-built railroads that were laid out in a north-south pattern. Building the roads in this fashion facilitated the export of goods, particularly natural resources, to the United States—and only secondarily were these roads connected with Mexico's economic heartland (an objective of British and French railroads in their colonies). In the immediate postwar period no fewer than 350 foreign-owned companies, most of them American, took advantage of the propitious investment climate and set up shop in Mexico. During the 1950s the American economic presence predominated in a number of areas, as pointed out in a 1953 *Yale Review* article:

> Many of our big corporations, like General Motors, General Electric, Ford, International Harvester, and Du Pont, have branches in Mexico. Current American investments in Mexico, which compose about 70 percent of all foreign investments there, are concentrating in industry, rather than in oil and mining, as they once did.[4]

One could add many more names to this "who's who" of major American corporations, including Monsanto, Anaconda, B. F. Goodrich, Westinghouse, Sears, Anderson Clayton, and banks such as Pan American Trust, Chase Bank, National City Bank, J. P. Morgan and Company, Bank of America, and the Export Import Bank.[5] Gradually, Mexico became a debtor nation, drawn into programs allegedly designed to develop Mexico economically but ultimately leaving it under the sway of foreign banks and investors.

A second theme concerns the bracero program itself, which expressed one variation of what then amounted to a half-century of Mexican migration and of the migrants' integration as labor within the heart of the U.S. economy. The bracero program was established at the behest of the United States, and under its oversight, the two nation states managed and organized an ongoing migration. Elsewhere it has been argued that the continuing migration that began in the first decade of the twentieth century comprises one social consequence of U.S. economic domination.[6] Rather than viewing Mexican migration as a classic supply-and-demand "push-pull" affair (the conventional model) as well as newer versions of push-pull, which hold that migration is "self perpetuating" based on "social networks that sustain it," migration here is explained through acknowledging the critical impact effected by U.S. imperialism upon the demography and social organization of the Mexican nation.[7] Explaining migration in this fashion is virtually unheard of today, even though the vocal critic of the bracero program, Ernesto Galarza, understood as early as 1949 the transnational forces leading to Mexican migration. He explained that the Mexican migrant "is forced to seek better conditions north of the border by the slow but relentless pressure of United States agricultural, financial, and oil corporate interests on the entire economic and social evolution of the Mexican nation."[8] These migrations, generated by the economic expansion of the United States into Mexico, manifested first as internal migrations that eventually continued into the United States and ultimately led to the ongoing formation of the modern ethnic Mexican community.

Finally, convention has it that the roots of Mexican migration are much like those of the majority of other migrations coming to the United States, most often compared to European migration. The heated rejoinders to the publication of Samuel P. Huntington's "The Hispanic Challenge" are a good case in point.[9] Huntington deplores what he contends is an emerging cultural divide in the United States between bilingual Hispanics and English-speaking America, and in response a chorus of critics counter that Mexican immigrants are undergoing experiences having much in common with previous European immigrants. Rather than using the European migrations to the United States as a "one size fits all" model for explaining Mexican migration to the United States, the present study emphasizes the neocolonial status of Mexico as the precondition for migration to the United States and for the subsequent Mexican immigrant experiences within the United States.

In addition to describing the bracero program as an expression of U.S. economic domination over Mexico, this study analyzes the marked similarities between colonial forms of labor and the bracero system. For example, several students of the bracero program have pointed out parallels with Spanish colonial forms of labor.[10] However, a more important comparison is that between the Indian and Algerian labor migrations (during their colonial periods) and the Mexican bracero program. That is, whereas the Spanish system evokes similarities, the British and French colonial labor systems and Mexican migration in its varied forms exhibit well-defined parallels, thus implying that Mexican migration is a manifestation of colonial labor migration rather than an independently spurred migratory flow similar to European migrations.

Interestingly, parallels with Roman imperial labor allocation have also been found. In their defense of bracero usage, agricultural entrepreneurs presaged by several decades the current imperialistic neoconservative outlook.[11] Indeed, many years earlier, at a 1958 congressional hearing on migratory labor, advocates of the bracero program were queried regarding the need for braceros. Their response, offered in a moment of unusual candor, ironically reflected the colonial character of the bracero program: "The same thing was true even in the Roman Empire. When they reached a stage of civilization they had to reach out to other areas where there was a lesser standard of living to bring in those people to do the menial tasks."[12]

Agriculture and Seasonal Harvest Labor

The vast majority of braceros worked in agriculture in a setting that had been well established for several generations before their arrival, and the heaviest users of bracero labor were Texas and California. Agriculture had developed to become the region's principal economic sector and one dominated by large-scale enterprises. Early in Texas's and California's agricultural development, a system evolved for securing labor through contractors hired by growers or grower associations to recruit a specified labor force. These contractors hauled workers to the work site for the harvest and performed the service of foreman. Growers seldom paid workers directly; instead, the contractors determined each worker's earnings and paid wages accordingly. Rarely if ever did workers come face to face with an employer or their representatives, and once the task was finished the labor force dispersed. With the next harvest, the cycle repeated, although workers were sometimes distributed to new farms from day to day. The only consistent factor in the organization of labor, and the main avenue available for farm workers to seek work, was the contractor system.

Throughout the history of southwest agriculture, tradition and sheer appropriation of power allowed growers to dictate wages, working conditions, work schedules, and standards in grower-supplied housing. That power secured the lowest wages in any industry and guaranteed extreme forms of poverty. Working and living conditions were abysmal, and health problems among farm workers and their families were common. It was into this historic context that braceros labored; the abilities and work habits accorded to braceros, as well as their placement in agriculture as seasonal labor, had been firmly established by two generations of Mexican laborers who, by then, had dominated the labor supply. The arrival of the braceros did not alter this historic legacy; indeed, the treatment that harvest labor had been subjected to fell upon the braceros with even greater intensity. Within this setting, braceros represented one variation on the theme of Mexican migration that entered into key sectors of the southwestern economy and society beginning in the early 1900s.

Reviewing the Bracero Contract Labor Program

Over the past several years the Bush and Fox administrations have engaged in highly publicized discussions over establishing a new guest worker program. Officials from both nations have met on numerous occasions to hammer out an agreement that has yet to bear fruit.

However, the Fox-Bush discussions do not represent the first attempt at creating an international agreement to import Mexican labor. By reviewing the bracero program we can begin to understand the proposed Bush guest worker agreements. An estimated 450,000 Mexican males worked in the United States as temporary laborers under this program from 1942 until 1964—an export of labor considered by some observers to be one of the largest mass movement of workers in history. Under the auspices of a binational agreement, men (and only men) were recruited, processed, and transported from dirt-poor farming villages in remote sections of Mexico and, to a lesser extent, from urban centers to work as cheap, controlled, reliable, experienced, and easily-disposed-of laborers.

During the war, braceros were employed mainly in agriculture but also as railroad maintenance workers. Upon the termination of the contract, which lasted from six weeks to eighteen months, the men were immediately returned to Mexico. The war's end did not signal the end of the program as agriculturalists lobbied successfully for annual extensions without recourse to allegations of "labor shortage." After a series of extensions, a new formal agreement was negotiated and Public Law 78 was signed in 1951. This legislation, which codified a temporary labor importation program exclusively for agriculture, continued with minor modifications until the bracero program ended in 1964.

Over the course of the bracero agreements, the United States served as a labor contractor, Mexico served as the labor recruiter, and both worked for the employers: large-scale agricultural interests. The bracero program provided a huge subsidy for agriculture by supplying ideal labor at taxpayers' expense. Braceros were readily available and disposable, effortlessly controlled and efficient, and, best of all, cheap. As if that was not enough, braceros lowered the wages of the nonbracero workforce and in some areas, such as the citrus industry, virtually eliminated the domestic labor force. Perhaps more important for agribusiness, the program provided a formidable obstacle to the formation of agricultural labor unions. Throughout the twenty-two-year span of the bracero program, no labor union ever seriously threatened agricultural interests.

Administered over the years by various Washington agencies and their regional affiliates, the program was publicly and loudly celebrated by administrators—particularly by the same agricultural corporations that grew to depend on seasonal imported labor. Proponents lost no opportunity to reiterate alleged benefits to Mexico, declaring that the program contributed to Mexico's economic development and that the men were returning with pockets overflowing with dollars, sporting not only new apparel but also the wisdom that comes with modern ideas. Over the life of the program, the bracero program was said to be of a piece with the Good Neighbor Policy, the Point Four Program, the Alliance for Progress, and even the Peace Corps. Bracero program advocates (like the proponents of globalization forty years later) contended that the program lifted all boats equally, although in relation to Mexico no evidence ever appeared to buttress such contentions.[13] However, those who chose to critique the program faced the combined opposition of growers and of federal and state authorities charged with managing the program. Two prominent examples illustrate the clear linkage of economics with political power. (1) Ernesto Galarza, in his opposition to the program, researched and authored a severely critical overview of the bracero program, *Strangers in Our Fields,* which prompted grower associations to lobby federal officials to prohibit its publication.[14] Fortunately for Galarza and opponents of the bracero program, the growers' efforts were unsuccessful. And (2) UC Berkeley researcher Henry Anderson lost his position at the university after California growers learned of his critical opinions regarding the bracero program.[15]

The Contemporary Migration Phase

With the end of the bracero program in 1964, the demand for Mexican labor in the United States continued and, contrary to some prognostications, mechanization failed to decrease the required labor in agriculture. Consequently, the flow of undocumented labor filled the places formerly held by braceros and by the end of the century comprised one-half of all agricultural labor in California. Subsequently, with the disastrous decline of the Mexican economy that began in the early 1980s and nose-dived after the implementation of the North American Free Trade Agreement (the archetypal expression of the neoliberal model), the flow of undocumented and documented labor reached epic proportions in the 1990s. During this period of unrelenting migration a chorus of voices in opposition to undocumented migration resulted in such programs as the Clinton administration's Operation Gatekeeper, California's Proposition 187, and Arizona's Proposition 200—the latter two intended to deny public-welfare benefits for the undocumented.[16] Nonetheless, the conditions driving migration worsened.

While undocumented laborers are blamed for causing drug trade, crime, and poor public education and accused of poaching welfare funds, the free investment policy that goes by the innocuous acronym NAFTA has resulted in the mass desertion of vast areas of rural Mexico and the placement of hundreds of thousands of people on the migratory trail, a migration that began in the early twentieth century. To this day, U.S. economic expansionism into the heart of the Mexican economy continues to tear Mexico's society apart. Farmers cannot compete with the "open door" to imports of U.S. corn, soy, beans, rice, beef, pork, chicken, and much more, which have come to dominate the Mexican marketplace since NAFTA lowered the bar to U.S. imports and, taking advantage of cheap labor, vastly increased the numbers of maquilas (foreign-owned manufacturing plants located mainly along the U.S.-Mexico border) to produce goods for consumption in the United States.[17] Today, Mexico has lost its ability to feed itself, a fundamental tenet of national sovereignty. Sociological studies have found that thousands of people—farmers and their families—leave the countryside annually and move to cities, many arriving at the border seeking poverty-guaranteeing jobs at maquila plants where women comprise nearly 70 percent of laborers.[18]

The countryside is being abandoned across Mexico. Between 1995 and 2000, 1 million people or more migrated from Mexico's central and southern sections to the northern border towns, which are growing at a record pace and where 80 percent of maquilas are located. In the 1990s, Tijuana, for example, increased its population by nearly 7 percent annually; 56 percent of the city's population were born elsewhere, many comprising a floating population intending to cross the border.[19] The maquila plants, which offer employment, are little more than export platforms disconnected from the rest of Mexico's economy and therefore have no "spin-off" effects; they are islands of U.S. production on Mexico's soil. If migrants cannot find a maquila job, they find a route across the increasingly dangerous border—with or without a *coyote* (smuggler). People displaced by the actions of U.S. imperial capital will seek work, legally or illegally, across the border regardless of guest worker agreements, Operation Gatekeeper, or Proposition 187. Not even the extreme dangers of border-crossing (several hundred migrants die each year) deter men and women who have no other options.

The bracero program is a strategy designed to transport indentured labor from an underdeveloped country to the most powerful nation in history and, as such, comprises a labor policy whose contemporary parallels can be found in colonial labor systems such as those implemented by the British in India and the French in Algiers. The same parallel can be drawn with respect to the currently proposed guest worker agreements between the United States and Mexico, a system of state-controlled migration of cheap labor that replicates the bracero program in its fundamental details. If we are to understand the various guest worker proposals put forward during and shortly before the 2004 presidential elections, we need go no further than a thorough analysis of the former "guest worker" agreement and the currently tendered proposals for such worker agreements.

Policies falling under the mantle of free trade have not borne the benefits promised; if anything, conditions in those countries undergoing neoliberal reforms, including the United States, have moved backward.[20] Poverty throughout the Third World has increased rather than decreased since the onset of free trade, and the distance between the First and Third Worlds is growing steadily. Mexico is an example of free trade that has lowered the standard of living for peasants, workers, and even the middle class, and official prescriptions to solve poverty seldom go beyond promoting "guest worker" emigration to the United States, remittances, and more free trade.[21] On the other hand, Mexico's farmers, students, workers, and teachers have taken actions against NAFTA in street demonstrations, even stopping shipments of U.S. goods that compete with small Mexican producers.[22] Such demonstrations against free-trade policies have taken place throughout Latin America—in Ecuador, Bolivia, Colombia, the Dominican Republic, Argentina, and Peru. A battle line is being drawn within nations and across continents. The people versus free trade and its varying identities—such as free markets, globalization, the Washington Consensus, and neoliberalism—has emerged as a key political battle of the twenty-first century.

Ernesto Galarza was the first to identify the actions of U.S. capital as the cause of conditions leading to continual migration from Mexico;

but his suggestions for resolving the crises that spur migration need to be heard again. In particular, he argued that

> [u]ntil Mexico can offer a far larger degree of economic security to its people, thousands of them will seek relief by migrating over the border, legally or illegally. Thus it becomes of primary importance to determine whether the economic policy of the United States is fostering or hampering the chances for creating a Mexico able to employ, feed, house, clothe, and educate its workers on a rising standard of living. To ignore this basic premise is to overlook the roots of the problem.[23]

Galarza addressed this very issue when in the same essay he pointed to the actions of U.S. capital as a principal cause of Mexican migration. Unfortunately, his prescription for initiating a review of the actions of U.S. capital and its relation to the migration question has been long overlooked; yet the first step in understanding Mexican migration requires that we, too, address this issue. Galarza further contended that the bracero program was "a palliative, a national narcotic" that postponed the great need for a fundamental alteration of Mexico's political and economic institutions. Exported labor only concealed the fundamental economic problems facing the nation, which could be resolved through a revolutionary change that eliminated Mexico's "reactionary elements, who perpetuate the bracero program."[24] Thus two objectives were foremost in Galarza's mind for explaining Mexican migrations: first, that we identify the social consequences of U.S. economic expansionism, which in itself is the cause of migration; and, second, that we recognize the Mexican elites' collaboration with that economic domination by promoting migration.

This study explores the actions of U.S. capital in relation to migration—the bracero program, in particular—from a perspective in which the United States is acknowledged as a quintessential expression of imperialism. The imperialist character of U.S.-Mexico relations and its significance for explaining Mexican migration and, hence, Chicano history remain on the margins in academia and among liberal reformers. By examining the Bracero Agreements within a context of imperialist domination, we can engage more realistic explanations regarding the U.S.-Mexico relationship and its offspring—migration—and thereby establish valuable approaches to the more important aspects of Chicano history. Simultaneously, we can explain the political struggles now taking place domestically (the anti-WTO demonstrations in Seattle and Miami come to mind) and internationally (Cancun and Genoa) against the very policies that have led to migration. This study seeks to contribute to that objective.

Notes

1. See, for example, Erasmo Gamboa, *Mexican Labor and World War II: Braceros in the Pacific Northwest, 1942–1947,* Austin: University of Texas Press, 1990; and Barbara Driscoll, *The Tracks North: The Railroad Bracero Program of World War II,* Austin: University of Texas Press, 1999.

2. John Mason Hart, *Empire and Revolution: The Americans in Mexico Since the Civil War,* Berkeley: University of California, 2002; Robert Freeman Smith, *The U.S. and Revolutionary Nationalism in Mexico, 1916–1932,* Chicago: University of Chicago Press, 1972; and Gilbert G. Gonzalez and Raul Fernandez, *A Century of Chicano History: Empire, Nations and Migration,* New York: Routledge, 2004.

3. Smith, *The U.S. and Revolutionary Nationalism in Mexico,* p. 34.

4. David L. Graham, "The United States and Mexico: A Reluctant Merger," *Yale Review,* vol. 43 (December 1953): 238.

5. Hart, *Empire and Revolution,* pp. 414–415.

6. Gilbert G. Gonzalez and Raul Fernandez, "Empire and the Origins of Twentieth Century Migration from Mexico to the United States," *Pacific Historical Review,* vol. 71, no. 1 (2002).

7. On the "self perpetuating" model for explaining Mexican migration, see David Jacobson, *The Immigration Reader: America in Multidisciplinary Perspective,* Malden, Mass.: Blackwell Publishers, 1998, p. 11; Robert S. Leiken, "Enchilada Lite: A Post-9/11 Mexican Migration Agreement," Center for Immigration Studies, available online at http://www.cis.org/articles/2002/leiken.html; David M. Reimers, *Still the Open Door: The Third World Comes to America,* New York: Columbia University, 1985; and Douglas Massey et al., *Worlds in Motion: Understanding International Migration at the End of the Millennium,* Oxford: Clarendon Press, 1998. Massey and his cohorts write: "[T]he absence of well-functioning capital and credit markets creates strong pressures for international movement as a strategy of capital accumulation. The manifold links between various market failures and international migration are illustrated by the following examples" (p. 22); these include crop insurance markets, futures market, unemployment insurance, and retirement insurance. In short, the sending countries do not have what the receiving countries have, a gap that migrants seek to close by migrating. It all sounds very much like "push-pull" in new dress.

8. Ernesto Galarza, "Program for Action," *Common Ground,* vol. 10, no. 4 (Summer 1949): 31.

9. Samuel P. Huntington, "The Hispanic Challenge," *Foreign Affairs* (March-April 2004).

10. In particular, see Henry Anderson, *Harvest of Loneliness: An Inquiry into a Social Problem,* Berkeley: Citizens for Farm Labor, 1964, ch. 4; and Richard Hancock, *The Role of the Bracero in the Economic and Cultural Dynamics of Mexico,* Stanford, Calif.: Stanford University Hispanic American Society, 1959.

11. See, for example, Greg Grandin, "The Right Quagmire: Searching History for an Imperial Alibi," *Harper's Magazine* (December 2004).

12. Ernesto Galarza, *Merchants of Labor: The Mexican Bracero Story* (Boston: Houghton Mifflin, 1964, p. 259.

13. See, for example, Verne A. Baker, "Braceros Farm for Mexico," *Americas,* vol. 5 (September 1953). The author writes: "At the start it may have seemed to Mexico that the U.S. employers were the principal beneficiaries of the international hiring plan, but now it turns out that Mexico is the long-term winner" (p. 4). And later: "So the agricultural improvements introduced by the workers who went north legally on contract may in the long run be a big factor in solving the problem of their unauthorized fellow migrants" (pp. 4–5). See also the following: J. L. Busey, "The Political Geography of Mexican Migration," *Colorado Quarterly,* vol. 2, no. 2 (Autumn 1953); D. S. McClellan and C. E. Woodhouse, "The Business Elite and Foreign Policy," *Western Political Quarterly,* vol. 13, no. 1 (March 1960); A. R. Issler, "'Good Neighbors' Lend a Hand," *Survey Graphic,* vol. 32 (October 1943); and Richard H. Hancock, *The Role of the Bracero in the Economic and Cultural Dynamics of Mexico: A Case Study of Chihuahua,* Stanford, Calif.: Stanford University Hispanic American Society, 1959.

14. Ernesto Galarza, *Strangers in Our Fields,* Washington, D.C.: Joint United States-Mexico Trade Union Committee, 1956.

15. In an interview conducted by Henry Anderson for his study, which was summarily terminated by the University of California (and discussed in Ch. 4), Anderson found that others beside himself were victimized for criticizing the bracero program. His interviewee stated: "A friend of mine back East had prepared a manuscript in which he was highly critical of the Department of Labor. His treatment was critical, but fair. He said a number of things that badly needed saying by someone. He submitted the manuscript to a publisher—one of the national magazines. Would you believe it? The editor sent the manuscript to the Department of Labor for evaluation! My friend has never been able to get the darn thing published." See Anderson, *Harvest of Loneliness,* p. 718.

16. Richard Marosi, "Arizona Stirs Up Immigration Stew," *Los Angeles Times,* November 6, 2004.

17. On the failed promises of NAFTA and its negative consequences for Mexico, see John J. Audley et al., *NAFTA's Promise and Reality: Lessons From Mexico for the Hemisphere,* New York: Carnegie Endowment for International Peace, 2004; Michael Pollan, "A Flood of U.S. Corn Rips at Mexico," *Los Angeles Times,* April 24, 2003; Hector Tobar, Sam Howe Verhovek, and Solomon Moore, "A Scourge Rooted in Subsidies," *Los Angeles Times,* September 22, 2003; and Victor Quintana, "The Mexican Rural Sector Can't Take It Anymore," in Gilbert G. Gonzalez et al., eds., *Labor Versus Empire: Race, Gender and Migration,* New York: Routledge, 2004.

18. See Alexandra Spiedoch, "NAFTA Through a Gender Lens: What 'Free Trade' Pacts Mean for Women," *Counterpunch* (December 30, 2004); Carlos Salas, "The Impact of NAFTA on Wages and Incomes in Mexico," in Economic Policy Institute, *Briefing Paper* (Washington, D.C., 2001); and Juan Gonzalez, *The Harvest of Empire: A History of Latinos in America,* New York: Viking Press, 2000, ch. 13.

19. San Diego State University Institute for Regional Studies of the Californias, Tijuana, Basic Information, available online at http://www-rohan.sdsu.edu/~irsc/tjreport/tj3.html(p. 1).

20. Paul Krugman, "The Death of Horatio Alger," *New York Times,* January 5, 2004; Aaron Bernstein, "Waking Up from the American Dream," *Business Week,* December 1, 2003; Jeff Faux, "NAFTA at Seven: Its Impact on Workers in All Three Nations," in Economic Policy Institute, *Briefing Paper* (Washington, D.C., 2001). Faux writes that maquila plants "in which wages, benefits, and workers rights are deliberately suppressed—are isolated from the rest of the Mexican economy. They do not contribute much to the development of Mexican industry or its internal markets, which was the premise upon which NAFTA was sold to the Mexican people" (p. 2).

21. Lisa J. Adams, "Fox Acknowledges Dire Poverty in Rural Mexico," *Orange County Register,* February 6, 2003; Solomon Moore, "Mexico's Border-Crossing Tips Anger Some in the U.S.," *Los Angeles Times,* January 4, 2004; Olga R. Rodriguez, "Mexico Failing to Slow Migrant Smuggling," *Orange County Register,* July 27, 2004; and Olga Rodriguez, "Book Called Aid to Illegal Entry," *Orange County Register,* January 6, 2005.

22. Susanna Hayward, "Thousands Protest Fox's Address," *Miami Herald,* September 2, 2004; Ginger Thompson, "Fox Vows to Pursue Genocide Charges," *New York Times,* September 1, 2004; Mark Stevenson, "Workers Protest Fox's Economic Policies," *Orange County Register,* September 1, 2004; Chris Kraul, "Mexico on Right Path, Fox Says," *Los Angeles Times,* September 2, 2004; and "Protesters Attack Fox's Car in Mexico City Border City," *New York Times,* October 22, 2004.

23. Galarza, "Program for Action," p. 35.

24. Quoted in Anderson, *Harvest of Loneliness,* p. 617.

Chapter 2

Imperialism and Labor: Mexican, Indian, and Algerian Labor Migrations in Comparative Perspective

ONE OF THE ENDURING CONVENTIONS of the literature on Mexican migration to the United States is the tendency to equate European and Mexican migrations. Indeed, virtually every study of Mexican migration since the theme first appeared in the early twentieth century has interpreted that migration to be an example of various European peoples escaping harsh economic conditions particular to their homelands and moving to the United States to enjoy its benefits—as in the mythical "American Dream." While some scholars contend that Latinos may not be as successful as their European counterparts, the majority argue that Mexican migration largely replicates the critical features of European migrations. For instance, a 2003 Rand Corporation study conducted by economist James Smith described as "unfounded" arguments contending that Latinos are "not sharing in the successful European experience."[1] A highly regarded scholar of Mexican American history, Mario Garcia, affirmed in his study of the political history of the Mexican American community that

> the history of the Mexican in the United States coincides with the history
> of other immigrants in the process of becoming Americans. This is a
> history rooted in the relationship between the labor needs of industrial
> capitalism and the displacement of millions of people of Eastern and
> Southern Europe, Mexico, and to a lesser extent Asia, owing to changes
> in the world economy and their need in order to survive.... Mexican

15

Americans in the twentieth century form part of an expansive new addition to the American national experience.[2]

At the core of this theoretical approach is the rarely challenged "push-pull" convention used to explain migration from Europe and Mexico. "Push" refers to poverty, unemployment, political rebellion, or lack of resources from within the sending country, whereas "pull" refers to demand for labor.

Unfortunately, the parallels drawn between Mexican and European migrations are superficial at best. Yet Europe remains the model for explaining Mexican migration and the subsequent immigrant experience. The present chapter addresses this widely accepted misconception and argues for an alternative explanatory approach—namely, that Mexican migration, along with its causes and general features, finds greater parallels with migrations from European colonies than with those from European nations and, further, that the push-pull model cannot account for these migrations.

To demonstrate this commonality, the chapter examines salient factors shared by Mexican, Indian, and Algerian migrations, in all of which foreign domination is fundamental. Indian and Algerian migrations are analyzed in the context of the epochs of imperialist domination exercised by Britain and France, respectively. Explaining Mexican migration places economic domination by the United States since the late nineteenth century, a domination tantamount to colonization, at the center of that migration.[3] In short, the present study contends that imperial domination served as the fundamental condition for labor migrations from India and Algeria, and that this condition continues to apply in the case of Mexico as it proceeds under the cloud of the North American Free Trade Agreement (NAFTA).

In drawing the parallels linking the three migrations, the study will emphasize those social and economic conditions that were imposed upon the colony from abroad or, in the case of Mexico, the economically dominated nation, those that played critical roles in propelling and shaping migration. In pursuing this line of analysis, few will object to defining India and Algeria as one-time colonies of Britain and France. However, arguing that Mexico is a colony—specifically, an economic colony of the United States as well as contending that the United States is an imperialist nation will surely raise vigorous dissent and, at the very least, serious questioning.

In fact, within the past few years, a handful of neoconservatives have opened a dialogue defending the United States as an imperialist power, proclaiming that the U.S. version is benign, liberal, humanitarian, and democratic, distinct from all previous imperialist expansions. Despite spirited discourse, this dialogue has remained beyond earshot of most Americans, and certainly most political figures, academics, and students of U.S. history, who seldom address the United States as an imperialist power.[4] However, there is substantial evidence in support of the argument that shortly after the Civil War the United States initiated a classic imperialist policy in relation to Mexico, and undoubtedly so in the militaristic acquisition of Puerto Rico, Cuba, and the Philippines as well as the artificial creation of Panama.[5] Nevertheless, most interpreters of U.S. history, as Amy Kaplan has so eloquently argued, prefer to identify the United States as a nation that respects the sovereignty of other nations and deals with all of them on the basis of equality and reciprocity.[6] However, this study argues, as others have done, that since the late nineteenth century the United States has implemented an imperialist agenda (and not the humanitarian agenda that neoconservatives would have us believe) and it is this agenda, as applied to Mexico, that has led to over a hundred years of migration.[7]

As mentioned above, there is no question that India and Algeria served as colonial outposts for Britain and France, the two most prominent European colonial powers through most of the nineteenth and into the mid-twentieth centuries. Both colonies served as reservoirs of cheap and easily controlled labor as well as sources of raw materials and outlets for manufactured goods and surplus capital from the colonial powers. In the case of India, this study will examine indentured migration to the sugar plantations on the British Caribbean colonies of Guiana and Trinidad, a state-managed migration that began in the late 1830s and reached peak levels between 1870 and its termination in 1917. Algerian migration began in the early twentieth century and lasted past independence (granted in 1962) and into the 1970s. We are concerned here with Algerian labor migration during the colonial era, when French government agents recruited thousands of migrants as contract labor, and during other periods when industrial corporations actively recruited immigrant workers while some voluntarily migrated (legal and illegal).[8] In the case of Mexico, finally, the comparison will emphasize indentured labor known as the bracero program to work in agriculture and, to a far smaller extent, on railroads—though with less attention paid to actively recruited labor and voluntary migration (legal and illegal).

Each of these distinct labor migrations share a number of conditions that serve to initiate the respective migrations and propel them forward. These circumstances, which are consequences of foreign domination, include the managed dissolution of communal peasant economies and the forced mass uprooting of peasants from traditional villages to form a surplus population—that is, a "colonial reserve army" living in dire poverty and amenable to migrating as labor. These conditions are contextualized within a modernization process administered by the colonial power characterized by export-oriented extractive industries that limit national economic development to lesser forms of production and an absence of national industrialization. These varied conditions, in turn, propelled internal migrations that eventually led to emigration administered by the respective receiving states.

Colonized peoples serve first as cheap labor in the colony and subsequently as cheap labor within the colonial power or in other colonial outposts, as with the Indians in Trinidad and Guiana. Other parallels will be highlighted as well, including systems of recruitment and repatriation, concentration in unskilled labor ranks, meager wages, wholesale violations of work contracts, substandard working and housing conditions, and subjection to social and political relations defined by the enterprises employing them. It will be shown that these parallels are more than coincidental or superficial and that the migrations originate in economic conditions resulting from subordination to a dominant foreign power—that is, imperialism.

The following discussion consists of two parts. First, I examine the assault on peasant subsistence economies in each of the cases under analysis and the coerced internal and cross-border labor migrations. Second, I analyze in some detail the distinctive parallels of the emigrant worker experiences within the confines of the foreign power.

Breaking Down Peasant Systems of Production

In Mexico, Algeria, and India, the radical alteration of their respective productive traditions and demographic patterns, which had been in place for centuries, led to the major social consequences of imperial domination. In the case of Mexico, and to a larger extent India and Algeria, peasant populations underwent radical demographic transformations as they were wrenched from traditional farming villages through decrees that caused wholesale land expropriation, population redistribution, and drastic declines in health and well-being. In India specifically, peasant production systems were seriously undermined by taxation codes, privatization of landholdings, and the introduction of British manufactures (e.g., cotton cloth), which undercut village cottage industries and ruined artisanal production. Likewise, Algeria and Mexico underwent a massive reconstruction of their traditional economic base. Let's examine each case more closely, beginning with Mexico.

Mexico

Before the first decade of the twentieth century, Mexican migration involved little more than sporadic border crossings to the United States and was of little significance compared to European migrations. By the second decade the trickle had grown to considerable proportions. Most historical studies contend that the 1910 Mexican Revolution caused the first waves of migration. However, it has been shown that migration preceded that revolution by at least five years and that the migration had its roots in the economic expansionism into Mexico by U.S. corporations and investors. It is important to examine the events of the late nineteenth century, for it was during this period that imperial-minded U.S. investors under the aegis of U.S. foreign policymakers moved into Mexico on a large scale and captured the main pillars of the economy including railroads, mining, oil, and significant segments of agriculture.[9] An internal migration flowed first to foreign-owned industrial sites within Mexico, during which the demographic pattern began to reconstruct and conform to these sites, and later the same migration entered the United States.

Events leading up to that economic takeover help to explain why the domination of Mexico by U.S. investors and corporate entities took place. In the post–Civil War period a widespread and vocal groundswell of businesspeople argued for the forced military occupation and annexation of Mexico. The *New York Herald*, for example, demanded that the United States "take all of Mexico" and establish "a protectorate over Mexico." A critical response to those voices emanated from the then-minister to Mexico (and an investor in Mexico's railroads), William Rosecrans, who answered that the absorption of Mexico ensured more problems than benefits. On the contrary, he confided, there existed an alternate method for realizing the benefits of "taking all of Mexico" while avoiding the negatives. He argued that by dominating Mexico economically, a policy that he termed "peaceful conquest," investors from the United States would eventually realize the promises of occupation without the drawbacks of having to control a population of 12 million, most of them indigenous people. An advocate of that policy offered a corollary: "If we have their trade and development we need not hasten the other event [annexation]."[10]

By the end of the nineteenth century the policy of "peaceful conquest," with the active collaboration of Mexico's pre-capitalist landed elites, had become the core of U.S. foreign policy toward Mexico and, later, all of Latin America. The first application of "peaceful conquest" came in the form of railroads, followed by mining and oil production, all of which fell under the sway of American capital. By 1900 dominant U.S. monopolistic capitalists such as J. P. Morgan, Daniel Guggenheim, J. D. Rockefeller, and Jay Gould, as well as near-monopolies like Southern Pacific, Union Pacific, Atchison Topeka, and Santa Fe, had come to control the Mexican economy, dominating oil, mining, railroads, and vast sections of agriculture. Each sector had an effect on the peasants, redistributing them through an active labor recruitment leading to internal migrations and later emigrations to the United States.

Major U.S. railroads led the "peaceful conquest" in the early 1880s and by 1910 had constructed 15,000 miles of roads, an investment totaling $500,000,000. Rail lines originated from the U.S. border southward, a veritable extension of the U.S. system that brought Mexico into the range of the northern economy. Rather than serving as a system that united Mexico's economy and thereby promoted the home market, railroads above all else connected Mexico with the United States. Like the railroad systems for the British and French colonies, railroads in Mexico functioned as a system for the export of raw materials and the import of finished goods. The first social consequence of railroads was the removal of peasants from lands officially conceded to railroad corporations by the Mexican government under the iron-fist dictatorship of Porfirio Diaz (who proved a staunch ally of the United States). Second, sensing an opportunity to profit from the roads, elite landholders envisioned transforming subsistence lands into agricultural fields yielding goods for export via the railroads. Realizing that potential gains were in the offing if they traded agricultural products on railroads, Mexican elites then enforced decades-old laws, long ignored, requiring peasants to provide documentation that the lands were legally acquired—a requirement nearly impossible to fulfill. Applied almost exclusively to peasants, the law had disastrous consequences for the peasantry. Communally held peasant properties across Mexico were legally confiscated—in essence, privatized—and sold or handed to foreign entities and landed elites. American investors reaped huge tracts of land at bargain-basement prices. For example, New York financier Edward Shearson and a partner acquired 990,950 acres, after which Shearson joined with a second set of partners to acquire another tract measuring 890,000 acres. Not to be outdone, newspaper magnate William Randolph Hearst purchased a hacienda measuring 1,192,000 acres.[11]

The combined result was the mass eviction of more than 300,000 peasants from traditional farmlands, the first large-scale population redistribution in Mexico's history.[12] Suddenly, 90 percent of the peasantry, more than 80 percent of the population, held no land whatsoever. Not surprisingly, the majority of removals occurred along the planned or constructed rail lines. Historian Michael Johns notes that "railroads and the expanding haciendas [landed estates] threw so many off their lands in the 1880s and 1890s that nearly one-half of the city's five hundred thousand inhabitants ... were peasants."[13] Confined to towns and cities, uprooted peasants (largely from the central highlands) became a large labor surplus that railroad companies tapped into to construct and maintain the roads, leading to the redistribution of the former peasants northward along the tracks.

Railroads also led to the ruin of many thousands of mule-packers who at one time functioned as a transportation system but ultimately could not compete with the faster and cheaper rail systems. Overwhelmed as well by the effects of the "peaceful conquest" were artisans of various kinds, including soap makers, weavers, shoemakers, and others who could not compete with the goods being imported from the United States. As the handicraft and tradesmen systems slowly disintegrated they, too, entered into the labor pool, with the vast majority centered in and around Mexico City. Historian John Mason Hart summed up the fate borne by the dispossessed: "[T]hey had to choose between performing labor in estate agriculture or emigrating in search of employment."[14]

But railroads led to more than land dispossession and the ruin of artisans. Mining companies followed shortly after the completion of rail lines, which allowed access to rich mineral and metal deposits into remote areas of northern Mexico, transforming railways into principal conduits for ores and machinery. By 1910 U.S. concerns had modernized the mining industry, investing $300 million, two-thirds of the total invested in mining, while Mexican concerns, minor partners for sure, held but $15 million. These mining operations then tapped into the surplus labor supply and recruited them northward to form an internal migratory flow complementing the migration created by the railroads and "legal" land dispossession. By 1910 some 140,000 laborers were working in mining operations; another 30,000 labored for the railroads, and many more thousands worked in the oil extractive regions and the henequen plantations. In the Tampico oil fields, for example, at least 7,000 laborers were recruited mainly from the central highlands.

Foreign investment was the driving force behind the Mexican economy and, as such, depended upon the availability of Mexican labor. One journal editorial accurately noted in 1924 that "practically all the capital invested in industrial enterprises in Mexico is foreign while all the labor employed in these enterprises is Mexican."[15] (The same could have been said of India and Algeria at the time.) One outstanding feature of this radical reconstruction of the Mexican economy and society was the formation of company towns along the rail lines and in the oil and mining camps. Segregation separating Mexican laborers and their families from American administrators and managers—along with terms like "Mexican work" and "Mexican wage"—made their debut. However, labor recruitment and segregation did not stop at the border. Books, journals, and articles by American businesspeople, travelers, missionaries, journalists, and academics offered to American readers a cultural expression of colonial authority, portraying Mexicans as a pathological tangle of cultural and genetic inferiority that required a civilizing agent (i.e., Americanization) to develop their potential.[16]

While modernization spread over the Mexican countryside, the previously self-sufficient nation found itself for the first time feeding on imported goods. Having long supplied its own foodstuffs, including beans and corn, it could no longer feed itself. Indeed, for over three centuries of Spanish colonialism and nationhood Mexican peasants had fulfilled the population's nutritional requirements. Within two decades of the "peaceful conquest," however, Mexico became a net importer of foodstuffs and manufactured goods from the United States and an exporter of raw materials to the same country. Between 1877 and 1910, the era of the Diaz dictatorship and shelter for U.S. investors, corn production decreased by 50 percent and beans by 75 percent.[17] Food costs skyrocketed to the point where daily consumption dropped significantly during the "free trade" and open-investment epoch. Meanwhile, Mexico's trading partnership with the United States as exporter of raw materials and importer of finance capital, technology, and finished goods was firmly established and would last throughout the twentieth century to the present.

Internal migration provided the first step in migration to the United States as the same monopolistic concerns operating in Mexico recruited their labor across the border to work in their U.S. operations. Villages underwent a slow depopulation of once-industrious communities, a migratory process that would continue into the twenty-first century. In 1908, a U.S. Department of Commerce and Labor study recounted that "[e]ntire villages have migrated to other parts of Mexico, where employment has been found in the mines or on the railways," adding that

> [t]his has carried the central Mexican villager a thousand miles from his home and to within a few miles of the border, and American employers, with a gold wage, have had little difficulty in attracting him across that not so formidable line.[18]

The result was that by 1910 more than 60,000 Mexicans were migrating annually to the United States. Mexicans became the prime source of railroad maintenance labor and farm labor across the Southwest and, soon after, the prime source of mining labor in Arizona. This same migration continued into the 1920s as border patrol agents ignored, and thus encouraged, the mass crossing, legal or otherwise. When a practically open border failed to bring in the required laborers, employers secured their labor under the umbrella of the state labor importation programs, and from 1917 to 1921, 83,000 workers were imported for temporary labor. Not until the eve of the Depression did migration dwindle, supplanted by wholesale deportations to rid the welfare roles of unemployed immigrants—the very people who previously had been eagerly recruited to work for railroad, mining, and agricultural corporations.

However, the migratory hiatus was short-lived. Migration resumed with the onset of the highly controlled state-managed "guest worker" bracero program, designed to import workers for large-scale agribusiness, mainly in Texas and California, under conditions of indentured servitude bordering on slavery.

India

As in the case of Mexico, foreign economic intervention undercut the viability of Indian peasant production, creating social conditions ameliorated through internal migration and eventually, under the stimulus of British rulers, emigration. From the first landing of the British East India Company and the initiation of the export of manufactures within areas limited to Calcutta, Madras, and Bombay, the internal political and economic structure of India began to undergo significant alterations. These slowly emerging alterations were greatly enhanced by the territorial acquisition of Bengal in 1757 and the defeat of French claims to India in 1763.

British imperialism wrought disastrous modifications in traditional forms of production, with parallel consequences for the peasantry. As Walton Look Lai points out:

> One of the lasting consequences of the changes thus introduced in the nineteenth century was the erosion of the traditional Indian village community, with its high degree of self-sufficiency and its delicate balance of agriculture and handicraft industry which had served well for centuries.[19]

The British sought to plow the ground, so to speak; it sought to prepare for its own vision of the role of India in the British Empire. First, the British, like the French in Algeria (as we shall see below), established a "land taxation and revenue system," which caused greater economic hardship in village communities than was previously the case under the Mogul rulers. The responsibility for tax collection accrued to the local chieftains who, although they diligently returned those taxes decreed by their British overseers, also retained personal allotments for themselves. Previous to the British, taxes took a modest sum from the peasants and were seldom excessive; that system changed and "made [taxation] more efficient and more brutally extractive" than ever before.[20] Second, elite landlords serving as intermediaries for the British were granted private property rights to those lands under their control upon which peasant tenants lived and worked, thereby transforming the Moguls into landlords in the capitalist sense.

In designing policy from a classic imperialist script, the British attacked communal property rights and initiated the primacy of private property as the foundation for the land system. Those communal lands held under the Mogul system soon became the means of subjecting peasant tenants to myriad forms of cash rents. This turned one-time nominally free peasants into debtors, who then became dependent on moneylenders to survive the foreign installed economic regimen. As villagers fell into deeper debt, bankruptcy and then landlessness followed across the regions controlled by Britain. A system of communal land use, in place for centuries, gave way to a mix of feudal lords holding private property utilized for the production of commercial crops destined for the market.

With the abrogation of traditional peasant rights to land as well as the repayment of debts cushioned by custom, seizure of peasant plots became a legal right for collecting debts. Similar in important respects to what occurred in Mexico, the landed class took advantage of their newly ascribed privileges and began to appropriate lands based on newly recognized legal privileges. Customs that once protected peasants from disenfranchisement were overshadowed by legal protections for private ownership enforced through the colonial court system. Landlessness soon became a common feature of the countryside, and many sought relief by migrating to cities. Again, the words of Walton Look Lai capture the moment:

> Village debtors were often at the mercy of their creditors. The result was frequently bankruptcy and eviction, in a process that constantly multiplied the numbers of landless laborers living on the edge of starvation in a generally depressed and nonvibrant agricultural milieu.[21]

More than just land expropriations followed on the heels of British colonialism as manufactures from British factories entered the colony on a massive scale, to the ruin of cottage artisanal production. The British practiced free trade when it benefited their manufactures, but denied the same to Indian artisanal goods available to export to

Britain. Thus, the British exported to India factory-produced textiles protected by free-trade privileges, virtually destroying the production of fine silks and other cloths and resulting in the ruin of millions of artisans. The governor-general of India, Lord William Bentinck, described the appalling situation in 1834 as one in which "misery hardly finds a parallel in the history of commerce. The bones of the cotton weavers are bleaching the plains of India."[22] With the onset of railroad construction in 1853, the introduction of textiles reached into every corner of the colony, exacerbating the ruinous conditions that confronted the once-flowering domestic handicraft industry and domestic market. Neither agriculture nor artisanal shop production would suffice for the burgeoning flood of dispossessed people entering cities in search of livelihood.

More destruction would follow as the disruption of agricultural production led to periodic crop failures and famines, throwing more people onto a migratory course. Labor began to flow toward employment opportunities that presented themselves, appearing in the textile mills; coal mines; coffee, tea, and cotton plantations; government public works; and railway construction. The latter two employed thousands of laborers. From these initial employments a wage labor force emerged that was dependent on the British colonial system for its livelihood.

While India was undergoing colonial subjugation, Britain secured colonies in the Caribbean, including Trinidad, Guiana, Jamaica, and several others. Beginning in 1838 these small sugar plantation islands, deprived of slave labor after the British proclaimed emancipation, would welcome several hundred thousand indentured workers recruited from Calcutta, Madras, and Bombay. As historian Hugh Tinker observes, "It was India's role, within the British Empire, to furnish a supply of cheap and disposable labor. Units of production, not people, were exported across the seas to supply the demand."[23] Walter Rodney clarifies the impact of imperialism on the creation of a "colonial labor supply," arguing that the "push"—that is, a surplus labor supply available to migrate—originated from the very economic policies designed and enforced by the colonial masters. He writes:

> The overseas migrations are to be seen as an extension and overflow of an internal labor fluidity within the colonial Indian economy itself, as it adjusted to the British imperial impact, and not as a separate phenomenon.[24]

The same could have been said of Mexican migration.

Not surprisingly, the Indians' status as colonial subjects and the consequent rebellion against colonialism contributed to the migration flow into the economic heartland of the colonial power. A major impetus to migration followed the unsuccessful anticolonial rebellion that occurred in 1857–1858. The defeated forces—composed of elites who had lost their social standing, mutinous soldiers rebelling against the British army, and displaced peasants—rose together to challenge the British but were finally defeated after an eighteen-month battle. The rebellion and its defeat resulted in great loss of life and further population displacement. Defeated militants sought escape, and emigration as indentured workers offered many a way out. However, an additional condition entered into that colonial experience: Indenture was intended as a replacement for freed slaves but more often than not replicated slavery.

Algeria

In 1830 France undertook the military conquest of Algeria, the North African territory bordering the Mediterranean populated by tribal communities of Arab herder nomads and sedentary Berber highlanders. During the next 130 years the native economy and society based on subsistence peasant production would undergo tumultuous changes and alter the society in fundamental ways. These alterations would form the foundation for subsequent mass migrations that would continue beyond Algerian independence in 1962. Indeed, these changes would, in numerous ways, mirror the experiences both of Mexican peasants during and after the Diaz dictatorship (particularly during the era of NAFTA) and of Indian peasants during British colonialism.

As the first salvos of the First World War exploded, about 13,000 Algerians made a trek to France. By 1930 at least 130,000 Algerians had crossed the Mediterranean and landed at Marseilles to labor mainly in mining and tire and automobile manufacturing. However, before this emigration began, Algerians worked in mines, vineyards, and other agricultural enterprises owned by *colons* (French settlers). It is important to review the economic and social changes wrought by French colonialism, the precursor to migration. It is here that the key to explaining Algerian emigration is to be found.

French colonial expansion into Algeria began with the capture of the major cities; soon thereafter, forcible transfers of land to the *colons* became the order of the day. Proclaiming liberty and the "civilizing" of the peoples of Algeria, the occupying power decreed "through innumerable arbitrary measures" the

> sequestration, confiscation, expropriation, cantonment and the application of various property bills devised to establish presumed "incommutable individual property" to transform the soil into a commodity."[25]

As lands were privatized the next step was to have them exchanged on the market, and French speculators moved in to cash in on the bargains. Their objective was successfully achieved. Between 1830 and 1850, the initial period of colonization, 365,000 hectares of land were transferred via legalities designed by French authorities for the benefit of French settlers. As the years progressed the expropriations continued without abatement. Foreign travelers and government officials witnessed the forced transfer of land. In 1868 the English consul reported on a 6,500-acre "concession," which in fact amounted to a typical expropriation:

> A concession of this forest was originally given to a French gentleman for a period of 40 years … extended to 90 years. In terms of this he was to enjoy the right of stripping the cork trees over the whole extent; and of cultivation and pasturage over about 225 acres of cleared land. From the latter portion the Arab occupants were ejected, much against their inclination.… Subsequently, the right of pasturage over the whole forest was assumed by the concessionaire, the claims of the Arabs were ignored, and they were only permitted to pasture their flocks within the forest on payment of rent to the concessionaire.… What I have described as having taken place … was going on all around.[26]

The post-1870 period witnessed the largest forced land transfers: 1,912,000 hectares were transferred to private owners between 1891 and 1900, 2,581,000 during the following two decades, and nearly 3,500,000 hectares from 1921 to 1940. Eric Wolf summarizes that policy as one that made of common lands a potential commodity and even booty—a policy that "threw all land held by Muslims upon the open market, and made it available for purchase or seizure by French colonists."[27] The prize was for the French and only the French to seize.

Only the highland sedentary peasantry who farmed harsh and difficult terrains remained relatively free of the level of expropriation aimed at the nomadic herding tribes who plied the plains regions.[28] For the Algerian peasants of the plains the expropriations were devastating; their centuries-old traditional way of life largely based on tribal communal forms of property was systematically eroded. Meanwhile, French settlers reaped the harvest. By the 1950s, 11 million hectares were in *colon* hands compared to only 7,133,000 hectares in Algerian hands, though French settlers comprised but 8 percent of the total population. More, the French acquired the best, most fertile lands and forced the peasants, particularly those of the plains regions, into the hinterlands and less favorable regions. Not content with expropriation, the French sought to destroy the tribal system itself and to reconstruct a demographic pattern conforming to the colonial economic design. The social consequences that ensued were depressingly inevitable.

The slow undermining of the Algerian subsistence economy left peasants in increasingly dire straits. Whereas in 1871 the average peasant utilized 83 ares for cultivating, by 1948 that figure had fallen to 24 ares. And annual per capita peasant production of basic grains fell precipitously from five hundred kilos in 1872 to fewer than two hundred in 1951.[29] The peasant element of the population slowly began to disappear while dispossessed laborers increased in number; the latter increased by 29 percent between 1929 and 1954 while the peasantry decreased by 20 percent.[30] Where peasants could continue to work agricultural lands, their labor was transformed from subsistence production to mainly cash crops, subject to the *colon*-controlled marketplace; in order to solve the inevitable "vagaries of the marketplace," even landed peasants became a source of harvest labor on *colon* lands as they sought to supplement their income.

The mass of dispossessed peasants barely able to scratch out a living became the good fortune of the *colons,* providing the main labor supply in the form of wage laborers and sharecroppers for the continually increasing colonial agricultural and extractive enterprises. As early as 1851, during the first phase of the colonization process, an observer noted that "since a long time ago almost all the big concessionaires of land … in the civil territory have been using indigenous laborers for cultivation of their estates. They recruited them from everywhere."[31] Indeed, without plentiful labor the vast agricultural developments engaged by the *colons* would have been impossible to achieve, particularly the plantation-like, labor-intensive vineyards that measured 400,000 hectares in total in 1940.

Resettlement programs acted to remove the land-deprived former peasantry who had formed new communities—dense pockets of poverty comprising "huts built of reeds." Faced with disappearing supplies of food and obligated to labor for meager wages, the peasants turned to borrowing, which led them into debt and hastened the sale of remaining minifundias.[32] As a student of the Algerian colonial history comments:

> The huge mass of rural poor lived in the most abject poverty. They were described at the turn of the century by European observers as working endlessly from dawn to dusk in the full heat of the day and without pause. Their meager diet consisted of wheat or barley griddle cakes, whey and a few dates or figs and, on rare occasions, couscous and meat.[33]

Across the traditional and national divide the French communities became a source of second-hand pickings and garbage scouring by the mass of dispossessed Algerians. As expected in a colonial situation, those French laborers who found their way to the colony earned wages well above those paid to the colonized, creating in effect a "dual-wage" system conforming to the conventional French perspective on Algerians—a people "less than the lowest French citizen."[34]

Importantly, the available emigrant population was largely determined by the needs of the *colons* for cheap and abundant labor. Consequently, in order to limit regional migration, drastic legal measures were instituted to enforce a system for controlling migration from immediate regions. Former nomadic peasants who served as sharecroppers and harvest hands, and who found themselves in desperate straits, were systematically denied migration and virtually indentured to the *colons*. However, people from the rough highlands escaped such restrictions and were granted permission to leave the immediate area and carry on their traditional trading migrations. In short, the imperative of local labor needs restricted the exit of large numbers of Algerians but offered the French recruiters operating in behalf of the homeland's manufactures access to highland folk during the initial phase of migration. In the later post–World War II phase, the lowlanders would seek escape on a truly massive scale.

In marked similarity to the Indian and Mexican cases, railroads were a means of importing French manufactured goods and exporting raw materials to France. In mining regions such as Bone, the construction of ports and railroads was undertaken more for the export of "minerals than for the transport of people." Among the minerals mined were iron, copper, and phosphates. Throughout the colonial period, manufactured goods from abroad were the mainstay of the marketplace. As one French historian observes:

> The most ordinary piece of sheet metal, the smallest pair of tongs, the most ordinary ball of thread, the smallest nail, the thinnest candle all come from abroad.... Algerian exports are characterized by the over-whelming preponderance of raw materials which constitute 96 percent of its exports in value.[35]

More than land theft deprived peasants of an independent livelihood. French factory-produced goods forced local producers, particularly those devoted to long-distance trading, to compete with French goods—with critical consequences. Parallel to the situation in Mexico and India, French imported manufactures took its toll on Algerian artisanal production.

As is the case in every imperialistic endeavor, the debasement of all things related to the colonized—in this case, the Algerians—was embedded within the colonizer's cultural outlook. Largely in order to legitimize the colonization as well as the use of the colonized as cheap labor, French imperialists depicted Algerians as backward and ignorant children requiring the intervention of a Western civilizing agent. With the proper upbringing—that is, French acculturation—Algerians could very well "assume the full political rights of an adult."[36] From the Algerians as they currently existed, little was to be expected.

The Colonial Heartland and the Demand for Labor

In each case of imperialism discussed here, the colonized peoples served as cheap labor in their respective homelands and within the colonial nation itself or areas controlled by it. Indians were chosen to supplant freed slaves in the Caribbean islands colonized by Britain and for eighty years provided an annual supply of fresh recruits to serve as indentured labor. In this section we consider the laborers transported to British Guiana and Trinidad. In the example of Mexico, desperately poor dirt farmers working on minifundias, as sharecroppers, or under other labor arrangements responded eagerly to the call for recruits to serve as temporary agricultural laborers across the United States. One program that paralleled the British indentured program was the bracero program, which brought 450,000 workers from 1942 to 1964 to work primarily in agriculture (in what was known colloquially as "stoop labor") and, to a lesser extent, in railroads. In the case of Algeria, early immigrants—that is, those leaving at the start of World War I—were either recruited as indentured contract workers through government auspices, recruited by paid agents of industries, or motivated by "social networks" that traveled on their own. Algerians who were drafted into the French army and served in France also provided an impetus for others to follow their footsteps.

Mexican Indentured Labor Migration

The First Indentured Labor Program, 1917–1921. The very first contract-labor program directed at Mexican labor was enacted in 1909, functioning only briefly; although little information has materialized regarding that operation, it presaged what was to come in the future.[37] Before a decade had passed, agricultural interests returned to what would become a favorite theme—namely, importing temporary contract labor. Shortly after the United States passed an immigration act in February 1917 that severely limited Mexican migration (by imposing, among other things, a literacy requirement), Southwestern agribusiness interests lobbied successfully to have the restrictions lifted. Supposedly a wartime labor shortage required an increase of laborers, and Mexican men were selected to fill the void. Cotton and sugar beet growers lobbied to have the legislation waived until the "wartime shortage" could be solved. The U.S. government complied on the basis of authority to allow "temporary admission" of "inadmissible aliens."[38] On a strictly unilateral basis, the United States administered a labor importation program that was designed to benefit agricultural interests and, later, extended to a wide number of economic branches. As with the subsequent bracero program, clear protections and standards were to be observed. According to the U.S. Labor Department, employers were obliged to rigorously abide by existing wage levels and housing standards in areas where contract workers were to be employed.

On the other hand, contracted workers were obligated to work only for a designated employer; if they quit in order to work for another employer, they faced apprehension, arrest, and deportation. In order to ensure compliance, the Labor Department included in the contract a "wage withholding scheme" that required employers to withhold 20 percent of each worker's wages for the first two months, 15 percent for the next two, and 10 percent for the final two months. The workers were to receive the withheld wages only upon their return to Mexico. (Later, the withholding amount was fixed at $100.) Nevertheless, an estimated 21,400 men broke their contracts and settled, largely unnoticed, into the existing Mexican immigrant community.

By 1918 contracted workers were allowed to labor in mining, railroads, and construction work as well as agriculture. The program was publicly presented as a response to wartime labor shortages, yet the war's end did not terminate the program. Notwithstanding the previous arguments for initiating the program, agricultural interests once again, in 1919, lobbied successfully to extend the program; in 1921 it was extended for the final time. No fewer than 81,000 men were imported under the program, but the Arizona Cotton Growers' Association reaped the largest benefits when it contracted more than 30,000 Mexican workers. However, the program not only guaranteed sufficient labor but provided excess labor such that wage levels nosedived across the board, raising profit levels.

Over the course of the program the U.S. government "tried to do all it could to provide employers with temporarily admitted workers." Immigration officials' reports found that little control was being exercised over employers who purportedly respected federal guidelines "very lightly." The program proved a boon to employers who, it was said, "were burdened with few responsibilities" while utilizing a formidable supply of cheap and easily disposable labor.[39] The Arizona Cotton Grower's Association was certainly not alone when it reported substantial benefits from the temporary labor program, which saved the Association "$28 million in picking costs." As for the indentured laborers, as soon as jobs became scarce "many found themselves stranded without funds" and consequently were ordered deported.[40]

The Second Indentured Labor Program, 1942–1964. Braceros entered into a labor system that had become firmly implanted in the corporate agriculture. For generations, seasonal harvest labor composed largely of migrant workers from distinct nationalities filled agribusiness's needs.

A tradition evolved over the previous fifty years that differentiated the alleged qualities of the various ethnic groups—Filipinos, Blacks, Whites, and Mexicans—regarding types of labor suitable for each group. Subjected to pitiful wages, farm workers were the most exploited labor force in the United States. Braceros fit the ideal type previously reserved for Mexicans, in that they were dependable, efficient, cheap, and well suited for "stoop labor." In California, where one-half of all braceros were assigned, the men worked in several agricultural regions, including tomatoes, lettuce, citrus, cotton, sugar beets, and cantaloupes. Here they comprised 95 percent of the harvesters of tomatoes; 90 percent, lettuce; and 80 percent, citrus.[41] As harvesters of the melon crop in Yuma, Arizona, braceros formed 95 percent of the workforce; they also comprised 75 percent of Michigan's pickle cucumber harvesters and 90 percent of New Mexico's cotton pickers.[42]

Braceros commonly worked under miserable conditions, and protections such as health benefits, housing standards, and wages guaranteed to braceros under the terms of the agreement were generally ignored. Braceros were regimented in barracks and other quarters housing several thousand men; these overcrowded, squalid, and segregated camps were kept hidden from the outside world. Critics were quick to point out the nature of many of these camps in California. Ted Le Berthon, for example, wrote:

> While in a sense the imported braceros are an invading army, their status more clearly resembles that of prisoners of war. In the camps and fields, lest any run away, there are armed guards. Theoretically, these Mexican nationals have certain, not inconsiderable rights. In practice they have few.[43]

Another vocal critic and astute student of the program, Ernesto Galarza, bitterly condemned bracero housing, which he described as "far below the legal standard."[44] And as Berthon further reported after a summer 1957 visit to a bracero camp:

> Twelve hundred and twenty Mexican men had eaten and washed up after picking tomatoes for twelve hours, much of the time in the broiling sun. These imported braceros looked tired, perhaps too tired to talk. For they were quiet as deaf mutes as they sprawled on the ground outside a row of raw, ugly, oblong barracks, covered over with

blistered and peeling tarpaper, in which they would sleep.... [M]ost were homesick.[45]

Bracero wages varied from the legal minimum to below minimum; but whatever the amount, it was determined arbitrarily by collaborative grower decisions. Again, Galarza's fieldwork indicted the program: "[A]s far as wages are concerned, the protection afforded to the Mexican National [bracero] on paper adds up to weak guarantees in practice." Many men earned a pittance and not a few returned to Mexico penniless, and in some cases, men actually owed their employers at the end of the contract.[46] For the first seven years of the program, as a means of ensuring that the men would return to Mexico at the end of the contract, 10 percent of their wages was placed into a special bank account accessible upon their return. However, the majority of men never recovered their deducted wages, the disappearance of which has never been brought to light; undoubtedly the funds disappeared into the pockets of authorities managing the program.

Ample evidence demonstrates conclusively that under the terms of the bracero agreements, bracero labor was identical in many respects to traditional forms of colonial labor exploitation, in that the braceros were systematically controlled and denied the right to organize, to bargain over wages individually or collectively, to protest, and to change residence or employer. If a worker chafed at his workload or wages he ran the risk of being returned to Mexico—in which case he was blacklisted. In practice, agricultural corporations were given a free hand to manage their braceros as they saw fit and to disregard the formal agreements, which supposedly governed the rights of bracero laborers. Although Mexican consuls were given the charge of investigating bracero grievances and ensuring that the protections were observed, in practice they did very little. One sociologist researching the bracero program in 1958 wrote: "In the past year and a half I have observed every major rule touching upon the bracero program widely—sometimes systematically—violated."[47] In short, managers dealt with their bracero labor as they pleased, as one bracero testified in 1958:

We had a foreman ... who did not pay us for all the hours we worked. Our wages were short. I asked him about it. He said if I gave him some money, he would check on it. I gave him all the money I had, which was $3.80. He went away, saying he would find out what the trouble was. I never saw my money again, and I never found out why we had been getting short wages.[48]

A bracero working in cotton described another typical management policy: "When we complain ... we are told that if we don't like it here we can go back home. Several of the men have gone back home ... because they are robbed of pounds when they weigh [cotton] in." Growers were reluctant to hire "slackers." To ensure that only dependable labor was hired, a six-week contract was instituted so that managers could evaluate the braceros as they labored, repatriating the unreliable—the "complainers"—after six weeks (or sooner, if possible) and keeping the rest.[49]

The earnings of the majority, who worked an average of three months per contract, amounted to very little. One study of 398 braceros randomly selected in California showed that each earned an average of $14.77 a week, or $2.11 per day.[50] From this amount he sent his family a remittance, paid back loans, and bought supplies to meet his daily needs. These practices prompted Henry Anderson, who studied the bracero program under a National Institute of Health grant in 1958 (see Chapter 6), to describe the program as a system of "exploitation more heartless than chattel slavery."[51] His charge was not an exaggeration.

Despite controlled wages, braceros were able to send $30 million in the form of remittances in 1954, said to be "the largest source of income to Mexico after mining and tourists."[52] That figure at first blush appears impressive, but it averaged out to only about $73 per bracero. Consequently, remittances never led to economic development or social change in the sending villages, and rarely benefited the men involved; in all probability the money filled the pockets of lenders (and thus, indirectly, of bribe takers). In a few cases, remittances did enable poverty-stricken farming families to purchase food and clothing or repair a house; for the rare lucky ones, perhaps the money led to the purchase of a small plot of land, a tool, or a work animal.[53] But on the whole, by exporting its best laboring men to work as "stoop labor" for the benefit of agricultural giants across the border, Mexico neither ended its poverty nor diminished its extent.

Not surprisingly, the domestic agricultural labor supply, composed mainly of Mexican immigrants, was forced to compete with the work conditions and wages accorded to braceros and was gradually eliminated from the agricultural labor market. Studies demonstrate conclusively that the "native inter-state migrant, about whose peripatetic misery a copious and sympathetic literature had accumulated, was close to extinction."[54] In the citrus region (citrus being a main agricultural product, second only to oil production in California), growers informed their field bosses not to hire from the local labor supply if braceros were available. Often, however, growers simply let a weighted "supply and demand" model work for them, as this domestic citrus picker testified in 1957:

> [N]ow you won't find more than a handful of local fellows still working in the lemons. You want to know why? I'll tell you one of the biggest reasons: these poor Nationals [braceros] ... [t]hey'll go in there, no matter what the orchard looks like. They won't say a word. They think they're lucky to get it.[55]

Braceros thus served to replace rather than to shore up the existing agricultural labor supply. Hence they traversed the same migratory path as that taken by the first wave of Mexican migrants who, between 1910 and 1930, were recruited across an open border, moved into agriculture, and, in doing so, supplanted the Chinese and Japanese labor supply.[56] Now it was the braceros' turn; but this time, indentured Mexican immigrants competed with the ethnic Mexican laborers and virtually drove them out of agriculture. But such was not the fault of the braceros per se; rather, it was the consequence of a federal labor policy instituted at the pleasure of agricultural giants.

However, the end of the bracero program merely changed the form of Mexican labor migration. No sooner did bracero recruitment cease in 1964 than the migration of "illegals" began on a large scale. Agribusiness adjusted to the "New Deal," which it could not refuse, and incorporated illegals into its labor force on a large scale so that by the 1980s undocumented workers comprised at least one-half of all farm labor in the American Southwest. Not surprisingly, Mexicans of all legal categories and ages made up 90 percent of the agricultural laborers in the Southwest. Indeed, Mexican immigrant labor, whether bracero, legal, or illegal, supplied key sectors of the American economy—particularly the service, agriculture, and construction industries—with a virtually inexhaustible supply of reliable, efficient, and easily replaced workers laboring for pitiful wages that guarantee poverty.[57] The communities that immigrants formed were far from the "American Dream." The observations that celebrated novelist Hart Stillwell recorded in 1950 certainly applied when the bracero program was terminated. As he pointed out, agricultural worker communities comprised a "foreign population living under conditions which simply cannot be reconciled with any American concept of the barest minimum of a decent standard of living."[58]

The fates of braceros and of illegal and legal Mexican immigrants have intertwined in the larger history of the ethnic Mexican community. Since the end of the bracero program, Mexico has undergone economic stagnation; more recently, "free trade" policies have uprooted small farmers and ranchers from slowly dying villages and placed them on the migratory path. An accessible pool of cheap labor for U.S. corporate capital has indeed emerged from imperialist policy, replicating the experiences of Algerians and Indians during their respective colonial eras.

Indian Indentured Laborers

Although Mexican and Indian migrants underwent similar experiences, one distinction needs mention: Indian women and men served as indentured laborers. Representatives of industries based within the respective dominant powers heavily recruited both nationalities. Initially, industries developed by the dominant power stimulated an internal migration; later, recruiters working for the colonial power coordinated emigration. The case of Indian migration as indentured labor is particularly evocative of the Mexican experience with bracero labor. Both labor programs responded to a need within the dominant power to supplant an existing labor supply that had become undependable and even rebellious, thereby solving a serious labor problem.

Nearly 430,000 people were transported to the British West Indies, in ships holding 400 to 800 passengers each, under the terms of a five-year indenture to replace former slaves who after manumission refused plantation work, fled to surrounding regions as free wage labor, and became "unreliable" and "undependable" workers. As Walter Rodney points out, former slaves learned the art of politics reflected in "protracted sugar strikes in 1842 and 1848, which strengthened the determination of planters to secure immigrant laborers whose conditions of indentured service excluded the right to seek out new employers and whose wage rates were also statutorily restricted."[59] The overall goal was to seek an easily controlled labor force that would take the place of freed slaves who had turned to farming, who numbered 17,500 in Trinidad and 70,000 in Guiana. As Eric Williams concludes, Indian migration "led to the introduction of an entirely new population in Trinidad, *which converted* the island from a society of small farmers into a typical plantation society."[60] Indenture freed planters from relying on the labor of former slaves and provided an inexhaustible supply of cheap, dependable labor.

Beginning in the late 1830s, licensed recruiters working directly for colonial administrators, but indirectly for the plantation owners, plied their trade at various places in India (Calcutta, Madras, and Bombay were principal centers). Often an officially licensed recruiter would assemble a team of recruiters to comb through the streets of villages. In 1912 an opponent of the indentured system described the method used to recruit indentured laborers for passage to the Caribbean:

> [T]he victims of the system—I can call them by no other name—are generally simple, ignorant, illiterate, resourceless people belonging to the poorest classes of this country and ... they are induced to enter ... [—]entrapped into entering—into these agreements by the un-scrupulous representations of wily recruiters, who are paid so much per head for the labour they supply and whose interest in them ceases the moment they are handed to the emigration agents.... [A] system so wholly opposed to modern sentiments of justice and humanity is a grave blot on the civilization of any country that tolerates it.[61]

In order to enter into a contract, prospective recruits needed permission to emigrate from local authorities. Once permission was secured, they were then able to sign a contract. An obligatory inspection at the recruiter's office rounded out the process. Hugh Tinker captures the evaluation process of the aspirant "once in the Emigration Agent's net":

> He was supposed to check their muscles, and to inspect their hands for evidence of manual toil. But the agent needed to fill his ship, and if the vessel were delayed demurrage fees must be paid, so nobody looked too closely at the hands of the itinerant musician or the barber who was cozened to going overseas.[62]

One witness who testified in a proceeding investigating Indian emigration stated that he did "believe the present recruiters in

India care twopence whether the men are good men for agriculture or not so long as the get their commission."[63] Nonetheless, planters demanded and received the specific kind of labor that more than filled the need.

Between 1851 and 1917 a total of 238,909 Indians were indentured to Guiana, whereas 143,939 sailed to Trinidad during the seventy-year span of the program (most were transported after 1870).[64] In marked contrast to the migrations from Mexico and Algeria, not just men but also women and even children were recruited to migrate, although women were limited to about 30 percent of the total. As Madhavi Kale points out, aside from their ability to labor, women served "as symbols of legitimacy and authority ... of the bourgeois-colonial state and its nationalist challengers" by making the system appear to satisfy the anti–slave reformers' concerns for the "moral and material welfare of Indian indentured migrants."[65] Accordingly, planners of the indentured system thought that women would "do the cooking and the washing—for Indian males."[66] Kale quotes a witness at a hearing on indentured labor held in 1910 who assessed the role of women:

> A great many of them [women] don't work, but all the sensible planters as a rule told me that they did not care whether the women worked or not. The great idea was that the presence of the women kept the men more contented and they did not force them to work. If they did not care to work they left them alone.... [T]hey are very ambitious, but they are not forced to work.

Women were generally allotted chores that had been limited to men deemed "weaker," while boys and girls were assigned the "less arduous" planting and harvesting tasks. Nevertheless, for all practical purposes, indentured laborers were generally understood to be males; women and children were there "due to the planters' need for a resident labouring community, with a settled population."[67] Moreover, to foster a resident labor pool in the face of a sparse colony population, Indian men and women were encouraged by bonuses to marry "within the first three or four years of the contract," thus resolving the long-term need for a permanent plantation labor supply.[68] Of course, a resident labor force was secured by other practices as well; even as contracts expired, indebtedness to the planters obliged many newly released indentured workers to remain, under the terms set by the planters.[69] In addition, if the indentured individuals returned to India upon termination of the five-year contract, they had to pay the return fare. If they re-signed for another five years, however, their passage was guaranteed at the planters' expense—an enticement that must have kept more than a few in the plantation work force, creating awkward distinctions within the indentured force.

Indentured laborers, belittled by the racially prejudiced and colonially legitimized term "coolie," worked toward one principal goal established by their overseers: to handle the same functions formerly performed by slaves under nearly identical conditions. The two systems, slavery and indenture, may at first glance appear unrelated; but in practice they were quite similar, in that "the slave system laid the foundations upon which the coolie system was later erected."[70] Indentured labor kept the traditional plantation system securely in place, in more ways than one. Not mentioned in the contract were local provisions that obligated indentured workers to observe the terms of the contract under threat of imprisonment, which paralleled the system of slave control. The indentured workers were required to carry an identification card issued at the time they signed their contracts and were obligated to present it when asked by overseers or constables. If they wished to venture beyond the confines of the plantation, they required permission from the administrator or overseer. Absences from work or charges of misbehaving—for example, by leaving the work site or housing without permission, skipping off to another plantation, or, worst of all, organizing workers to rebel—were grounds for punishment and even imprisonment. Planters, however, rarely received anything other than fines for contract violations, although such violations occurred often and were rarely brought to justice.[71]

The contract carefully outlined such terms as guaranteed wages, free and adequate housing, medical care, and other protections—all of which were generally ignored. Contracted workers were covered by the Masters and Servants Ordinance of 1846, which supposedly protected indentured laborers. However, as Kusha Haraksingh confirms: "Minimum wage provisions were rendered largely ineffective in practice.... Short payment and worse—the complete withholding of wages[—] ... were frequently encountered." Haraksingh further describes how wages found their way into the pockets of others, by the use of chits redeemable at a company store and local shops: "Overseers and shopkeepers sometimes colluded to deduct money at the pay table from the wages of customers to satisfy shop accounts.

Deductions were also made to set off the expense of work-place accidents." But perhaps the most-used system of "recovering wages was
the imposition of fines for small offenses in the adjudication of which
the employer was both complainant and judge."[72] The system worked
nearly perfectly to satisfy the interests of the plantation owner to
keep production costs at a minimum, particularly during periods of
economic depression. Ultimately, the reliance on indentured laborers
not only secured a low-cost, easily controlled, and effective workforce
but also ensured secondary benefits when, upon termination of the
contract, the majority chose to remain and in so doing tied themselves
once again to the plantation workforce.

As a contract term expired and an indentured worker became a
"free" wage laborer, working conditions and wages were determined
by the price paid to incoming indentured workers. Thus, for those
whose indenture expired, their place in the economy and society
varied little from their experiences as indentured laborers. In the
early years of the program, indenture made "the former slaves more
tractable by reducing their bargaining power."[73] As the program
matured, the indentured laborers made those formerly indentured
"more tractable by reducing their bargaining power." Consequently,
as the indentured laborers fulfilled their contracts and settled into
communities, their identification as "coolies" remained, thus "le-
gitimizing" their second-class status and confinement at the lower
levels of the occupational hierarchy. The nonindentured wages and
working conditions anchored to those of the indentured laborers,
the lowest paid of all workers. Indenture, then, proved more than a
legal contract; it became an integral component of the cultural and
economic practices of the society.

Algeria

Algerian migration occurred in two main periods, the first lasting from
roughly 1905 to 1929 and the second from 1946 to the 1970s. The
Great Depression and World War II divided the two migration streams.
The first waves of emigrants came largely but not entirely from the
highland Berber region and were overwhelmingly men. However, in
the post–World War II period and up until independence, the people
leaving were largely families from the impoverished and dispossessed
Arab population. Previously, Arabs had been denied permission to

emigrate by the local *colons,* who depended on the Arab labor supply. In both migratory periods, the conditions bred by imperialism fostered the emigration.

Before the first wave appeared, highland Berber traders plied their handicrafts in the coastal regions of France; however, their numbers were not significant and they were not strictly speaking immigrants. Soldiers drafted and recruited into the French army in response to the rising tensions of World War I comprised the next group to enter France. During the course of the war 83,000 conscripted and 87,000 volunteer soldiers served in France. There, special policies pertaining to the Algerian military presaged the treatment of those who later migrated to labor either as indentured workers or as free immigrants recruited to work. Algerian soldiers, for example, wore easily identified special uniforms, lived in separate quarters, and were routinely assigned lesser tasks; moreover, French female nurses were removed from military hospitals treating Algerians lest perverse romantic relationships occur. Taken together, these French policies served to segregate Algerian soldiers "as far as possible" from the French.[74] Interestingly, a segment of the French army itself was treated as a separate entity, untrustworthy and ridiculed.

However, wartime labor needs quickly mounted and Algerians stepped into the breech, but not altogether voluntarily. In 1914 French policy legalized an "open border" that allowed 20,000 male workers to enter France, but restrictions were reimposed the following year and immigration was placed under a central administrative unit charged to supervise a controlled Algerian migration. The latter unit successfully centralized the regulation of migration by regularly assessing public and private labor requirements and organizing and supervising recruitment in Algerian villages and towns. Immediately, recruiters arrived to stress the "golden opportunities" that awaited the potential migrant. Exaggerations flowed freely, impressing men, and only men, with the assured benefits of emigration. An anonymous novelist recreated the recruiters' siren call: "[T]he orator would promise amusements, women, lights, promenades, something to satisfy all the appetites."[75] An estimated 120,000 men answered the call by 1918.[76]

In transit while in Algeria, the men were placed in "collection centres" and organized into military-like "labor units." As they alighted at Marseilles, they were housed in "a huge camp of wooden barracks, given medical inspections, photographed for identity cards, and organized into work detachments." Each brigade, composed of several hundred men, was then transported to various work sites (primarily those related to war industries in France) to labor in unskilled occupations. In terms of wages, the returns were negligible. Horrendous conditions led to an unusually high death rate among the men. Typical of such conditions were those at the Sete sawmill, where nearly a thousand men "lived in sheds ... which were without floors, water supply, toilets or cantines." Controls over the men extended from their communities to the workplace. If men refused any assigned task or job, they risked a military tribunal.[77] The quarters were policed by agents hired because of their experience as *colons* and, hence, expected to know the "ways" of the Algerians; as Neil MacMaster has shown, they "reproduced the 'native management' techniques" used in the colony.[78] As in the case of the Algerian soldiers, the military-like labor organization served to segregate Algerians from the general working-class population of which they had become a part.

Not surprisingly, as with the Mexican braceros, thousands of men "jumped their contracts" and surreptitiously entered into society armed with forged papers. These men joined with the nonindentured Algerian workers who had entered before the wartime recruiting and lived in dense settlements of apartments and boarding houses rented at "exorbitant rates" near their work sites. The community of Algerian workers, regardless of their location in France, became "an excluded and essentially masculine population."[79] These settlements would serve as centers for future migrants who would arrive in the 1920s and, later, in the post–World War II period.

Like the bracero migrants, the indentured Algerians did not form permanent settlements at the end of the war; instead, they were rounded up and returned to Algeria. Nonetheless, approximately 4,000 Algerian workers illegally blended in with their fellow Algerians. Shortly after the end of the hostilities, the barriers to Algerian migration were removed, the immigration gates were opened, and a surge in free migration began. A significant transition occurred in that Arab nomadic peoples accompanied the highland Berbers in the migration stream. As stated above, the Arabs underwent extreme economic assaults, resulting in the "disintegration of the pre-colonial social structures." In his work on Algerian migration, Neil MacMaster writes: "Most emigrants came from rural societies in which a shortage of land, heavy taxes, low wages, debt and massive unemployment or underemployment meant that most peasants were living in abject poverty."[80] Deprived of land upon which to eke out a living, and forced to become a source of labor for the *colons,* the Arabs began to uproot on a much larger scale than ever before. In addition to the classic consequences of colonialism, a major famine affected wide swaths of the lowland countryside in the postwar era, rapidly increasing the number of Arabs seeking to resolve their immediate condition through migration.

In 1920 a mere 22,000 workers migrated, but by 1924 that number had risen to 71,000. We should recognize that migration to France was a costly affair and that the poverty-stricken Arabs found the expense overwhelming. The postwar migrant was largely on his own, each paying his way through the bureaucratic process; first he needed to travel to the immediate provincial processing centers, then he had to get to the port, and finally he needed to pay for passage to France. As with the Mexican braceros and the Indian indentured workers, borrowing became one means of raising funds. Selling land or an animal in order to borrow from a "village usurer" became another means.[81] Migrants traveled by ship and were relegated to accommodations at the lowest level, segregated from the other passengers. As the ship unloaded, the Algerians alighted last. One migrant captured the fate experienced by thousands: "On disembarkation the humiliations began," he said. "[T]he 'superior' race got off first; as for us, the 'inferior' race, we were kept back until the customs officers and police had searched us in a revolting manner."[82] Industrial agents recruited men as they landed at Marseilles, and those who signed on were quickly routed to their employment site. Many sought their way to an Arab quarter, and still others were directed to a remotely located "Reception Center" for Algerians composed of filthy barracks once used for military purposes.[83]

As the migrants arrived they settled into communities populated by Algerian men who more or less understood the "system" in which they now lived. Once a sizable number of Algerians were employed in a particular industry, they served informally and, at times, formally as recruiters and encouraged the migration of relatives and village acquaintances. Their letters to relatives and friends motivated new migrants. And when these new migrants returned for a temporary visit with exaggerated stories of the metropolis and bags filled with new clothes, new recruits came forward. Companies realized this multiplied valuation of their Algerian labor: Their most "trusted workers ... were dispatched to their home area" to persuade others to migrate. Likewise, Algerian workers served as an informal network that drew workers when work was available.[84]

However, the experiences of the Algerian emigrants in France were hardly idyllic, nearly duplicating those of indentured workers. They lived in bleak shack towns derisively labeled *bidonvilles,* composed of overcrowded, sparsely furnished barracks, dormitories, and hostels. And nearly all Algerians labored in unskilled occupations, the worst jobs available in which industrial accidents and diseases was commonplace. With the war's end, one task available to Algerians (because the French refused to do it) was to clear the land of live ammunition, including unexploded shells discarded after the war. A well-known practice among employers was to pay Algerians less for the same work allotted to French workers (i.e., the dual wage)—as we have seen, a fate experienced on a wide scale by Mexican and Indian laborers as well.

During periods of economic upturn Algerians were eagerly recruited and readily available; during downturns Algerians were easily removed from their jobs and barriers to migration were raised. And so when the Depression hit, many Algerians became targets of harassment and were rounded up (illegally, given the rights of the Algerians as French subjects) and sent home. Migration practically came to an end. As one migrant recounted, "Here in France they throw you away like dross.... [A]n Algerian is like a lemon: they squeeze it, to take the juice, leaving the skin, which counts for nothing. Go back home now that you are buggered."[85] By the end of the Depression an estimated 130,000 Algerian men were living in France, very disproportionately affected by unemployment. Even after having worked in France for decades, the typical Algerian remained a temporary migrant worker, an Algerian villager at heart. For him, France was never home but, rather, a place to work and support his family with what little remittances he could muster.

Meanwhile, despite the Depression the population of Algeria increased significantly, from 5.5 million in 1931 to 7.6 million in 1948. Economic conditions had worsened, and migration had become a greater means of countering the continuing economic disintegration now impacted by overpopulation. With the breakdown of social and economic structures in most of the peasant areas, migration began to take on a distinct definition. Family migration (and by this is meant *extended* family migration), rather than male migration per se, made its appearance in the postwar period on a rather large scale.

In terms of occupations and living standards, little would change relative to the wartime migration; the die was cast. The unskilled work and commensurate wages relegated to Algerians remained. By the mid-1950s, 400,000 Algerian men were employed "in occupations deserted by the European workers ... or in the hardest, the dirtiest and the most dangerous tasks."[86] The *bidonvilles* expanded and living conditions worsened as families from the colony occupied the poverty-stricken zones on the outskirts of cities like Paris and Marseilles. Historian Gary P. Freeman sketched an image of the typical *bidonville,* where the "most reprehensible social conditions of any group of workers in Europe" could be found:

> Unable to secure adequate shelter at a price they could pay, the migrants, often with families, congregated in and around industrial centers, throwing up shanty towns built of tin cans and cardboard.... Here they lived in unbelievable squalor, without plumbing, heat or medical care.[87]

As Algerian migrants entered France their status as colonized subjects, as virtual indentured workers, limited them to economic, political, and social niches that adhered to them and shaped their relations with French society. Indeed, their status as colonized peoples defined them well beyond the colony. Public and private policy affecting all Algerians in France coordinated with colonial policy in Algeria and, as noted, paralleled the experiences of Indians and Mexicans.

Conclusion

In the preceding pages evidence has been presented to demonstrate that the general practice among academicians that equates Mexican migration with the European migrations of the nineteenth century ignores the far greater parallels between Mexican migration and colonial migrations. For nearly a century, commentators have argued that Mexican migration has been touted as nothing more than a variation of European migrations that are triggered by adverse conditions within the home country, and that the receiving country, the United

States, has been sounding a siren call, the "American Dream," that pulls people into its civilizing web. The present chapter presents an entirely distinct approach to understanding Mexican migration—in particular, the contract labor migration commonly referred to as the bracero program.

Instead of applying the "push-pull" model and its various versions, this chapter explains Mexican migration by acknowledging the United States as an imperialist power. After examining the economic relationship between the United States and Mexico, it concludes that this relationship is one of domination tantamount to colonialism. It also presents evidence demonstrating the parallels among three migratory streams: Mexican, Indian, and Algerian. In each case, foreign domination resulted in extreme economic and social transformations, which satisfied the interests of the foreign power but resulted in severe hardships and deprivation in the dominated region or nation. Also in each case, a traditional peasant economy and a centuries-old demography underwent drastic alterations caused by the measures applied by the colonial power. Perhaps the most important alteration was the widespread dispossession of the peasantry from communal subsistence farming plots. This mass uprooting, resulting in a reconfiguration of the demographic mapping, was followed by internal migration, new work patterns, and community redistribution and reconstruction. As foreign corporations gained a foothold and then proceeded to dominate a particular branch of the economy, the surplus population that had emerged from among native peoples deprived of subsistence lands become the source of labor and was recruited to the foreign-owned and -managed work sites.

At some point, the internal redistribution of the population assumed an "international" character as it became a source of cheap labor within the colony as well as within the colonial power itself. Emigration from the colony to the imperialist power became a tradition, albeit one sanctioned by the state and managed by it. One method utilized by each imperialist relationship under review was to construct a temporary worker program, an indentured labor program, managed by the respective states. In each case the labor programs were gendered. In India, the program recruited males and, to a lesser extent, women; in the cases of Algeria and Mexico only males were recruited for their contract labor program. However, outside of the contract system, women were involved in the migrations. Again, the evidence points to a large number of parallels. Workers were perceived as colonial subjects—as people in need of cultural reformation designed by the dominant power—and were treated as such. For Mexicans, Americanization was the prescription most highly recommended; for Algerians, French acculturation; and for Indians, Western ways. In each case, indenture was legitimized as a means of modernizing the "uncivilized."

In contradiction to the desire for cultural reformation, work conditions, housing, wages, and labor rights were far below minimal standards; indeed, the standards guaranteed by legislation or worker contracts, such as they were, were simply overlooked and in most cases consciously violated. Employers and state officials charged with oversight defined standards on the basis of whatever they considered appropriate at any given time. Moreover, workers were segregated near their place of employment and lived virtually separate lives. What Ernesto Galarza said of braceros could well have been said of Indians in Guiana or Algerians in France:

> Hundreds of Nationals [braceros] are parceled out in small groups, ranging from two or three up to 15 and 20. These men are installed in tents, barns, huts, and bungalows, and while they remain there they are practically lost to all the purposes of inspectors and regulation. Ranchers sometimes hire a single National or handyman. Living in a tent, a shed, or a garage this bracero will work out his contract, his relationship to the employer being more that of a ward to a patron than that to two equal contracting parties.[88]

It is not surprising that a student of Indian indenture, Hugh Tinker, titled his work *A New System of Slavery* while a student of bracero labor described the program as a "captive labor system"; another described Algerian labor migrations as "an aspect of colonial policy." Each interpretation applies to the three cases of migration examined here. Perhaps the main difference among them is that the indentured system has continued to this day in the United States under the federally supervised H2-A. Known colloquially as the "guest worker" program for importing labor from Mexico, the Caribbean, and Central America, H2-A annually brings approximately 43,000 workers into the United States. Research undertaken in 1999 by the Carnegie Foundation found that forms of labor control similar to the bracero program are institutionalized within the H2-A. The Carnegie study reported that "[blacklisting] of H2 workers appears to be widespread, is highly organized, and occurs at all stages of the recruitment and employment process. Workers report that the period of blacklisting now lasts three years, up from one year the previous decade." Other investigations found that H2 "[w]orkers pay their way to get off the blacklist."[89]

With the implementation of free-trade policies under the mantra of globalization and its particular manifestation, NAFTA, the "peaceful conquest" of Mexico, begun in the late 1880s, has continued into the twenty-first century. The erosion of small-scale farming caused by the "open door" for U.S. agricultural products and financial capital intensifies peasant uprooting and removal across Mexico today. Widespread village desertion, internal migration, and emigration that began in the late nineteenth century, ancillary to the economic expansionism into Mexico by large-scale capital, continues into the twenty-first century at levels never seen in the past. The bracero system still functions, albeit in altered form under the H2-A, and the Bush administration and the Democratic Party each discuss what kind of new bracero program, or "guest worker" program, should be instituted. Indenturing as many as 300,000 workers per year has been discussed in some quarters. Seemingly, little has changed.

Notes

1. James P. Smith, "Assimilation Across the Latino Generations," *American Economic Review,* vol. 93, no. 2 (May 2003): 315. The opening lines of the Immigration Policy Center study captures the methodology that the vast majority of students of U.S. immigration, particularly Latin American immigration, are applying: "Latinos experience substantial socioeconomic progress across generations compared to both their immigrant forefathers and native Anglos. But, this fact is lost in statistical portraits of the Latino population, which don't distinguish between the large number of newcomers and those who have been in the United States for generations. Advocates of restrictive immigration policies often use such aggregate statistics to make the dubious claim that Latinos are unable or unwilling to advance like the European immigrants a century ago." And later: "A question that arises repeatedly in the immigration debate is whether or not the children and grandchildren of modern-day immigrants from Latin American are moving up the socioeconomic ladder like the descendants of European immigrants who came to the United States in the late 19th and early 20th centuries" (Walter A. Ewing and Benjamin Johnson, "Immigrant Success or Stagnation? Confronting the Claim of Latino Non-Advancement," *Immigration Policy Brief* [October 2003]: 1). A nationally syndicated news columnist applied the conventional comparative template to conclude that "there is not much difference between the immigrants who crossed the Rio Grande to get here and those who had

come across the Atlantic" (Ruben Navarrette, Jr., "Latino Immigrants Have Done Just Fine in Pursuing Dreams," *Los Angeles Times,* May 28, 2003). A number of volumes describe the Mexican immigrant within the European model, including the following: Leo Chavez, *Covering Immigration: Popular Images and the Politics of the Nation,* Berkeley: University of California Press, 2001; Camille Guerin-Gonzalez, *Mexican Workers and American Dreams: Immigration, Repatriation and California Farm Labor, 1900–1939,* New Brunswick: Rutgers University Press, 1994; David Jacobsen, ed., *Immigration Reader: America in a Multidisciplinary Perspective,* Malden, Mass.: Blackwell Publishers, 1998; David M. Reimers, *Still the Golden Door: The Third World Comes to America,* New York: Columbia University Press, 1985; and David E. Hayes-Bautista, *La Nueva California: Latinos in the Golden State,* Berkeley: University of California Press, 2004.

2. Mario T. Garcia, *Mexican Americans: Leadership, Ideology, and Identity, 1930–1960,* New Haven: Yale University Press, 1989, p. 296. Liberal pundits have also joined the chorus praising Mexican migrants for searching for the "Dream." For example, the late associate editor of the *Los Angeles Times,* Frank del Olmo, wrote that Mexican immigration is a manifestation that "the American Dream is alive and well" and, furthermore, that "the nation is absorbing yet another people into its rich and re-markable mix." See his appropriately titled article "Mexicans Are Keeping the Dream Alive," *Los Angeles Times,* May 13, 2001.

3. Raul Fernandez and I explain in detail the relationship between Mexican migration to the United States and the economic domination exerted by the United States in *A Century of Chicano History: Empire, Nations and Migration,* New York: Routledge, 2004.

4. In the pages of the *Orange County Register* (California), Jay Bookman wrote, "The concept of America as world empire, so controversial as to be almost unsayable just a few months ago, is now close to conventional wisdom. The topic is featured regularly on the covers of national news-magazines, is discussed in popular books and is celebrated on some op-ed pages.... In fact, some of those who once shied from the word 'empire,' even as they advocated policies to that effect, now embrace the label with varying degrees of fervor" ("Now, Open Talk of Empire," *Orange County Register,* May 11, 2003). One more example will suffice to round out the evidence of a discourse on imperialism. In the *New York Times,* journalist Emily Eakin wrote, "Americans are used to being told—typically by resentful foreigners—that they are imperialists. But lately some of the nation's own eminent thinkers are embracing the idea. More astonishing, they are using the term with approval. From the isolationist right to the imperialist-bashing left, a growing number of experts are issuing stirring paeans to American empire" (Emily Eakin, "'It Takes an Empire' Say Several U.S. Thinkers," *New York Times,* April 2, 2003). Among the many political figures who have "outed" the United States as an imperialist power we find Max Boot, Henry Kissinger, William Rusher, Charles Krauthammer, and Ben Wattenberg.

5. See, for example, John Mason Hart, *Empire and Revolution: The Americans in Mexico Since the Civil War,* Berkeley: University of California Press, 2002; and my own work, *Culture of Empire: American Writers, Mexico and Mexican Immigrants, 1880–1930,* Austin: University of Texas Press, 2004.

6. Amy Kaplan, "'Left Alone with America': The Absence of Empire in the Study of American Culture," in Amy Kaplan and Donald Pease, eds., *Cultures of United States Imperialism,* Durham, N.C.: Duke University Press, 1993.

7. See Gonzalez and Fernandez, *A Century of Chicano History*.

8. The use of Algerians to serve French economic and political interests is a complex issue. For example, the French army drafted Algerians for military service during the First World War.

9. See chapters 6 and 7 of Robert Freeman Smith, *The United States and Revolutionary Nationalism in Mexico, 1916–1922*, Chicago: University of Chicago Press, 1972.

10. David Pletcher, *Rails, Mines and Progress: Seven American Promoters in Mexico, 1867–1911*, Ithaca, N.Y.: Cornell University Press, 1958, pp. 38, 79–80.

11. Hart, *Empire and Revolution*, pp. 177–179.

12. Moises Gonzalez Navarro, *Historia Moderna de Mexico: El Porfiriato*, vol. 4, Mexico City: Editorial Hermes, 1957, p. 25.

13. Michael Johns, *The City of Mexico in the Age of Diaz*, Austin: University of Texas Press, 1997, p. 64.

14. Hart, *Empire and Revolution*, p. 200.

15. "Mexican Labor and Foreign Capital," *The Independent*, vol. 112, no. 3869 (May 24, 1924), p. 275.

16. The work of Wallace Thompson repeats many a writer's assessment of Mexican culture. Indeed, Thompson was not a lone voice when in 1921 he wrote: "The depth of Mexico's ignorance, in childhood and in adulthood, in life and business, literally passes comprehension. The active, curious minds of the Indian youngsters grow quickly into sodden stupidity; the keen and vivid intelligences of the children of the middle and upper classes expend their growing forces in sensuality and plunge themselves and their country into debilitating excesses—because there is no training to give a life above the animals" (*Trading With Mexico*, New York: Dodd, Mead and Company, 1921, p. 129).

17. Johns, *The City of Mexico in the Age of Diaz*, p. 14.

18. Victor Clark, *Mexican Labor in the United States*, U.S. Department of Commerce and Labor, Bureau of Labor Bulletin no. 78 (Washington, D.C.: U.S. Government Printing Office, 1908), pp. 470–471.

19. Walton Look Lai, *Indentured Labor, Caribbean Sugar: Chinese and Indian Migrants to the British West Indies, 1838–1918*, Baltimore: Johns Hopkins University Press, 1993, pp. 20–21.

20. Ibid., p. 21.

21. Ibid., p. 22.

22. Quoted in Look Lai, *Indentured Labor*, p. 23.

23. Hugh Tinker, *A New System of Slavery: The Export of Indian Labor Overseas, 1830–1920*, London: Oxford University Press, 1974, p. 38.

24. Walter Rodney, *A History of the Guyanese Working People, 1881–1905*, Baltimore: University of Maryland Press, 1981, p. 26.

25. Mahfoud Bennoune, "Impact of Colonialism and Migration on an Algerian Peasant Community: A Study in Socioeconomic Change," Ph.D. dissertation, University of Michigan, 1976, p. 12.

26. David Prochaska, *Making Algeria French: Colonialism in Bone, 1870–1920*, Cambridge: Cambridge University Press, 1990, p. 73.

27. Eric Wolf, *Peasant Wars of the Twentieth Century*, New York: Harper and Row, 1969, p. 213.

28. On this issue, see Neil MacMaster, *Colonial Migrants and Racism: Algerians in France, 1900–1962,* London: Macmillan Press, 1997.

29. Bennoune, "Impact of Colonialism," p. 116.

30. Ibid.

31. Quoted in Bennoune, "Impact of Colonialism," p. 106.

32. Ibid., p. 142.

33. MacMaster, *Colonial Migrants and Racism,* p. 31.

34. By 1850 the dual-wage system was well entrenched in Algeria, as a colonial official reported at the time: "I have indicated what is more important and it is easy to judge the enormous difference in the sum to be paid for the employment of an Arab labourer in contradistinction to that offered to a French labourer.... It is sufficient to ensure that the price paid to the indigenous worker will not ordinarily exceed the fourth of that which we are obliged to give the European worker" (Mahfoud Bennoune "Impact of Colonialism," p. 106).

35. Quoted in David Prochaska, *Making Algeria French: Colonialism in Bone,* p. 97.

36. MacMaster, *Colonial Migrants and Racism,* p. 154.

37. Manuel Garcia y Griego, "The Importation of Mexican Contract Laborers to the United States, 1942–1964," in David G. Gutierrez, *Between Two Worlds: Mexican Immigrants in the United States,* Wilmington, Del.: Scholarly Books, 1996, p. 47.

38. Mark Reisler, *By the Sweat of Their Brow: Mexican Immigrant Labor in the United States, 1900–1940,* Westport, Conn.: Greenwood Press, 1976, p. 27.

39. Ibid., p. 39.

40. Cecilia Razovsky Davidson, "Mexican Laborers Imported into the United States," *Interpreter Releases,* vol. 20, no. 38 (October 18, 1943): 299.

41. Paul Garland Williamson, "Labor in the California Citrus Industry," M.A. thesis, University of California, 1947, p. 55.

42. "Fight Brews Over Mexican Worker Law," *Congressional Quarterly Weekly Report,* vol. 19 (March 31, 1961): 538.

43. Ted Le Berthon, "At the Prevailing Rate," *Commonweal,* vol. 67 (November 1, 1957): 123.

44. Ernesto Galarza, *Strangers in Our Fields,* Washington, D.C.: Joint United States–Mexico Trade Union Committee, 1956, p. 29.

45. Le Berthon, "At the Prevailing Rate," p. 122.

46. Galarza, *Strangers in Our Fields,* pp. 38–39.

47. Henry Anderson, "Social Justice and Foreign Contract Labor: A Statement of Opinion and Conscience," typed manuscript, Department of Special Collections, Stanford University Libraries, 1958, p. 3.

48. Henry Anderson, *Harvest of Loneliness: An Inquiry into a Social Problem,* Berkeley: Citizens for Farm Labor, 1964, p. 247.

49. One bracero had this to say: "I can read the contract and I know that several of the clauses are not observed.... We talk about the clauses among ourselves in the camp. But nobody would make a complaint for fear of being sent back to Mexico. When you are sent back, you are sent back in a hurry. They give you the notice in the morning, or maybe at noon, or when you get back from work. You tie up your bundle and they put you in the truck to go back to the Association" (Ernesto Galarza, *Strangers in Our Fields,* p. 66).

50. Anderson, *Harvest of Loneliness,* p. 247.

51. From the "Introduction" to Henry Anderson, *The Bracero Program in California,* New York: Arno Press, 1976, n.p.

52. "Manpower: Wetbacks in the Middle of a Border War," *Business Week* (October 24, 1953), p. 64.

53. Recent studies have shown that remittances only "tide over" people for short periods of time, rather than moving them vertically along the class order. On this issue, see Rafael Alarcon, "Nortenizacion: Self-Perpetuating Migration from a Mexican Town," in Jorge A. Bustamante, Clark W. Reynolds, and Raul A. Hinojosa Ojeda, eds., *U.S.–Mexico Relations: Labor Market Interdependence,* Stanford: University of Stanford Press, 1992, p. 305.

54. See, for example, Ernesto Galarza, *Merchants of Labor: The Mexican Bracero Story,* Charlotte: McNally and Loftin, 1964, pp. 94–95.

55. Anderson, *Harvest of Loneliness,* p. 245.

56. In the 1880s Chinese laborers were the targets of small farmers who opposed Chinese immigration because they were utilized by large farmers to compete with the smaller outfits. In the 1890s Japanese laborers initially supplanted the Chinese laborers and subsequently organized quasi-union organizations. By 1910, however, the Japanese were personae non grata, and Mexican immigrants were recruited on a large scale to replace them.

57. During periods of downturn such as the early 1920s and the 1930s Depression, Mexican immigrants (legals as well as illegals) were rounded up en masse and repatriated back to Mexico. In the 1930s, an estimated 450,000 were repatriated.

58. Hart Stillwell, "The Wetback Tide," *Common Ground,* vol. 9, no. 4 (Summer 1949): 7.

59. Rodney, *History of the Guyanese Working People,* p. 32.

60. Quoted in Madhavi Kale, *Fragments of Empire: Capital, Slavery, and Indian Indentured Labor in the British Caribbean,* Philadelphia: University of Pennsylvania Press, 1998. p. 60.

61. Quoted in Madhavi Kale, *Fragments of Empire,* p. 167.

62. Tinker, *A New System of Slavery,* p. 51.

63. Rodney, *History of the Guyanese Working People,* p. 28.

64. Ibid., p. 33.

65. Ibid.

66. Kale, *Fragments of Empire,* p. 171.

67. Patricia Mohammed, *Gender Negotiations Among Indians in Trinidad,* London: Palgrave, 2002, p. 103.

68. Ibid., pp. 96–97.

69. O. Neil Bolland, *The Politics of Labour in the British Caribbean: The Social Origins of Authoritarianism and Democracy in the Labour Movement,* Kingston, Jamaica: Ian Randle Publishers, 2001, p. 61.

70. Tinker, *A New System of Slavery,* p. 4.

71. Ibid., p. 106.

72. Kusha Haraksingh, "The Worker and the Wage in a Plantation Economy: Trinidad in the Nineteenth Century," in Mary Turner, *From Chattel Slaves to Wage Slaves: The Dynamics of Labour Bargaining in the Americas,* Kingston, Jamaica: Ian Randle Publishers, 1995, pp. 234–235.

73. Bolland, *The Politics of Labour,* p. 58.

74. MacMaster, *Colonial Migrants and Racism,* p. 61.

75. Ibid., p. 71.

76. Bennoune, "Impact of Colonialism," p. 204.

77. Ibid., p. 204.

78. MacMaster, *Colonial Migrants and Racism,* p. 63.

79. Ibid., p. 64.

80. Ibid., p. 69.

81. Bennoune, "Impact of Colonialism," p. 151.

82. MacMaster, *Colonial Migrants and Racism,* p. 74.

83. Ibid., p. 75.

84. U.S. railroads relied heavily upon Mexican workers in the first decades of the twentieth century and encouraged migrants to act as informal recruiters. This they did by supplying paper, envelopes, and stamps so that Mexican workers could write to relatives and friends urging them to come and work on the railroads.

85. MacMaster, *Colonial Migrants and Racism,* pp. 80–81.

86. Bennoune, "Impact of Colonialism," p. 206.

87. Alan P. Freeman, *Immigrant Labor and Racial Conflict in Industrial Societies: The French and British Experience, 1945–1975,* Princeton: Princeton University Press, 1979, p. 78.

88. Galarza, *Strangers in Our Fields,* p. 66.

89. "Unfair Advantage: Workers' Freedom of Association in the United States Under International Human Rights Standards," *Human Rights Watch* (August 2000), available online at http://www.hrw.org/reports/2000/uslabor/, p. 51.

Chapter 3

Recruiting, Processing, and Transporting Bracero Labor to the United States

Within a few years of the bracero program's inauguration a host of liberal critiques raised a long list of serious charges regarding the treatment of the braceros, including wholesale corruption, ramshackle and overcrowded housing, unsafe work conditions, wage cheating, unsafe transportation, nonexistent health protections, and few opportunities for recreation. Moreover, bracero labor undercut wages for domestic workers and, worse, sent them to the unemployment lines. Among the critics of the bracero program none stand out more than Ernesto Galarza, whose several works have exposed the program's multiple layers of cruel exploitation and oppression.[1] The glaring gap between the legal protections for braceros incorporated into the international agreement and the reality of a virtual *laissez faire* exploitative system has compelled progressive-minded people to criticize the program severely. Eventually, the program was terminated, but only after nearly a half-million men were transported to labor in the production of the United States' field crops, fruits, and vegetables—the most arduous and least compensated work available in the nation.

Since the vast majority of criticisms have focused on conditions within the United States,[2] the bracero program within Mexico—that is, the system of recruitment, processing, and transporting of men to the border—has attracted little attention by those discussing the bracero program and "guest worker" proposals. It is the contention of this study, however, that the bracero program's intensely exploitative and injurious nature was transnational in scope. Many adverse conditions associated with the bracero program within the United States also affected men in Mexico as they sought a bracero contract in recruiting centers established in Mexico. Unfortunately, the abusive treatment exposed by the critics of the bracero program overlooked similar and, in some instances, worse consequences affecting men in the process of becoming braceros in Mexico. It will be argued here that the bracero program, like all "guest worker" programs, are not merely national in scope and therefore need to be examined from a transnational perspective. Again, the analysis will maintain that the bracero program exemplified several basic characteristics of a colonial labor force derivative of U.S. economic domination over Mexico.

Recruiting Systems

The bracero system as defined by the international agreement left the responsibility for determining the numbers of braceros required for a harvest season to the individual grower or to associations of growers formed principally to coordinate requests. Generally the largest agricultural corporations determined the necessary labor force for a coming harvest season.[3] The bracero agreement stipulated that only when an imminent domestic labor shortage threatened production were growers enabled to submit requests to the central offices in Washington, D.C., for a specific number of workers (although it was well known that shortages seldom, if ever, existed; growers defined their needs without government oversight). Washington then informed authorities in Mexico City who then advised state and local officials to inform area residents of potential bracero employment channeling them into the recruitment pipeline. Mexican officials *and* American authorities managed the remainder of the recruitment process, which included evaluating and selecting the assembled candidates and securing the prescribed number of workers for shipment to the United States. Mexico's management of the initial phase in the recruiting process met the approval of agricultural corporate headquarters. In a 1963 article in the *California Farmer*, a semi-official journal for California's farming enterprises, great satisfaction was expressed for the work performed by the Mexican government:

> The Mexican government makes every effort to have men available when they are needed. According to the agreement between the two

countries, our government must give the Mexican Government 30 days' notice when requesting braceros. As a practical working measure, Mexico will supply braceros on two weeks' notice if necessary. In some cases, such as last summer when a sudden change in the weather ripened the California canning tomato crop overnight, workers have been supplied on one week's notice.[4]

On paper the system operated according to established bureaucratic guidelines, which were violated in wholesale fashion. U.S. officials forwarded requests to *Gobernacion,* roughly the Department of the Interior, which established a quota for particular states and informed the state governors. The governors assigned each municipio, village, and town a quota based on the *Gobernacion's* state allotment. The governors then relayed the message to municipio (county) authorities who informed the mayors of villages and towns. Rural farming districts were targeted with the expectation that the ideal laborer fitting the employers' requirements resided in these locales.

Those men choosing to become braceros then voluntarily stepped forward, at which point local authorities performed the first phase in the selection process and identified the men for the next step. Those approved for candidacy received a *permiso,* an official identification card verifying that the individual had served his military service and was a law-abiding citizen; as merely the very first legal requirement, this rendered him a bracero candidate and nothing more. After the village, municipio, or state quota was filled, no more IDs were assigned. Those gaining proper papers were responsible for their own transport to an assigned processing site.

Over the first three years of the bracero program, the Mexico City soccer stadium served as the initial processing center where recently arrived men from villages and towns, official IDs in hand, gathered with the hope to be called to enter into the examination process. (After Public Law 78 was ratified, several sites were selected across the northern interior of Mexico.) If the bracero hopefuls passed muster at the first processing center, they then traveled to the next center at the U.S.-Mexico border where the second selection process would take place. No one was guaranteed a work contract; in Mexico City 20 percent of those reporting were rejected, as were 7–10 percent of the men at the border reception stations.

This recruiting process may at first blush seem little more than an international technical entanglement resulting in the production of the required mass of laborers on short notice. In reality, however, it entailed much more than merely putting the word out for workers, rounding them up, and shepherding them to the border. Not only was the process corrupted systematically (more of this later), but it had much in common with colonial methods of organizing labor, particularly the Spanish colonial practice known as the *repartimiento*.[5] More than coincidence marked this parallel between the two labor systems.

For example, under the Spanish colonial system, Indian villagers were forced to fill a quota of male workers, and only males, to labor for a week or more at a time on a hacienda. In marked resemblance to the bracero program, Spanish aristocrats holding royal land grants had authority to utilize the labor of indigenous peoples. The colonials petitioned authorities for indigenous laborers living in subsistence agricultural villages for use as labor for a specific period of time. The requests would then be forwarded to an official responsible for administering the process, the *juez repartidor*, who set a quota for selected Indian villages to provide men to labor for the petitioning Spanish colonials. After the call was sent out, village men were selected by the *juez*, assembled in a central location, and then delegated to an assigned hacienda. The number of Indians allocated to the Spanish colonial depended on the request formally submitted.[6]

From the central location, men were gathered into groups to travel on foot to the assigned hacienda, often over very long distances without rest; many arrived exhausted and ill. The men had no choice as to which landed aristocrat they would work for, nor any control over wages, work conditions, housing, or work-period length (this last was fixed at one week or more). Moreover, the Spanish-feudal tributary system encouraged bribery and other forms of corruption that seldom favored the villagers. Each man was obligated to pay the *juez repartidor* a half-real for his fees! Once on the hacienda, the men were subjected to methods that had evolved for making them stay on the job and preventing them from engaging in rebellious activities. For example, work tools brought by the men were confiscated and returned only upon their completion of the work period. If men left the hacienda before finishing the assigned work period, they faced arrest and a whipping at the central market. In the final analysis, according to Thomas Gage, the men indentured through the *repartimiento* were virtual slaves for a set period of time and were frequently obligated to repeat the process.[7]

Obviously, not every facet of the *repartimiento* and the bracero program can be compared, but a number of practices and activities associated with both systems deserve more than passing mention. These important parallels can be summed up as follows: the announcing of required laborers requested by employers and the subsequent quotas assigned to each village; selection of the men (and only men) by government officials; allocation to an employer (amounting to an indenture), and travel over long distances to the work site; systematic control over the laborer during the work period; a nearly free hand given to the employer to manage the laborers; and widespread corruption. That the *repartimiento* required the men to labor while the bracero system simply asked for volunteers appears to be the main difference between the two systems.

The most critical similarity, University of California investigator Henry Anderson concluded (as did Thomas Gage when he personally observed the *repartimiento*), is that the bracero program was in some respects "worse than chattel slavery."[8] A Los Angeles Spanish language weekly, *El Angelino*, repeated the charge in a 1949 article on braceros under the headline "Esclavos Modernos" (Modern Slaves).[9] Let us now turn to a detailed examination of the bracero recruiting system as administered in Mexico, because it was here that this process of an indentured labor system "worse than slavery" began.

Prospective Braceros and *Permisos*

Once the village or town elders announced the labor opportunity that existed, a surplus of men generally appeared, eager to procure *el permiso*—the official document affirming that the holder was a citizen in good standing and gave the person the right to enter into the selection process. In some instances the *permisos* were handed out in a fair and honest fashion, such as occurred in one area of northwestern Zacatecas state. One hundred and forty men were selected on the basis of a lottery from nineteen farming villages.[10] However, the common practice differed greatly from that of northwest Zacatecas. The great poverty in the small-scale subsistence farming districts there, and images of a good wage (or any wage at all), prompted huge numbers of men to apply, many more than the quotas allowed. An oversupply of men and an undersupply of *permisos* stimulated a number of corrupt "cottage" industries, beginning with the selling of *permisos* at the village level.[11] Men opting to purchase their *permiso* needed money to pay the official, prompting locals—usually merchants with cash on hand—to lend to the eager candidates.

Studies reported that in 1955 no fewer than 75 percent of all braceros paid from 150 to 300 pesos for the initial papers, the much-hoped-for *permiso*, solicited from local authorities.[12] Most men held very little property to offer as collateral, perhaps only a small farming plot or work animal; but this they frequently did. These men then incurred a heavy debt in order to take the first step in becoming a bracero. But borrowed money, often lent at a usurious 5–10 percent per month, needed to cover more than just the purchase of initial papers. Once the required papers were secured, those men fortunate enough to hold them needed to find transport to the processing station. The amount borrowed was expected to cover the cost of travel to the processing center, food and board, and more documentation if necessary as the men waited to be called up into the reviewing center and, luck forthcoming, to receive a bracero contract. Still, there were no promises; the bracero candidates themselves incurred the costs of becoming a bracero.

From 1942 to 1945 the Mexico City soccer stadium served as the first processing point from which all those seeking a bracero contract would be chosen; subsequently, various sites around the nation served as the initial processing station. It was common during the recruiting season to see huge throngs of anxious men hoping to be called into the processing center. Literally thousands of men swarmed around the center, and not every job seeker would be accommodated. One day in 1943, 5,000 men crowded into the stadium but only 3,000 names were scheduled to be called.[13] In a book of his experiences as a bracero, published in 1948, Jesus Topete paints an evocative image of the processing center:

> In the streets, the sidewalks were insufficient for the numbers of aspirants who with a bag of clothes and a blanket on a shoulder, walked about in groups, hotly discussing the possibilities of leaving for the United States on such and such a date; and of the money coming from their distant village or ranch, in order to continue in the capitol, which for the majority was a "*via crucis.*"[14]

The "way of the cross" became the common metaphor used by braceros for describing the recruitment process and work experience—and for good reason. As one bracero recollected, "It is understood that there will be much *sufrimiento* [*sic*] when one ventures to come to the United States as a bracero."[15]

One visitor to the scene recounted that most "of the candidates were poor ... from remote villages and ranches expecting enrollment to take only a few hours."[16] Many simply had no notion of what to expect and took their chances to travel to the recruiting center without papers. Mr. Topete recalls "immense lines ... huge crowds of desperate men, struggling for a contract, which, for the aspirant, seemed something like a gateway to paradise."[17] After their names were called, the men stepped into long lines of four abreast around the recruiting offices, waiting for hours, sometimes days; here they slept and, in order not to lose their place, relieved themselves where they stood or nearby. Food stands sprouted, selling favorite fare to the often-underfed men, while merchants hawking water, drinks, and snacks walked up and down the lines. For those who waited in the formless crowd to be called into line, borrowed money slowly dwindled as the days became weeks; for many, a month or more passed without a call into the center. Even when their few pesos ran out, they stayed, and appeals for public charity became commonplace.[18] Soon the term "braceropolis" seemed perfectly suited for describing the stadium.

With so many strangers, a virtual army of uprooted peasants, arriving seemingly overnight in Mexico City, concerns over crime became a critical issue. Police patrolled the several thousands of men with far greater intensity than was the case with the general population. Armed with truncheons, pistols, rifles and, as a precaution, tear-gas grenades, the police waded into the crowds, attempting to keep order but often provoking disturbances and ill-will. Every now and then a scuffle broke out over a perceived injury, and as men jostled for a better place in line fights inevitably followed, with the usual barrage of shouts, insults, and condemnations. Some of these incidents became large-scale battles, with dozens of men injured. Rather than functioning as a source of protection, some police sensed an opportunity for extortion as they ordered angry men to the rear of the lines—men who, for a small fee, the traditional "*mordida*," might return to their previous spot.[19]

The immensity of the throng, called by many an "invasion," promoted an array of widespread frauds such as the selling of "insider" contacts for accessing a quick bracero contract. The interminable waiting was enough to prompt weary men to seek any means to earn a contract. Many men, perhaps most, were barely schooled and with funds fast disappearing comprised an army of naïve customers for crooks selling fraudulent papers that supposedly provided an inside track for a quick contract. Others sold memberships in sundry organizations that promised to act on the buyer's behalf to secure a contract.

For a variety of reasons, thousands of men with the hope that work was still available appeared at the centers without initial papers from their local authorities. Sufficient numbers of men like these meant that the charlatans' business would be brisk. Prices for a "secure" contract ranged from 100 pesos to as much as 500 pesos, according to one newspaper report.[20] As Celedonio Perez, who served several stints as a bracero, recalled:

> I borrowed 500 pesos from a friend who lived in a nearby town.... It was very common for men to borrow from others with very high interest rates. The charge was 280 pesos in order for the contracting center to continue with the process.[21]

The Mexico City newspaper *Excelsior* informed its readers that every year 90 million pesos were fleeced from the bracero candidates. These funds were over and beyond the sum that each aspirant had to spend in food and transport while navigating the *via crucis*. One study carried out at the University of California found that, on average, each bracero incurred a debt of 1,200 pesos, equivalent to the hefty sum of $120, in order to labor in U.S. agriculture.[22] Even the thousands of men who never received a contract nonetheless spent vast sums, leaving them deep in debt without means of repayment.

Government officials, too, practiced systematic corruption. One group of bracero aspirants delivered a protest to a Mexico City daily alleging that they were victims of crimes committed by government employees and the police. They testified:

> Some employees of the Department of Labor continue selling approval papers to go onto the border processing station and ... either he or the police who are guarding the door will forcibly remove the papers, telling them that they are false, but ten minutes later will sell them back for fifty pesos.[23]

Such conditions existed throughout the duration of the bracero program.

In 1946, the recruiting stations were assigned to outlying states, but the results were the same. One news account in Leon, in the state of Guanajuato, described a scenario nearly identical to that witnessed earlier in Mexico City. The bulletin reported: "The situation of the braceros found in Leon, according to information, is desperate; many have waited various weeks to be called up and the economic conditions are precarious."[24]

Anxious, destitute, and tired men seeking work—many going hungry and unable to pay their way home—began to protest. In March 1944, for example, men organized a protest in Mexico City that "ran through the main streets, and leading to the National Palace"; their request was that the president grant them authority to become braceros.[25] Later that month 1,500 men demonstrated in the capital's streets, which terminated at the offices of the Department of Labor, protesting against the fraud and corruption that accompanied the recruitment process.[26] Even after the recruiting center had been removed from Mexico City, uninformed men seeking to become braceros continued to arrive, and, before long, in the spring of 1946, 1,000 were protesting loudly and hoisting banners and signs pleading to become braceros; naturally the police were called in to restore order.[27] Later that year, in Leon, hundreds demonstrated "in tumultuous fashion" in front of the Municipal Palace to demand the same privilege.[28] Two years after that, in Mexico City, news reports described a mass protest by 5,000 bracero hopefuls who had become dispirited but were still holding the

> illusion of a contract to go to the United States. [They] invaded the area near the [offices of the secretary of *Gobernacion*] and attempted to enter into the interior.... [T]he police were opportunely advised and arrived to prevent the Secretariat from invasion.[29]

Similar protests occurred frequently throughout the duration of the program. However, order was to be maintained at any cost, if necessary, as the men sometimes relieved their pent-up emotions among themselves.

The Empalme Recruiting Center

After the signing of Public Law 78 in 1951, which institutionalized the bracero program for over thirteen years, three and sometimes four recruiting stations operated in Mexico. Migratory stations, as the U.S. officials referred to the recruitment centers, were established in Empalme (Sonora), Chihuahua, and Monterey. These stations completed the initial screening procedure, and the second (final) review of the candidates was concluded at a border "Reception Center." Above all else, the men were judged on their potential to perform various forms of back-breaking seasonal farm work, or "stoop labor," the term commonly applied to seasonal agricultural labor.

The official account of the recruiting in Mexico published in the United States portrayed a well-run operation, efficient, effective and, above all, fair.[30] The reality was another matter altogether. The Empalme station located in a scrubby, rustic village—unlike urban Chihuahua and certainly far from the likes of Mexico City—served as the western first stop in the bracero recruiting process in the mid-1950s. Getting to the station for many, if not most, was a costly, often painful and difficult routine. One man traveling to Empalme by third-class bus recalls being on the road for thirty-five hours, riding on "steel bouncing on steel, the hard straight-back seats providing little cushion between bodies and highway."[31] But bus travel was possible only if the men had enough funds. Many men walked for days, when necessary, and camped out on the roadside as they made it to the center. A journalist recorded one bracero hopeful's journey of 825 miles to Empalme on foot; as often as possible, he hitched rides, and in the evenings he slept in the roadside brush. Upon arriving at the center he became just one more in a "huge mob of men standing or sitting closely packed about a fence."[32] The writer found that a great many of the men had no *permisos* from their respective local authorities to proceed to the center; nonetheless, they held out hope that somehow they might find a way—by means of a *mordida,* if necessary—to become a bracero.

As had happened in Mexico City twelve years earlier, the arrival in Empalme of throngs of men easily distinguished by their clothing and "general appearance" overpopulated the town. One observer described the vast crowds at the Empalme station as having a "carnival atmosphere," with street hawkers "selling everything from plastic cases for documents to tortillas and tacos." Prostitutes, "gaudily dressed," peered from doorsteps about the village.[33] Food stalls alongside the waiting men competed with ambulant venders selling their wares, who, together with residents who rented beds (more often a floor space, a garage, or front porch) on a nightly basis, brought an economic upswing to the unattractive town. The migration created a lively informal industry in which "many citizens earn their livelihood from the presence of the braceros."[34] A traveler testified that men paid a peso per night for sleeping space, and that

> [a]s the dawn broke ... the men who had curled up under porches and sheds or hunched against buildings and in doorways struggled to their feet and numbly made their way to the station compound.... [M]ore than 5,000 were crowded around the calling area under the watchful eye of soldiers garrisoned nearby. In every mind there was a single thought. The burning hope that today they would hear their names called over the station's loudspeaker.[35]

Another visitor to the center estimated that, during his stay, crowds varied from 1,000 to 10,000; a third estimated one day's crowd at 20,000. (At the Chihuahua station the number at times exceeded 20,000.[36]) The waiting could run into months; some days only 50 men would be called on, while on other days perhaps 300 were; and in the summer, temperatures and humidity often rose to searing levels, yet the luxury of seeking shade could not be attempted lest one's name is called. Nerves frayed and tempers flared; conflict was inevitable as "big crowds, fights, brawls, disorder" prompted police to infiltrate the crowds, cracking rifle butts and truncheons on heads and shoulders. As one man stated, "[T]he soldiers don't use the guns to shoot with. They just hit people with them."[37]

Men began to slowly starve and grew emaciated, illnesses became commonplace, and some who experienced more than their bodies could withstand died alone in the surrounding brush. As one former bracero testified: "We suffered much at Empalme. At first, we had a little money to eat with. After that was gone, we had to beg for food." Another recounted that he "caught pneumonia from sleeping on the ground at Empalme, while waiting. .... [M]ost of the men are sick from not eating." Another recounted: "One time I met some friends at Empalme. They were from the same town I am: Nejapa, Guerrero. They had not eaten for nine days. Fortunately, I had some money, so I fed them for two weeks.... It seemed that they were never going to get contracts so I paid their way home."[38] One bracero was found dead under a palm tree; an autopsy revealed that he had nothing but banana skins in his stomach.[39] Appalled at the human suffering he witnessed while visiting Empalme, a priest was moved to write: "One doesn't have to go to India to see the masses hungry and with no future. One can go to Empalme."[40] Statements like his were not uncommon.

During a visit to Mexico in 1957, a Texas farmer and employer of braceros candidly noted conditions that called to mind the priest's India metaphor:

> Conditions in the Mexican cities where these recruiting centers are located became little short of nightmarish. Many, if not most of these men, have hoarded and done without for themselves and their families, and even sold all they possess to get to the recruiting center and to sustain themselves until admitted. All along the way, while securing the necessary documents for admission to the recruiting center itself, they are mulcted by systematic bribery—the mordida, the "bite." ... To conserve their meager funds or because their hoard has been exhausted, they sleep in the railway stations, in alleys and doorways. Theft and crime born of desperation are a dangerous commonplace. Health and sanitation conditions are worse than menacing.[41]

Nevertheless, and in spite of the seemingly endless waiting on the *via crucis,* thousands of men were eventually called by loudspeaker into the chambers of the recruiting center to undergo an evaluation to determine their worth as laborers. One American advocate of the bracero program put it bluntly: "[T]he braceros were not selected for their ability to represent Mexico's foreign policy, but for their capacity to work."[42] Those who did not demonstrate this capacity experienced the pain of rejection and had to make the sad, lonely return to their villages and families. But at least for a few days, weeks, or months, they'd held out hope of becoming a bracero.

All waited for their names to be called over a loudspeaker, and the number depended upon the workers requested on that day by growers in the United States. However, such a generous supply of laborers, in desperate straits and eager for work, provided local entrepreneurs and U.S. agribusiness interests in the region with an opportunity for exploiting the waiting men—an opportunity frequently taken advantage of over the duration of the program. While waiting at Empalme for their name to be called, men eager for a job were offered a place at the front of the list (and even an authorization document) if they were willing to take a different sort of job. For example, they might be asked to work for three days in the town proper in a street-cleaning crew or to help in town construction projects. One journalist for the *Saturday Evening Post* reported on the practice in a frank and uncritical fashion:

> To facilitate prompt issuance of such a *permiso* [entrance into the recruiting pipeline], it is suggested that the bracero work for the town for three days without pay. Hence, the streets and parks of Empalme are immaculate and a school is being constructed at relatively low cost to the taxpayers.[43]

One prospective bracero reported that after he had waited at Empalme for a month, an army colonel stationed at the center suggested an alternative to the selection process. "He told me," stated the candidate, "he would get me through if I worked for him for 15 days, and then I got through." On the other hand, more formal procedures were required for use of the floating labor pool. Recruiting officials commonly "requested" candidates to pick cotton for two or three weeks at a local cotton farm, allegedly in order to gain "practice" and "experience" as cotton pickers, thereby enhancing their "capacity to work" and their prospects for selection.[44] One former bracero recalled, "We had to pick 3,000 kilos of cotton to get the *carta de control* [verification of having labored] to get contracted in Empalme."[45] The director of the Empalme center, Clifford Burr (an American living in Sonora), described the practice as a win-win situation:

> Public relations of the migratory station is now accepted and recognized as an important and beneficial enterprise. Its operation in Sonora has helped to relieve that state's serious labor shortage. Its cotton and vegetable growers can employ the men who are awaiting selection for the later harvests in the United States. In the past two years, more than 50,000 out-of-state men have worked annually on Sonora's crops.

Burr added that working in cotton provided prospective braceros with funds to maintain themselves while waiting for selection and, furthermore, offered "preferential selection to workers who have already worked in Sonora's crops for 2 to 3 weeks."[46] Burr was not above using other corrupt methods. As one bracero testified, after rumors that the center needed work done were spread, several men approached Burr seeking a job. Another bracero disclosed that Burr suggested that if we brought our own paint, and cement, and other materials, and did the work, we would get contracts. We have been working eight days now. We work from dawn until we can't see any more. We are in a hurry to get finished, because we are not getting paid anything during this time.[47]

Not all were invited to perform labor in order to procure an inside track on a contract. Another bracero at Empalme reported: "During the time I was waiting, I had to work picking tomatoes at Ciudad Obregon.... They told us that if we did not do this, we would not get contracted."[48] In such cases would-be braceros were paid pitifully low wages, and as the above reports indicate, many received no wages whatsoever. Even after having performed obligatory labor, they had other means to enter the pipeline.

Of course, the benefits from working the sea of humanity accrued not only to the landowners and others in the region but also to a major corporation involved in U.S. cotton production, Anderson Clayton (AC). AC invested in the regional expanding cotton district, and its own offices and cotton processing plant were located adjacent to the bracero recruiting center. More than AC benefited as the farmers that surrounded Empalme secured financing through Nacional Financiera, Mexico's central financial agency, which in turn borrowed heavily from the U.S.-controlled International Bank for Reconstruction and Development and the U.S. Export-Import Bank.[49] In 1952 the assistant secretary for the Department of State's Inter-American Affairs, Edward G. Miller, proudly noted that approximately $400 million lent by the two Washington-based institutions to Nacional Financiera covered "the great bulk of this [west coast agricultural] financing."[50] The foreign-financed modernization in the region was described as a buzz of economic activities orchestrated by U.S. concerns in an article published in *Americas,* the journal for the Organization of American States:

> In the past few years the principal U.S. chemical and fertilizer companies have established agencies in the chief agricultural centers along the west coast of Mexico.... Sturdy U.S. farm trucks are seen everywhere on highways and side roads taking farm products, machinery, insecticides, and commercial fertilizers from one place to another. The big U.S. transport carriers are not yet in evidence, but they too will make their appearance just as soon as the highways are completed.[51]

Obviously, in terms of putting men to work on cotton and vegetable farms, the bracero program's returns to American agricultural and banking corporations began long before the braceros reached their labor camps in the United States. Still, even though some men were tapped to enter a virtually unpaid-labor phase of the process, there were no guarantees of a contract. Thousands of tired but alert men waited from day to day, separated from the center's entrances by wire partitions. One objective above all else occupied their minds: to hear their names called over the center's loudspeaker. Those who bought their contracts either with a *mordida* or with their labor stood the best chance. Each day between 200 and as many as 1,000 men were called. As a sequence of names blared across the crowd's hushed din, each man belonging to an announced name eagerly, if nervously, ran to the wire fence and at the desk presented his carefully protected and, by now, well-worn identification.[52] The fortunate job seeker merely entered the first step in that process organized along the lines of an industrial routine. From this point on he was constantly on the move. If his papers appeared to be in order, he was told to proceed to the next step. Still, no one was promising him a ticket to "paradise."

What this second step entailed was questioning and evaluation by officials of the U.S. Department of Labor and the U.S. Immigration and Naturalization Service. This would be the job seeker's first screening to determine whether he was worthy of "stoop labor." At Empalme (as well as at other recruiting stations) a former bracero with a *mica* (an expired bracero immigration visa) in hand, and whose name was not on a blacklist, received favorable treatment. A Labor Department official asked if he was experienced in agricultural labor. He then checked his attitude, size, and build; patted him on the shoulder or bicep to check his muscle tone; did a cursory examination to determine whether he had obvious disabilities; and, finally, looked at this hands to check for calluses, which were considered key evidence of farm-labor experience.[53] Overall, the immigration agent determined "admissibility" and ferreted out "undesirable aliens"—that is, previously deported immigrants and convicted felons, as well as security risks. Even though most braceros had known nothing but a hard life and few, if any, could ever pose a "security risk," the procedure was nonetheless conducted.

The candidate then moved on to the third step, the physical examination. Mexican doctors under contract with the U.S. government performed cursory health examinations for two pesos per man. Large

roomfuls of stripped-down men were lined up and each given a superficial examination lasting on average five minutes. Doctors peered
into the men's noses, ears, and throats; listened to their heartbeat; and
examined their genitals and anal area. Those too young or too old,
too tall or emaciated, disabled or afflicted with an obvious disease,
particularly venereal disease, were summarily rejected. Often growers' representatives would advise the station's officials of the "type"
of worker they were seeking from a day's selection. If the particular
candidate appeared to be an urban type, perhaps too well dressed or
speaking and acting as if he had had too many years of schooling, then
he too would be rejected. A *Saturday Evening Post* article contributed
by the former president of the Riverside (California) County Farm
Bureau, listed the primary concerns expressed by the growers:

> Will he be suitable for vegetables? Is he lean, small and young, suit-
> able for climbing forty-foot date palms? Leland Yost, manager of the
> Coachella Valley Farmers Association, says that since this sort of check
> was started efficiency has been increased ... largely from picking the
> right men to do the work.[54]

However, the men themselves were deeply offended by the examination. One said of the procedure that

> [i]n Chihuahua they would organize the transportation to the border
> as if we were cows. We arrived at Juarez and the worst was how we were
> treated at El Paso where we were dusted like animals. They made us
> take our clothes off and the doctors made sure that we had no illnesses.
> The examination was hard on us and the way they treated us made us
> want to go back [to Mexico].[55]

Braceros also complained about the harmful criteria by which they
were judged; as one put it, "I had a lot of trouble getting contracted.
The reason I had trouble is that they found out I had six years of
school. They only want dumb people."[56] Indeed, perfectly healthy men
found themselves rejected on grounds based entirely on employers'
requirements. And not a few were rejected for reasons relating to
poor health, possibly caused by the strain of waiting for a contract.
One rejected man described his experience:

> I waited at Empalme over a month. I, and many of the other men,
> became weak from not eating while we waited. I had to sleep on the

ground. Because of sleeping on the ground, I became sick. I have just been rejected for this sickness. They tell me I have pneumonia. This does not seem fair to me.[57]

One observer concluded that only one out of every ten job seekers ever attained bracero status.[58] In 1952 a total of 31,990 men were rejected at the processing centers in Mexico, compared to 21,000 in 1954 and 44,411 in 1955. Those rejected could either stay in town and continue to seek a contract with a *mordida,* return home at their own expense, or attempt to travel north to the border and illegally enter the United States to work as farm workers. Not a few chose the last route.

For those passing the initial review more interrogations and examinations would follow. Each man was fingerprinted and received a vaccination against smallpox. Although the international agreement stipulated that the selection for a particular grower or association was not to take place on Mexican soil, the selection frequently occurred before the men reached the border. At this point, the job seekers were lectured on the type of work they were expected to perform. A candidate could try to opt out of the job, but in practice he had little choice in the matter. If he agreed to the type of work, however, he received information concerning the details of the internationally negotiated work contract, how much he would be paid, and his rights under the contract—all of which he barely understood. Nevertheless, he now had good reason to believe that his long-sought goal had been reached.

In short, U.S. Labor Department officials had implemented a policy determined by one ultimate objective: finding ideal laborers. Mexican officials, including doctors, secretaries, and police, performed peripheral though important tasks toward this end.

For those men judged worthy but not selected at Empalme, this was but the first stop; one more would follow at the border. From Empalme the men comprising the selection of the day would be transported to the El Centro Reception Center for further processing. Usually candidates (the men were still not officially braceros) traveled overnight in converted boxcars refashioned with plank seats and arrived at the border around four o'clock in the morning. University of California researcher Henry Anderson witnessed several trips and took notes on one trip similar to that experienced by many thousands of men. "I have seen a ten-car freight arrive at the U.S. border," wrote Anderson, "carrying 1,200 prospective braceros from the recruiting station at Empalme, Sonora. During the thirteen-hour trip, the aspirants, 120 to a boxcar, were without toilet facilities, water, heating or cooling facilities."[59]

In speaking before a gathering of U.S.-Mexico border health officials, a Mexican doctor painted a similarly grim picture of men arriving at the Reception Center. "Another grave fault in sanitation," he stated, "is the lack of consideration given to the transportation of workers by railroad or by highway. We know of cases of movement of workers without any toilet facilities and no drinking water."[60] A photographer traveling through the region detailed analogous impressions seven years later: "It was another day and night before the train reached Mexicali. A day and night on wood-slatted benches, looking through dirty windows that would not open, twisting water spigots that long ago stopped working."[61]

An official for the Mexican Bureau of Migratory Labor also witnessed the demeaning treatment afforded the men. In an interview he recounted that

[m]any times there is no drinking water. There is no heat in the cars, and the trip lasts all night. There are no toilets in the freight cars. The men who have been before take tins with them, and go to the toilet in them, and then throw them out the door. But many of the men have to go to the toilet leaning out of the big sliding doors ... and it is dangerous. There have been times when we got trains with two or three men missing because they have fallen on the way.[62]

Upon departure each man was handed a paper-bag lunch of white bread sandwiches, which the men, unaccustomed to such food, often threw away.[63]

The cost of recruiting and transport to the border amounted to $34 per bracero; the growers contributed only $15 per man to cover transport from the border station to their labor camp, with the U.S. government paying the remainder.[64] The latter amount covered the recruiting, processing, and most of the transport to the border—a virtual subsidy to the growers, at taxpayers' expense. Upon alighting before daybreak in Mexicali, as many as 2,000 men per day walked to the border clutching their belongings, waited until daybreak, and then were bussed to the El Centro center at eight in the morning.[65]

The entire recruitment process, from his village to El Centro, brought the prospective bracero face to face with, as one visitor to the

Empalme center testified, "an ordeal equal to any he has experienced before."[66] After weeks, perhaps months, of traveling from their home and then waiting at the recruiting center, the physical toll on the men was pronounced. Witnesses commented on the stark appearance of the men as they crossed the border. One medical doctor with the Baja California Health Department observed that health conditions were precarious at best as the men moved from Empalme to El Centro, testifying that the

> [n]utrition of the workers in the Migratory Stations and on the way to the Reception Centers is so faulty that many workers have arrived in starving condition, and they are easy prey to the acute communicable diseases, or are victims of sunstroke in the summertime and freezing in the wintertime.[67]

A manager of a California growers' association bracero camp found similar conditions among the men delivered to work under him. "When we get a batch of men in here," he told an interviewer,

> they are usually nothing but skin and bones. The other night, for example, a group came in who had waited three months at Empalme before they could get their contracts. We get them here in a very run down condition. I would guess that on average our men will gain 10 to 15 pounds in their first few weeks with us.[68]

Upon arriving at El Centro, the stream of bracero hopefuls underwent further physical examination to check on their desirability as farm workers. They were not yet braceros. In a large room, a grower's representative spoke to them in Spanish regarding job possibilities. He identified the types of jobs available and asked those who wished to work for a specific employee at a certain wage to stand up. Those who stood were checked for stature, build, and size by experienced representatives of a grower or growers' association charged to get the right kind of men for a particular job. The representatives generally mingled with the men, moving close enough to eye them carefully, holding them by the arm or shoulder to check on muscles, and posing a few questions to gauge their attitude and inquire if they had experience in the line of work required by the employer. If they appeared to be of middle-class background, they would almost certainly enter the ranks of the rejected; as one former bracero recounted, he had a friend who was rejected "because he was wearing corduroy pants sent to him by his son who lived in the US." The officials refused to believe that the pants were a gift and thought he was lying.[69] After all the evidence had been weighed, selections were made; the majority remained while the "rejects" were sent out of the building.

Those who passed the growers' standards were sent out for another brief health examination. The men were stripped and told to enter an empty chamber resembling a large shower; here they were dusted with lindane, intended to rid them of body lice. Of all the measures that the men had to undergo, this spraying was considered the most unpleasant, possibly because they were dusted without masks and forced to breathe the poisonous mist. Next, the naked men were given a cursory diagnosis, this time by one or two U.S. Department of Health officials assisted by untrained staff. Attention was focused primarily on venereal disease, physical disabilities and deformities, and obvious health problems. Those judged too young were systematically rejected. Men with the appearance of venereal disease were given a blood test, and those who tested positive were vaccinated with penicillin. If they passed these examinations they were then moved to a radiological station for either a tuberculin skin test or an x-ray for tuberculosis. Because hundreds of men were being x-rayed in a short period of time, careful and effective diagnosis of each radiography was impossible; but the process continued. In fact, the perfunctory screenings overlooked many men with disorders, resulting in problems at the work site.

Finally, the men who made it through were photographed, presented a contract to sign, told of the work involved, advised of their rights and pay, and then informed that they had three days to make up their minds if they chose to consider the matter. Very few decided to wait; for the most part they signed at the first opportunity and received a *mica*, the official immigration ID that permitted them to work in the United States. Contracted men were then hustled onto buses and transported to their employer. One *Look Magazine* article accurately summed up the final step to becoming a bracero: "After passing immigration and health tests, *he is turned over to a California grower* for transportation to a farm."[70] The braceros had now become the property of a grower.

However, a few candidates were retained and were put to work at the Reception Center as a means of guaranteeing a contract—a clear violation of the international agreement. American-style *mordidas* sprouted in the desert Reception Center, as one investigator's critical statements confirmed:

> I have talked to braceros [*sic*] who paid bribes to employees of the U.S. Immigration and Naturalization Service, Public Health Service, and Department of Labor for routine services rendered during the contracting process. I have talked with a U.S. Department of Labor employee who made a bracero [*sic*] work on his home without wages for a week before granting him a contract.[71]

Each year one of every six men who entered the El Centro Reception Center was dismissed for a variety of reasons. Many thousands of unfortunate men were sent back across the border to Mexicali with bus fare to return to Empalme. Thereafter they had to fend for themselves and, if they chose return home, to pay their own way. Rejection amounted to humiliation and, for many, economic ruin, as this man explained:

> I and five of my friends have all been rejected. All of us are ruined, since all of us went deeply into debt in order to come here for a contract. I sold my *milpa* in Aguascalientes to raise money for the trip. My wife and six children are at home, waiting for me to send them money from the United States. Now there will be no money, and there is nothing for me to go back to. I guess my children will beg in the streets. I wish I were dead.[72]

Another man who had suffered the pain of rejection, and was found begging at the Reception Center, complained bitterly: "Why do they bring us all the way here to tell us we can't have the contracts? I spent my last money in Empalme. I do not have five *centavos* in my pocket. How do they expect me to get back home?"[73]

How he returned home was his problem; the U.S. and Mexican governments washed their hands of any responsibility for him and for the many thousands more in similar straits. Based on accounts of these firsthand experiences, one newspaper reporter drew a painful portrait not only of the men as they returned to Mexico but also of the dramatic population growth in the northern cities due to the settlement of rejected men, an internal northward migration (that often crossed the border) stimulated by the bracero program:

If you want my opinion as to what becomes of the men who are rejected, they simply accumulate in the cities across the border from the reception centers. This is one of the reasons these places, like Mexicali and Juarez, have doubled or trebled in population since the bracero program started, and one of the reasons why you will see so many sick people hobbling around there, and begging in the streets.[74]

The journalist added that those who are physically able simply "jump the fence," entering as undocumented workers (known by the pejorative term "wetbacks"). "The rest," he said, "just rot." According to Mexican government statistics taken in 1948, approximately 5,000 men in Mexicali were in desperate straits, sleeping in streets and begging for handouts; many others died from starvation.[75] An American medical doctor observed the dire conditions besetting the rejected men in that border city:

One of the biggest scandals of the whole bracero program is the way the rejection of the men is handled. They are simply dumped across the border, without even two bits for a meal. What do they do? Hell, what can they do? They scrounge in the garbage cans of Mexicali. Go down any alley of the town and you will see them. There are thousands of them. And Mexicali is a poor town. The garbage cans aren't full to start with. By the time the braceros get through, they are the cleanest garbage cans in the world.[76]

At this point the *via crucis* extended north and south of the border. While the rejected men attempted to put their lives back together as best they could, the contracted braceros traveled to work sites to perform "stoop labor" for anywhere from six weeks to six months. Those crossing without papers added to the growing number of undocumented laborers working alongside the braceros and domestic laborers, while other rejected men congregated along the border towns, swelling the ranks of the unemployed and desperate male population along the northern border states.

But between six weeks and six to eighteen months later, depending on the contract, the braceros returned to Empalme at the government's expense and to their final destinations at their own expense. Most arrived home with sundry newly purchased items—mainly clothes, but also perhaps a radio as well as a pedal-powered sewing machine and a new footlocker for storage. However, despite exemption from tariffs for returning braceros, the government *mordida* ate into the meager wages they had earned. One program administrator who witnessed numerous bracero return trips noted that

> the men were subject to inspection of their luggage in every state. It was crazy. Without any rhyme or reason, government agents would come through, slapping duties on things. Apparently, the amount of the duties depended on what they thought the traffic would bear. In other words, it was another case of the good old *mordida*. I saw one guy who had a footlocker full of clothing. An inspector went through it, and socked him with a duty on everything that was new.[77]

The higher his earnings, and the greater his purchases, the more the bracero was mulcted. Widespread and intense official bribery and fraud followed each step taken by bracero aspirants, bracero rejects, and eventual braceros; beginning at the recruiting stage, these crimes affected the braceros' every experience. In addition to state-managed migration, the bracero program exemplified systematic state-managed theft.

Conclusion

As we have seen, the bracero labor system, designed in Washington for the benefit of U.S. agricultural corporations, deeply affected the hundreds of thousands of men undergoing the bracero recruitment process in Mexico, as well as the families and villages these men left behind. Analyses and criticisms of the bracero program (and, for that matter, of all proposed "guest worker" programs) have yet to systematically assess the wholesale exploitation and suffering that ensue. Nor can we ignore the century-long history of imperialist domination by U.S. large-scale capital over Mexico that has propelled migration to the United States. Braceros were, in legal terms, indentured laborers, recruited and processed by the U.S. government with the assistance of the Mexican government and placed under the control of agricultural corporations for a specified period of time, after which the braceros would be disposed of—that is, repatriated. For twenty-two years this arrangement provided a near-perfect labor force for agricultural corporations. However, that system of indentured servitude did not originate on the northern side of the border; rather, it began in the sending villages and hometowns, long before the braceros arrived at labor camps in the United States. In short, the bracero program comprised one variation—in this instance, state-managed migration, of a hundred years of Mexican migration to the United States.

The bracero program, which today is cloaked under the euphemism "guest worker" program, served as a transnational system of controlled labor migration bearing marked similarities (e.g., the worker quota) to the Spanish colonial labor scheme known as the *repartimiento*. In both instances, poor Mexican male villagers served as a huge, cheap pool of labor indentured to wealthy strangers and foreigners. In the case of the bracero program, villagers were utilized for the benefit of U.S. corporate capital—a social process that began in the late nineteenth century under the flag of the "open door" and continues to the present day under the aegis of "free trade."

Notes

1. See Ernesto Galarza, *Merchants of Labor: The Mexican Bracero Story*, Charlotte, N.C.: McNally and Loftin, 1964; and *Strangers in Our Fields*, Washington, D.C.: Joint United States–Mexico Trade Union Committee, 1956.

2. See, for example, Galarza, *Strangers in Our Fields*; and Richard B. Craig, *The Bracero Program: Interest Groups and Foreign Policy*, Austin: University of Texas Press, 1971. Note, however, that Henry Anderson remains the one main exception to the lack of discussion on the recruiting and processing phase. His various works cited in the second chapter bear this out; he is also the subject of the fifth chapter.

3. George E. Coalson, "Mexican Contract Labor in American Agriculture," *Southwestern Social Science*, vol. 33 (September 1952). Citing a federal study, "Migratory Labor in American Agriculture," Coalson states: "[T]he demand for alien contract labor was continued by the relatively few but highly articulate growers who had come to rely upon this source of cheap and docile labor." He later quoted from the federal report itself: Migratory labor "is primarily a special concern of a small number of large and highly specialized farm employers" (p. 232).

4. Don Taylor, "How Mexico Feels About the Bracero Program," *California Farmer*, vol. 218 (April 20, 1963), p. 43.

5. See Henry Pope Anderson, *Harvest of Loneliness: An Inquiry into a Social Problem*, Berkeley: Citizens for Farm Labor, 1964, p. 82.

6. See the Introduction to Richard H. Hancock, *The Role of the Bracero in the Economic and Cultural Dynamics of Mexico: A Case Study of Chihuahua*, Stanford, Calif.: Hispanic American Society, 1959.

7. J. Eric S. Thompson, ed., *Thomas Gage's Travels in the New World,* Norman: University of Oklahoma, 1958, ch. 15. Thompson makes reference to "[s]howing the condition, quality, fashion, and behavior of the Indians of the country of Guatemala since the Conquest, and especially of their feasts and yearly solemnities."

8. Henry Anderson, *The Bracero Program in California,* New York: Arno Press, 1975.

9. Cited in Galarza, *Strangers in the Fields,* Washington, D.C.: Joint United States–Mexico Trade Union Committee, 1956, p. 11. The sub-headline reads: "In a century of liberty the Mexican braceros are the object of the most inhuman exploitation" (translation by the author).

10. S. W. Coombs, "Bracero's Journey," *Americas,* vol. 15 (December 1963): 7–8.

11. In 1942, in the port city of Tampico, hundreds of men congregated at the regional offices of the Department of Labor hoping that perhaps they could gain the first authorization papers. Unfortunately, few remained for distribution. According to news reports, the numbers of documents were very limited in comparison to the numbers soliciting the same ("Quieren Venir a E. U. Millares de Mexicanos," *La Opinion* [Los Angeles] October 9, 1942).

12. Galarza, *Strangers in Our Fields,* p. 36.

13. "Mexico: Estados Unidos Pedira Cincuenta Mil Braceros Mexicanos," *La Opinion* (Los Angeles), March 19, 1943.

14. Jesus Topete, *Aventuras de un Bracero,* Mexico City: Editora Grafica Moderna, 1948, p. 11.

15. Henry Anderson, "Fields of Bondage: The Mexican Contract Labor System in Industrialized Agriculture," mimeographed typescript (1963), p. 20.

16. Marco Almazan, "The Mexicans Keep Them Rolling," *The Inter-American,* vol. 4, no. 10 (October 1945): 21.

17. Topete, *Aventuras de un Bracero,* p. 12.

18. Almazan, "The Mexicans Keep Them Rolling," p. 21.

19. "Vil Explotacion a los Braceros Mexicanos," *La Opinion* (Los Angeles, CA), April 10, 1943.

20. "Robo a los Braceros en Mexico," *La Opinion* (Los Angeles, CA), January 4, 1945.

21. Interview with Celedonio P. Perez by Alicia Anaya, French Camp, California, January 6, 2004.

22. Anderson, *Harvest of Loneliness,* p. 105.

23. "Sigue Inicuo El Contrato de Braceros," *La Opinion* (Los Angeles), May 21, 1944; see also Wayne D. Rasmussen, *A History of the Emergency Farm Labor Supply Program, 1943–1947,* Washington, D.C.: U.S. Department of Agriculture, Bureau of Agricultural Economics (September 1951), p. 214.

24. "Un Motin de Braceros," *La Opinion* (Los Angeles), June 23, 1946.

25. "Manifestacion de Braceros," *La Opinion* (Los Angeles), March 8, 1944.

26. "Energica Protesta de los Braceros," *La Opinion* (Los Angeles), March 26, 1944.

27. "Queremos Ir a Trabajar en los EE.UU," *La Opinion* (Los Angeles), April 14, 1946.

28. "Un Motin de Braceros," *La Opinion* (Los Angeles), June 23, 1946.

29. "Motin de Braceros en Mexico," *La Opinion* (Los Angeles), April 23, 1948.

30. See, for example, Clifford F. Burr, "South of the Border," *Employment Security Review,* vol. 28 (January 1961). Burr served as manager of the recruiting station in Empalme, Sonora.

31. S. W. Coombs, "Bracero's Journey," *Americas,* vol. 15 (December 1963): 9.

32. Fred Aldridge, "Helping Hands from Mexico," *Saturday Evening Post* (August 10, 1957): 63.

33. Anthony Soto, "The Bracero Story," *Commonweal,* vol. 71 (November 27, 1959): 259.

34. Clifford F. Burr, "South of the Border," *Employment Security Review,* vol. 28 (January 1961): 38.

35. S. W. Coombs, "Bracero's Journey," p. 10.

36. Hancock, *The Role of the Bracero in the Economic and Cultural Dynamics of Mexico,* p. 64.

37. Anderson, "Fields of Bondage: The Mexican Contract Labor System in Industrialized Agriculture," p. 20.

38. Celedonio P. Perez, who worked for several years as a bracero, recalled: "Me and my friends had to sleep underneath the trees. Many of the men would go to nearby locals to eat if they had enough money. Others borrowed money from friends when they ran out of cash. My friends and I would only lend money amongst each other because there was trust and we were from the same hometown" (interview with Celedonio P. Perez conducted by Alicia Anaya, French Camp, California, January 6, 2004).

39. Anderson, "Fields of Bondage: The Mexican Contract Labor System in Industrialized Agriculture," pp. 19–23.

40. Ibid., p. 260.

41. Robert R. Cunningham, "North and South of the Border," *Americas,* vol. 97, no. 2 (August 17, 1957): 500.

42. Almazan, "The Mexicans Keep Them Rolling," p. 21.

43. Fred Eldridge, "Helping Hands From Mexico," p. 63.

44. Taylor, "How Mexico Feels About the Bracero Program," p. 43. The author writes: "Last year only those braceros from Sonora had to pick cotton before reporting to the recruiting center in Empalme" (p. 43).

45. Interview with Celedonio P. Perez conducted by Alicia Anaya, French Camp, California, January 6, 2004.

46. Burr, "South of the Border," p. 38. Cotton picking by prospective braceros occurred in Monterey, according to U.S. Department of Labor publications. In a 1959 Department report on farm labor, Labor Secretary Mitchell wrote that at the Monterey station those "[m]en who already had worked for 2 weeks on cotton farms along the Mexican side of the border . . . would get priority. (Mexico, too, has a problem of labor supply to pick cotton.)" See James P. Mitchell, *Farm Labor Fact Book,* Washington, D.C.: U.S. Government Printing Office, 1959, p. 169.

47. Anderson, "Fields of Bondage: The Mexican Contract Labor System in Industrialized Agriculture," p. 21.

48. Ibid., p. 21.

49. Soto, "The Bracero Story," p. 260; see also Craig L. Dozier, "Mexico's Transformed Northwest: The Yaqui, Mayo, and Fuerte Examples," *Geographical Review,* vol. 53 (October 1963).

50. Edward G. Miller, "Rewards of U.S.-Mexican Cooperation," U.S. Department of State, *Bulletin,* vol. 26 (March 31, 1952): 499.

51. Verne A. Baker, "Braceros Farm for Mexico," *Americas* (Journal of the Organization of American States), vol. 5 (September 1953): 31; see also J. C., "Mexico Today," *The World Today,* vol. 10, no. 3 (March 1954). The author writes: "The United States has naturally been the chief source of foreign capital in Mexico. By the end of 1952, the leading bank of the Mexican government had borrowed a total of $261 million from the United States Export-Import Bank, from the World Bank, and from a few private United States banks." And later, he or she writes: "The expansion of foreign investment in Mexico demonstrates that the Government has welcomed the entrance of capital from abroad" (pp. 117–118). A Department of Labor study published in 1966 reported that a "considerable amount of American capital" was invested in the region and that most of the fruits and vegetables exported to the United States through El Paso, Texas, were from American-owned firms ("Braceros, Mexico and Foreign Trade," *Farm Labor Developments,* Washington, D.C.: U.S. Department of Labor, Manpower Administration, Bureau of Employment Security [July 1966], p. 21).

52. Soto, "The Bracero Story," p. 259.

53. State of California, Department of Employment, "Mexican Nationals in California Agriculture," Sacramento: California Department of Employment (November 2, 1959), p. 14. The report states: "The U.S. Department of Labor also screens the candidates to select workers whose experience or qualifications, such as physical build, strength, manual dexterity, etc., make them most suitable for the types of work to be done" (p. 14).

54. Fred Eldridge, "Helping Hands from Mexico," *Saturday Evening Post* (August 10, 1957): 63. *Today's Health,* the journal of the American Medical Association, published an article on the bracero program in which it mentioned the measuring of bracero candidates for certain kinds of jobs. The article reported: "An interesting recent development in the examination of workers is the testing of their physical aptitude for different crops. The accident rate in working on date palms has been cut noticeably by using young men who work well at heights" ("They Help Feed America," *Today's Health,* vol. 35, October, 1957: 27).

55. Interview with Conrado Cardenas, Stockton, California, September 5, 2004.

56. Anderson, "Fields of Bondage: The Mexican Contract Labor System in Industrialized Agriculture," p. 27.

57. Anderson, *The Bracero Program in California,* p. 37.

58. Anderson, *Harvest of Loneliness,* p. 143. A respondent to Anderson's study stated: "Out of every thousand men perhaps only one-hundred will actually be chosen to come to the United States."

59. Anderson, "Social Justice and Foreign Contract Labor: A Statement of Opinion and Conscience," typed manuscript (May 21, 1958), p. 3.

60. Anderson, *The Bracero Program in California,* p. 19.

61. S. W. Coombs, "Bracero's Journey", p. 11.

62. Anderson, *Harvest of Loneliness,* p. 263.

63. Henry Pope Anderson, "Braceros Speak: A Contract Labor System in Theory and Practice," paper delivered at the annual meeting of the North American Labor Association, Detroit (2001), pp. 10–11.

64. Jean Begeman, "Sweatshops on the Farm," *New Republic,* vol. 125 (July 30, 1951): 17; and State of California, Department of Employment. "Mexican Nationals

in California Agriculture" (Sacramento: Department of Employment, November 2, 1959), p. 14.

65. The director of the Corpus Christi Reception Center noted with pride that, at Texas Reception Centers at the height of the 1955 season, "in one 20-hour period they processed 4,000 Mexican nationals" (Robert B. Lindsey, "Texas," *Employment Security Review,* vol. 22 [March 1955]: 21).

66. Quoted in Soto, "The Bracero Story," p. 260.

67. Quoted in Anderson, *The Bracero Program in California,* p. 19.

68. Ibid., p. 11.

69. Interview with Celedonio P. Perez, conducted by Alicia Anaya.

70. "A New Deal for the Mexican Worker," *Look Magazine,* vol. 23 (September 29, 1959): 55; emphasis added.

71. Quoted in Anderson, "Social Justice and Foreign Contract Labor: A Statement of Opinion and Conscience," p. 3.

72. Anderson, *The Bracero Program in California,* p. 53.

73. Anderson, *Harvest of Loneliness,* p. 352.

74. Anderson, *The Bracero Program in California,* p. 39.

75. "Pesima Situacion de 5,000 Braceros," *La Opinion* (August 14, 1948).

76. Anderson, *The Bracero Program in California,* p. 39.

77. Anderson, *Harvest of Loneliness,* pp. 296–297; see also "Explotan en la Frontera a Los Braceros," *La Opinion,* August 22, 1944. The latter article states that border officials were charging all returning braceros 30 pesos as they crossed the border and that an organization of former braceros was filing a legal grievance.

Chapter 4

In Defense of Indentured Labor

Following the implementation of the temporary indentured worker program with Mexico and the delivery of men to railroads and agriculture across vast sections of the United States there emerged an outpouring of publicity in celebration of the bracero program. The message reiterated during the war years centered on the importance of braceros to the war effort and of the program's value for the economic well-being of the braceros, their families, and Mexico. Not only were the war effort and Mexico's development a common refrain, but the program was hailed as providing "important forward steps in inter-American cooperation" on a par with the "Good Neighbor Policy."[1] Newspapers, magazines, popular journals, radio programs, public relations films, and photography exhibits produced by growers publicized the benefits of the program, particularly for the braceros, in glowing terms. Sometimes the publicity stretched credulity, as when it was reported that braceros en route to the United States were really trainloads of men experiencing an extended vacation, laughing, playing, and singing "Adios, Mariquita linda ... " while passing around a bottle of tequila.[2]

This positive spin was in keeping with the wartime political need to enlist allied support from Latin America, an objective delegated to the State Department's Office of Inter-American Affairs (OIAA), administered by Nelson Rockefeller. The OIAA's general agenda emphasized the cultivation of harmonious cultural and social relations between the Mexicans and Anglo Americans, as well as positive media coverage of Mexican Americans, in order to display an optimistic impression and thereby bolster war support from Mexican Americans, Mexico, and the rest of Latin America. The bracero program figured prominently within the OIAA's agenda.

Early in the deliberations over a contract worker agreement with Mexico, Carey McWilliams, a noted critic of discriminatory treatment affecting the Mexican community, warned Rockefeller that the agreement should include not only effective oversight but also strongly worded provisions protecting the workers.[3] In keeping with the overall goal of securing "Hemispheric Solidarity," the bracero program remained within the range of the organization's activities, though not central to it, resulting in wide community support for the program and resolving discrimination affecting braceros.[4] As part of the OIAA's activities the unit sponsored the journal *The Inter-American,* which on occasion highlighted positive articles dealing with braceros. (Note that McWilliams penned an article in *The Inter-American,* cited below.)

In sharp contrast to the long-standing discrimination and prejudice heaped upon the domestic Mexican community, including segregated public schools, residences, public parks, theaters, and restaurants, along with widespread police hostility, the braceros were treated to an appreciative welcome. During the second year of the program, while welcoming ceremonies greeted braceros, a virtual mass lynching known as the Zoot-Suit Riots was visited upon the Los Angeles Mexican community. Nonetheless, bracero laborers were brought into this context and, for the first three years of the program, were treated somewhat better than their Mexican immigrant predecessors—albeit only superficially so. Some argued that the braceros received special treatment, respecting them as individuals and not as cheap migrant laborers. However, that alleged distinction was in some degree a matter of staged publicity.

With the defeat of the Axis, the connection of braceros with the war effort soon dissolved, and the older stereotypes of all Mexicans once again regained their previous place. As the program entered into the late 1940s and 1950s the legitimate criticisms from liberals and progressives leveled at the harsh and abusive treatment of braceros moved the employers of braceros to circle their wagons, maintain the program's practices, and defend the program through numerous media channels. In the published literature, the brief wartime celebration of the bracero was soon followed by a defense of the program in which it was alleged that all boats were lifted equally. Optimistic contentions that the bracero program not only furthered U.S. foreign policy and aided Mexico's economic development, but also served to maintain the U.S. labor supply and agricultural output, took center stage. The phrase "mutual benefits"—what would later be termed a "win-win" situation—came to be widely utilized. It is useful to explore the literature that defined the braceros and the bracero program for the American public and to examine how the labor of indentured immigrants was defined, legitimized, and, given the gross violations of the program's contract provisions, covered up.

The War Years: Celebrating Their Arrival

Numerous cities and towns across the United States opened their doors wide to receive braceros as they arrived for the first time in their area. Noting this display, social critic Carey McWilliams commented, "In general, the imported Mexican workers have been well received. Many communities have staged fiestas upon their arrival, appointed welcoming committees, and endeavored to in many other ways to demonstrate their goodwill."[5] When the very first contingent of braceros to arrive in the United States reached their final destination (Stockton, California), officials from the Farm Security Administration (FSA), together with the employing ranchers and civic leaders, greeted them. The welcoming contingent joined with the braceros and sang a rollicking, if somewhat off-key, "El Rancho Grande." A similar welcome by FSA officials and Union Pacific representatives greeted braceros as they arrived in Los Angeles to work on the railroads; a banner reading "Bienvenidos los Trabajadores Mexicanos" brought smiles to the tired men.[6] The festivities were repeated across the state. One author wrote that in the towns of Santa Maria, Chico, Thornton, and Woodland, "[l]est nostalgia overtake the newcomers, there were fiestas, radio programs in Spanish [and] entertainments in which the boys take part."[7]

Even the Spanish-language press joined the groundswell of confidence. One article referred to the braceros as "Embajadores en Overoles" (Ambassadors in Overalls), noting that the men were very pleased to experience such displays of gratitude.[8] Another underscored the benefits for Mexico when they returned with new knowledge that would serve them as they applied it to their homeland.[9] A year after the first braceros arrived, a special bilingual radio program devoted to the program featured Governor Earl Warren and the Los Angeles Mexican Consul General Vicente Peralta. Warren exclaimed:

> I have the honor and the pleasure of extending this official tribute from the State of California to our neighbors, patriotic citizens who in such a wonderful manner have come to assist us to complete the harvests and as well to our own citizens for receiving the Mexican braceros as visitors and guests. We owe a special debt to President Avila Camacho.[10]

Officials repeatedly applauded the contribution to the war effort. The words of W. P. Parker, director of the Commission of Agricultural Production in California, expressed the prevalent view before the Congressional Budget Committee: "I must say the following. Were it not for the Mexicans we would have lost foodstuffs worth many millions of dollars."[11]

Given these welcoming receptions, it is not surprising that special endeavors were made to provide for the braceros' special needs. McWilliams mentioned that in some towns special night schools and recreational facilities had been established for the braceros' benefit. And another writer noted that at "various centers throughout the country...educational and recreational facilities have been provided for them."[12] The welcome mat extended by the town of Beaver Dam near Corning, New York, was just one example of the several educational offerings. When the townspeople discovered that the braceros who had come to work on the railroads were living in boxcars and spoke no English, a special English night class was instituted. The article underscored the Beaver Dam experience (and that of other communities as well) as an "effort of individual citizens to make life pleasant for the men sent to their communities."[13]

A similar effort in Napa Valley, California, sought to develop English skills as well as to impart knowledge of agriculture, farm tools and machinery, and sanitation and health as part of a state-sponsored educational project titled, appropriately enough, "Farm Labor Training Course for Mexican Nationals." However, since the men worked long hours "doing stoop work" and returned exhausted at night, only a few were willing to attend regularly.[14] Though sharply segregated from the majority population, Mexican communities, too, organized forms of assistance for the braceros, as exemplified by the activities prepared by these communities in Santa Maria, Guadalupe, and Betteravia. A women's group collected $64.00 for "cigarettes and other articles" and organized a welcoming dance, which was said to be a very successful endeavor.[15]

The friendly receptions for men arriving for the first time appeared throughout the country. In Sacramento, California, the men were greeted by a band and banqueted at employer expense. The Mexican consul exhorted them in Spanish to give their best effort to producing food for victory. There were loud *vivas,* for President Roosevelt, President Avila Camacho, and the United Nations. And the next day the good neighbors went to work.[16]

Meanwhile, in the railroad centers of Odinton and Cheverly, Maryland, not far from the Pan American Union headquarters in Washington, D.C., an upscale welcome mat was rolled out for the 150 braceros in that area. Among the dignitaries present were Mexican Ambassador Francisco Castillo Najera and Dr. L. S. Rowe, the director general of the Pan American Union. Rowe expressed his and the nation's appreciation to the braceros and promised that the Pan American Union would "assist them in any possible way." Castillo Najera emphasized the need for international cooperation and the importance of their labor to that goal. A musical program and presentation of a Cantinflas film followed, with refreshments completing the welcoming ceremony.[17]

As the war reached its final year, the growers' optimism generally continued, although the old social relations dividing Mexicans from Anglos never completely disappeared. For example, the townspeople of Yorba Linda, California, refused to allow the housing of braceros in their city, forcing the nearby town of Placentia to board them within the segregated Mexican *colonia.* Nevertheless, the groundswell of activities reflected a more or less friendly atmosphere, as in nearby Whittier, California, where a key rancher decided to sponsor a Cinco de Mayo celebration for the braceros, complete with fiesta, films, and a literary and musical program.[18]

The Bracero as a "Different" Mexican

Shortly after the large migrations from Mexico began in the first decade of the twentieth century and the modern ethnic Mexican community was set in motion, the English-speaking community began to draw a subtle distinction between "good" Mexicans and "bad" Mexicans. The latter retained their lifestyle and culture reminiscent of Mexico and were considered to be at odds with Anglo American culture in terms of lack of ambition and satisfaction with low social status. The "good" Mexicans, often called "different" Mexicans, were those who were deemed to dress, speak, and act like members of the English-speaking community, and to embrace the same values. That same method for distinguishing the braceros emerged as well. During the early years of the program, the users of bracero labor, along with government officials and the news media, constructed an identity for braceros that differentiated them from the entire resident Mexican community. In *Americas,* the journal of the Organization of the American States, an article repeated the charge: "Almost invariably the growers reported that they prefer the Mexican nationals to any other workers. They are more likely to work and less likely to quit in the middle of the day to visit the saloon in town."[19] Eventually, this description attached to the braceros. The *California Annual Farm Report,* the journal of the California Department of Labor Farm Placement Service, acknowledged a similar situation in the citrus industry. Braceros were vitally important because of the "continued reluctance of the other farm workers to accept jobs in citrus picking."[20] Many spoke glowingly of the solution to the labor shortage that braceros provided, one that smoothed the oft-fractious relations between agribusiness and seasonal farm labor; but also, and more important, they described the braceros as quality workers, comparing them favorably to the existing labor supply.

Lawrence Hewes, the western states' regional director for the Farm Security Administration, which administered the bracero program in the early years, reaffirmed the growers' preferences:

> I ... have never until now seen ranchers and their labor in such complete accord working in such harmony. I have not found one rancher who does not speak well of the imported Mexican workers."

Hewes added that "Mexican braceros are a valiant element in these times of war and I can say that we have received from them more than we could ever have expected."[21]

Hewes's observations of shared benefits were not unusual in that there seemed to be a concerted effort to underscore a new set of social relations that were allegedly in the process of developing. The author of an article appearing in *The Inter-American,* the journal of the State Department's Office of Inter-American Affairs, contended that there were "few cases of discrimination against braceros"; he then went on to qualify the good fortune bestowed upon braceros:

> For one thing, most of the workers minded their own business, having little to do with the mass of the local population. The gringos, for

their part, behaved well, perhaps because they realized the importance of Mexican help to the war effort. Their few direct contacts with the Mexican laborers were friendly.[22]

In a similar vein, another writer noted the better reception accorded the braceros compared to "most of our Mexican immigrants," even though culturally they were at the same level. She quoted, as an example, a rancher who confessed to a "distinct change of heart." The author asked what accounted for his "change of heart." Was it the Good Neighbor Policy? The braceros' labor? The Mexican government? She concluded that

> [w]hatever the reason, these boys have caught our imagination. We watch them on the street, notice how quickly they adopt American clothes while keeping their characteristic grace and swing. We dust off our few words of Spanish and are rewarded with flashing smiles. We like their music. We discover their color sense.[23]

This early optimism also appeared in special radio broadcasts. A New Haven radio station, for example, invited a group of braceros who often sang at their labor camp to perform on the *We the People* program.[24] Not surprisingly, the praise for braceros often reached hyperbole. One writer stated that

> their presence is helping to cement friendly relations between the two countries. Their goodwill and earnest determination to help win the war stamp them as true soldiers of production, and they have found ready recognition of that fact in the friendly attitude of the people of the United States.[25]

The braceros seemed, at least for the time being, the perfect Mexicans, perpetually referred to as "Good Neighbors."[26] Indeed, it was said that their presence was changing, for the better, the attitude of the dominant community toward the resident Mexican community. A spokesperson for an organization working to better the condition of immigrants in the United States lauded the bracero program, contending that

> the system is working so successfully in the various states which are employing Mexican nationals that many people advocate permanent development of this system for American migrant laborers when the war is over.[27]

However, as we shall see, these positive albeit qualified *bienvenidos* and distinctions would last but a few years.

Authors writing for journals related to hemispheric relations such as *The Inter-American* and the *Bulletin of the Pan American Union* emphasized the unique international bonds of friendship inspired by the program. In a 1943 article in *The Inter-American,* Carey McWilliams noted some very positive bracero experiences, despite the segregationist practices taking place in a nearby town. He interviewed three "typical" braceros who, according to McWilliams, were "in substantial agreement about their experiences" and "were greatly impressed with California . . . and intended to return."[28] Two years later, in 1945, another author noted that the old ethnic tensions were dissolving even as the "old problems started to come up." The author continued:

> [I]t was the way the laborers worked. The Mexicans would take their time about doing things. They couldn't understand why the foremen were in such a hurry. The foremen, on the other hand, thought the Mexicans were lazy until they discovered, to their amazement, that the little brown men could work for endless hours under sun, rain, or snow, once they had set their pace.[29]

Apparently, the "old problems" had never disappeared in the first place: Mexicans were still considered "little brown men" who could work endlessly under any conditions. Nevertheless, news articles repeated the assertion that social relations, at least where braceros were concerned, were undergoing a process of reformation.

An article in *Business Week,* for example, affirmed that braceros were "guaranteed no discrimination because of race, equal pay with U.S. citizens doing similar work, equal accommodations, round-trip transportation, and subsistence en route."[30] The subtle message here was that relations between the immigrant Mexican community and the majority community were improving due to the presence (and the exemplary behavior) of braceros. In conventional fashion, a manager of a lemon growers association lauded the braceros for, as he put it, "[having] saved the day for us."

> In a short time they have learned more than many U.S. workers. Their behavior is excellent. Their attitude is inspiring. Their cleanliness, their housekeeping, their self-discipline are amazing. We are most impressed with their production records. . . . And none of them ever saw a lemon grove before.[31]

In the literature on this subject, titles themselves often conveyed a positive image. Examples cited in this chapter include "Mexicans Assist," "Mexicans on the Job," "They Saved the Crops," "The Mexicans Keep 'Em Rolling," "Cantando Llegaron de Mexico" (They Arrived from Mexico Singing), and "Good Neighbors Lend a Hand."

On a par with such titles were the photographs accompanying the articles reviewed here. A number of photos pictured the men after they had signed up at a recruiting station in Mexico. One in particular showed them aboard a train ready to travel to the border; jovial faces peered out of the Pullman windows as families waved good-bye, with the caption reading: "Off to the United States: families crowd the station platforms as they bid God-speed to the farm workers."[32] At the labor camps, several photographs featured braceros at dinnertime in the mess halls. One was captioned: "By smiles and diligent knife-and-fork activity, Mexican track workers on the Southern Pacific R. R. demonstrate satisfaction with special cooks and menus."[33] The men were smiling and appeared contented; one caption of a grinning bracero dressed in overalls and kneeling before a box of fruit read: "Worker proudly displaying the results of his labors."[34] Another, featuring a group of young braceros, observed: "After working a week picking sugar beets [the] boys demonstrated satisfaction, working for $5 dollars a day."[35] And finally, a photograph in the Spanish-language *La Opinion* was captioned: "Typical and smiling Mexican workers who form a part of an agricultural work force come to work in the United States by virtue of the accord signed between the governments of Mexico and the United States."[36] Optimistic descriptions of braceros working and enjoying their newfound experiences found their way into the dominant news media as well. One UP journalist declared, for example, that "the Mexicans who have come to this country obtain good salaries, good food and above all a good education."[37] Obviously, the message delivered across the United States, in English and in Spanish, was that braceros were a special category of Mexicans, not to be confused with the domestic Mexican community.

Ranchers and officials charged with administering the bracero program often described braceros as a godsend—as workers superior to domestic Mexicans, who were alleged to have become less desirable. In this connection, an FSA official in the San Francisco region stated what many believed to be the case—that the bracero program was "the most efficient use of manpower ever worked out in agriculture."[38]

Benefits for Mexico

Among the beneficiaries of the bracero program, Mexico figured prominently within an "all boats lifted equally" perspective. Observers noted that their experience in the United States would change the men forever and that upon returning they would also change Mexico with better-educated outlooks and minds filled with new and modern ideas about farming techniques and perhaps even technology. "The benefits of the Mexicans' stay in the United States was not one sided," reported one writer. "They learned new methods in agricultural and railroad work."[39] Their newly acquired outlook, gained without formal instruction but through hands-on experience, would serve in the modernization of Mexico, particularly its agricultural system. An editorial in *La Opinion* repeated the assertion, contending that in a short time "these men will find a propitious field for their betterment, acquiring knowledge that will serve to improve their own country."[40] Along with knowledge gained writers cited remittances, the money earned and mailed to families, as a key measure of Mexico's improved welfare.

In 1944 an estimated $3.5 million were sent to families by braceros—an amount considered to be a major source of revenue for Mexico.[41] Three years later, in an article appearing in *La Opinion* entitled "El Exodo de Braceros es Conveniente" (The Exodus of Braceros Is Useful"), it was reported that braceros had returned 200 million pesos and that the funds were invested in the "betterment of their small inheritances and lands that they possess."[42] Moreover, the article asserted, bracero earnings are of major importance for the Mexican economy. The author speculated that the cash might also be used for purchasing new mechanical tools and supplies for farming. A separate article reported that a policy authorizing braceros to "buy agricultural tools and implements and other equipment, with which they could mechanize their farming or establish small industries at home," was under study by the Mexican government. Although it appeared that this proposal never reached the policy stage, the discussion that braceros worked for Mexico extended across the United States.[43]

The welcoming ceremonies that had once greeted braceros all but disappeared. The last celebration for incoming braceros occurred in 1952, when a reception was held in the rural farming community of Traverse, Michigan—an area known for producing 30 percent of the U.S. cherry supply. The mixture of braceros and a few Mexican migrants were said to be "the lifeblood of orchards and canneries." And so the townspeople gathered themselves together and hosted a cultural exchange: English classes for the laborers and Spanish classes for the townspeople, among other arrangements.[44] Such displays had become anachronisms; once popular, they were later abandoned and forgotten, even in cities that had previously made grand efforts to welcome the braceros.

The war was over within a few years after the first braceros arrived, but the growers and railroads using their services now claimed that they could not part with the most cost-effective laborers ever to work for them. Ultimately, however, only agricultural interests—mainly large-scale corporations—would benefit from the several program extensions that occurred after 1946. In the postwar years, the welcoming celebrations and praise for braceros faded into a distant memory, but the reliance on these men expanded significantly, largely owing to the argument that a labor shortage threatened production and that the United States and Mexico benefited equally.

The Postwar Years

For the first seven years of the bracero contract, 10 percent of wages were to be deducted and placed in an account at Mexico's National Bank of Agricultural Credit. As a sign of things to come, in May 1946 returned braceros formed long lines at the Mexico City branch, seeking to withdraw the 10 percent of their wages that had been withheld but that somehow had been lost and was unavailable. Former braceros discovered that bank managers were unable to identify any such account, which at that time was estimated at over 30 million pesos. This angered the braceros, who, it was said, were "profoundly disgusted with the delay" and threatened demonstrations.[45] Less than a month later a plane loaded with twenty-eight braceros who had violated their contracts and were being deported crashed in the San Joaquin Valley, killing all aboard. Only twelve could be identified. Earlier that year five braceros were killed and eighteen injured in a bus accident as they were being transported to the fields in California's Imperial Valley.[46] Charges of police brutality were also circulating; a year after the bus accident, braceros accused the city police in Oxnard, California, of harassment and unjustified monitoring of bracero activities.[47] Ultimately, allegations of gross violations of the work contract became commonplace.

For at least eight years Mexican men, recruited to work in the United States as seasonal agricultural labor, provided 10 percent of their wages to unknown beneficiaries. Few if any braceros would receive this money, while deadly accidents, isolation bordering on outright segregation, the poorest living conditions imaginable, and subjugation to employer power and more, continued to characterize the bracero experience. Meanwhile, agricultural representatives were successfully lobbying in Washington for the program's extension—an effort that would bear fruit in 1951 with the passage of Public Law 78, which legalized labor importation for the next fourteen years.

Into this context came the wartime supporters of the bracero programs, Ernesto Galarza and Carey McWilliams among them, who began to mount stinging critiques of the program for continuing beyond its original valid purpose and wholesale violations of standard labor rights. As labor representative for the Pan American Union, Galarza once greeted workers at a welcoming ceremony with kind words and promises that the Union would look after their interests; by the late 1940s, however, he had become fiercely critical of the program. He eventually accused the Union of being an "utterly useless instrument for the maintenance of inter-American standards of work and living." In his estimation, the continuance of the bracero program beyond the wartime emergency meant that the Good Neighbor Policy rang hollow, amounting to mere political symbolism. In 1949 Galarza depicted the bracero program as a profit-oriented "subterfuge," designed to serve as cover for "a new phase of the old quest for sources of low-cost, inexperienced, unorganized mass labor power." Finally, he argued, "the original intention of the agreements by some of the early advocates—the protection of wage and living standards as well as civil rights of imported workers ... has been sidetracked."[48] With the passage of PL 78, Galarza immediately rose up in strong opposition, labeling it a "corporate farm measure" that made possible the "rape of three million farm workers" now working in the United States.[49]

Carey McWilliams, another one-time advocate of the wartime measure, added his critical perspective at around the same time that Galarza leveled his opposition. Braceros, argued McWilliams, "are used not only to keep farm wages down but are a source of 'controlled' or 'stand-by' labor in the event of a strike."[50] Indeed, McWilliams's contention that farm-worker wages either stood still or decreased during the bracero program has been borne out by research: Between 1946 and 1955, these wages as a proportion of manufacturing wages fell from 47.9 percent to 36.1 percent.[51] Galarza naturally raised a similar charge—that for domestic workers "[h]ourly rates have been frozen or cut back ... and working time has been reduced." The Catholic archbishop of San Antonio, Robert E. Lucey—one of the more notable critics condemning the program—joined with Galarza and McWilliams to argue that the need for braceros was "artificially induced by the refusal of big corporate farms to pay high enough wages for an American worker."[52] Moreover, asserted Archbishop Lucey, PL 78 "provides scant protections to the braceros."

Perhaps the most effective of all the critical publications to appear during the course of the bracero program was Galarza's *Strangers in Our Fields* (1956), written under the auspices of the Joint United States–Mexico Trade Union Committee. *Strangers* appeared soon after PL 78 had matured into a major labor importation program, its outlines fully developed. The succinct eighty-page study conducted personally through visits to camp housing, and to fields as braceros labored, revealed a government-sponsored labor program entirely under the control of agricultural corporations that oversaw wholesale violations of the work contract. Galarza cited a bracero's frank assessment of the program for all to see: "The contract means nothing. It only keeps us from taking a job where we could get a better wage." Galarza himself summed up the experience that would eventually affect 450,000 men: "[The bracero] has encountered ignorance, prejudice, and discrimination; he has learned what loneliness in the midst of a crowd can be; he has suffered exploitation, abuse, and injustice."[53] There were, in short, no redeeming qualities in the postwar bracero program, designated by one critic (several years after Galarza's booklet appeared) as "The Grapes of Wrath, Vintage 1961."[54] Into the 1950s and 1960s, braceros were an out-of-sight labor force, largely ignored by the majority of U.S. population. Galarza's criticisms, however, would eventually bring the issue to the political forefront.

In Defense of Indentured Servitude

Immediately upon publication of *Strangers in the Fields,* agribusiness responded in kind to the scathing overview and a controversy arose as to the exact nature of the bracero program. Indeed, growers undertook "an intensive publicity campaign to discredit both the report and the author" and, not surprisingly, sought to have the distribution of the study halted by government intervention, which did not happen.[55] The program's advocates contended vociferously that the program was a model of its kind and that all shared the dividends equally. It was said that braceros and Mexico benefited significantly from the program and that abuses were rare. For example, a former administrator of the bracero program in Las Cruces, New Mexico, stated in a 1959 study of the program: "If there are abuses, they are the exception and not the rule. They stem more from the unfortunate but inexorable ethnographic and geographic facts of Mexican life rather than from the presumed rapacity of the United States farmer."[56] Agribusinesses welcomed such voluntarily proffered redemptions and, to be sure, delivered their own defenses as well.

During the war, several observers (as noted above) found that growers had declared braceros to be "different" Mexicans, preferable to the domestic Mexican community as a labor supply. That stereotyped optimistic outlook reemerged despite criticism of the bracero program. One academic study conducted at the University of California concluded that in California's Coachella Valley, a region of heavy bracero use, ranchers preferred braceros to local Mexican workers. A social scientist conducting a study asked the following of a random selection of ranchers in Coachella, California: "What are the chief advantages in the employment of Mexican nationals compared with any other supply of labor?" The ranchers responded that braceros were "dependable," "available," "not afraid of hard work," and "generally a superior type of person." Other reasons were written in, among them that "Mexican nationals will not strike."[57] In response to Galarza the old refrains had indeed reemerged.

"They Help Feed America," a photo story of braceros in California published in *Today's Health,* the journal of the American Medical Association, served as one of many privately published items in support of the bracero users' position. Sixteen photographs of smiling, contented, and happy men at work and at play filled several pages; a brief review of the bracero program accompanying the photos described a truly positive experience for the men. In so doing, the article attempted to answer the basic criticisms leveled by a host of opponents. Readers were told that the contract was rigorously enforced and thus all rights and privileges held by braceros were strictly respected and observed; that the program supplied a supplemental labor force that was truly necessary, given real labor shortages that threatened agricultural production; that the program not only was of great benefit to the workers but also maintained production of important foods at optimal levels; and, finally, that any violations of the work contract were immediately dealt with and resolved.[58]

So ideal was the experience that being a bracero was likened to winning a lottery. "These men have a chance to accumulate a nest egg with which to buy *la parcela,* or small farm," claimed the authors. Many acquired "small stores and other small businesses," and "others have been helped in their education for one of the professions."[59] In fact, one former bracero used his savings to start a clothing factory and "now employs more than 2000 workers." Another became "one of Mexico's outstanding young lawyers," and yet another was named one of the "top young executives in General Motors." Photos displayed men at a mess hall with food heaped on their plates, at well-equipped doctor's offices undergoing health examinations, and returning to Mexico wearing the latest garb popular in the United States.

The article emphasized rather pointedly that a bracero had a better life in the United States than in Mexico and that this experience "creates a good-neighbor benefit in Mexico by helping to bolster his country's economy." To convince the reader that all was well, the authors interviewed Ernesto Romero, the consul general at the Mexican Consulate in Los Angeles, who testified: "We are pleased with the steady progress that has been made in the migrant labor program in the last five years or so.... Our people report better facilities in these camps and higher financial returns." A citrus grower concurred and guaranteed that "these good workers" will be "treated in return with a fair hand and a warm heart."[60] Keep in mind that the role of the consulates was to ensure that the protections written into the international agreements would be strictly observed. In actuality, however, the consuls gave priority to the defense of the program over criticisms of men like Galarza and generally abandoned the defense of the bracero contract itself.

Critics rankled many a grower and were targets of heated responses. One Texas grower and employer of bracero labor penned an article based on personal observations in which he claimed that detractors failed to understand the benefits for Mexico. Braceros, he argued, earn in three days what they would earn in a month of labor in Mexico, which "results in greatly increased comfort and even comparative enrichment for his family." Moreover, the amount remitted "constitutes, after mining and tourism, that country's third-largest source of national income." Of all the lasting benefits to Mexico, remittances were considered the most important of all, and authors never lost sight of the topic. Numerous articles informed their readers that braceros earned a small fortune. For example, the author of a photo-article in *Look* magazine reported that for the average bracero the "fortunes awaiting him are as fabulous" as those during the old California gold rush. "With his savings," assured this author, "he can open up a small store—top status symbol in interior Mexico."[61] A *Saturday Evening Post* article underscored "the considerable benefit to Mexico" from the import of bracero earnings.[62] Allegedly, the money that was earned relieved unemployment and poverty.

Freely expended public funds were spent in a attempt to bolster the image of the bracero program. The State of California Department of Employment published "Mexican Nationals in California Agriculture" in 1959 to allay any doubts that the program was not a model of its kind. Readers were assured that all provisions of the work contract were designed to protect the interests of the bracero as well as those of the employer. Furthermore, all provisions related to wages, housing, work conditions, and grievance resolution were strictly observed. According to the publication all "corrective compliance" measures were implemented according to contract stipulations. Either all conditions shouldered by the employers were complied with or corrective actions were taken immediately to ensure compliance.[63]

A wing of the program's defenders admitted that abuses occasionally occurred, and one agreed that exploitation sometimes affected braceros. According to a bracero employer, any problems currently affecting the program were localized, and can and will be resolved through careful study and effective policy changes.[64] Despite the admission, most compared the situation of braceros in the United States to conditions in Mexico to defuse the criticism. One author claimed, "[I]f these conditions were not better than those prevailing in Mexico, there is no apparent explanation for the continuance of this voluntary migration. After all, he continued, "Mexico exports her labor and imports foreign exchange."[65] The argument that no matter the conditions under which braceros labored, and despite abuse and exploitation, they were better off in America than they would be in Mexico. Even at congressional hearings such relativistic defense was heard from time to time. In a 1957 discussion on bracero housing, one congressman criticized regulations on living quarters that promised each bracero a minimal space of six feet by a foot and three-quarters. "It seems to me," he argued, "that is an unusual amount of space for a human being to live in. . . . Does that give the person a chance to stand up or sit down in a chair or lie down in a bed?" A fellow congressman rose to his feet, challenged the remark, and defended the allotted living space. "Let me tell you something of what actually happens," he said. "Many of these people who come up into our country to work during the summertime never had a roof over them until they came. They have lived out of doors."[66] In other words, now that they have a roof, regardless of the space, they should be happy.

High school students, too, learned about the program through *Senior Scholastic,* a weekly news report that purported to inform teachers and students of current world and domestic issues. In its issue dated April 17, 1959, the publication advised its readers that most "braceros earn as much in an hour as they do in a whole day back home," which resonated with the congressman's contention that whatever the braceros' housing conditions, they're better than what can be had in Mexico. Moreover, bracero earnings turned into remittances said to total $30,000,000—"second only to that from American tourists." Finally, the matter of U.S.-Mexico relations entered the picture, with a confirmation that the bracero program was "an excellent—and efficient—way to cement good neighbor relations."[67] Several other *Scholastic* issues also contained articles on braceros, with similar optimistic interpretations of the program.

The Growers' Responses

Immediately upon the appearance of substantially researched analyses that exposed the glaring gap between theory and practice—indeed, revealed the actual practice—growers rose to their defense via state-sponsored publications and privately funded public-relations efforts. Every critical examination of the program and its conclusions was to be discredited—and to accomplish this goal, the growers lost no time. The annual *California Farm Labor Report,* the official organ of the Department of Employment Farm Placement Service (a public office

virtually under the control of agricultural corporations), lost no opportunity to defend the bracero program in each of its issues. In the 1954
issue, for example, the *Report* patted growers on the back, commenting
positively on all components of the program and their implementation. According to the issue editors, the growers held high opinions of
braceros, believing that each of them had proved time and again to be
"an industrious and serious worker, happy for the opportunity of the
American work experience and saving money to further his personal
objectives upon returning to Mexico."[68] The *Report* insisted that non-
compliance occurred mainly among those employers who were new to
the bracero program and had little familiarity with the regulations, but
that once a grower learned the rules, compliance was ensured.

In 1956 the *Report* resorted to a long-standing means of validating the
program in the public's eye—the testimony of Mexican consuls. According
to official reports submitted by the consuls to program administrators,

> the work experience ... continues to have a beneficial impact in Mexico.
> Returning men have not only advanced themselves financially, but
> they take home new standards of living, new knowledge, and better
> health, which have exerted influence for betterment in their home
> communities.[69]

The 1957 issue continued the defense, contending that braceros
"were well satisfied with their employment," and extended a rather
detailed description of the program in California. The "Mexican men
came and worked hard," began the section on braceros, and they
"were well satisfied. ... " It continued as follows:

> Most were well qualified, reliable workers who were serious in doing
> the job well and in benefiting themselves through the experience and
> earnings they would take home. Considering the large number of in-
> dividual Mexicans involved, there was remarkable orderliness in the
> conduct of the workers, on the job and in the communities where they
> worked. They elicited and won acceptance and friendliness of employ-
> ers and communities. They were appreciative of the efforts made for
> their comfort and recreation. Medical facilities were often located in
> or near the camps.

As in past years, all grievances were handled amicably through the
intervention of the Mexican consuls, who "were particularly helpful

in reconciling individual problems of Mexican workers." [70]

Perhaps the strongest grower effort to respond to these many criticisms came from the film *Why Braceros?* produced by the California Council of Growers in 1959. This public-relations project originated from a script written long before the film appeared, presenting a labor importation program that met all the provisions of the work contract and more. Again, the message was that no one was exploited and everyone earned their rightful due. The familiar mantras resurfaced, including those regarding the use of the Mexican consul to buttress the growers' arguments. Viewers were told that braceros were hired only because of the demonstrated scarcity of a local labor, that braceros earned no more or less than that paid domestic labor, and that the work contract was rigorously enforced. In order to make their contentions even stronger, the producers invited Mexican Consul Antonio Islas to provide his assessment. In a scene showing the consul chatting with a large Sunday gathering of relaxed, well-dressed and -groomed braceros (which contrasted with the usual condition of the men, who seldom dressed in anything other than work clothes), a voice-over recorded Islas offering his perspectives—which, of course, supported the growers' arguments. In Islas's opinion the operation of the bracero program was in full accord with the international agreement, the highest possible standards had been enforced, and very few violations were being committed. He added that the welfare of the workers was primary in the minds of the growers, guaranteeing that the men "were well treated"; that additional income flowed into the workers' pockets and indirectly into Mexico; and that upon arrival in the United States braceros wore old, threadbare clothing but upon returning to Mexico they were well dressed and pleased with their experience. Otherwise, "why would they come back?" asked the consul. In Islas's words, the program appropriated "mutual benefits" to Mexico and the United States. The Mexican government and the growers agreed: "Braceros are a must." [71]

Into the 1960s the growers' stance remained relatively unchanged, although there appeared to be more "indebtedness" toward the braceros than was normally the case. In the 1964 edition of the *Report,* prominent mention was made of the debt owed to "the thousands of friendly workers who have come from Mexico … to help out on our farms." Yet in keeping with the "mutual benefits" claimed by growers that validated the program, bracero' earnings were said to allow the workers to return with containers full of American products and to improve "their economic conditions at home in Mexico."[72]

Foreign Policy and Braceros

Federal authorities joined "shoulder to shoulder" with the growers in the latter's defense. In a U.S. Department of Labor booklet titled *Farm Labor Fact Book*, published in 1959, the bracero program was "recognized as an outstanding example of statesmanlike thinking." (Interestingly, the Department of Labor booklet and the film *Why Braceros?* appeared in the same year.) As expected, the matter of bracero grievances and contract violations was given due space. According to the federal authorities, there were bound to be difficulties and grievances, but these were "caused by differences in cultural and economic practices"—that is, by misunderstandings resulting from culturally based interpretations rather than from deliberate violations on the part of growers. The *Fact Book* also described the overall administration and operation of the program, as well as the average bracero's experience in the United States, as nothing short of ideal. Published with the approval of Secretary of Labor James P. Mitchell, it closed with the conventional references to U.S. foreign policy interests:

> Out of this international farm labor program, Mexico gains economically by acquiring through her people who work on U.S. farms a considerable practical knowledge of modern farming equipment, technological information which is later turned to use in the crop yield and management of Mexico's farms, and substantial acquaintance with the ways of living in a highly industrialized society.[73]

Combining the program with U.S. foreign policy became standard procedure among not only growers but also state authorities tied to the program. *The California Farmer,* a farmer publication, went to great lengths to validate the program, including an effort to link it with the Alliance for Progress in its April 1963 issue. Not content with merely connecting the two, the journal author contended that "the bracero program was the first real 'alliance for progress' between the United States and Mexico." He then went on to express what by then had become commonplace arguments: that the program provided an "important source of income to Mexico" and that returned braceros often used their money to "buy a small tractor, a mill to grind corn,

... improvements on his homestead or home or to buy a small business of his own." The result: "a tremendous impact on the economy of the smaller farming communities of Mexico." And whenever unemployment plagued a rural sector of Mexico "the bracero program really proves its worth" by relieving Mexico's unemployment problem, transporting them en masse to work on California's farms.[74]

Finally, the author assured his readers that "[t]here are no major problems in the bracero program now," and that the occasional complaints that came up were related mainly to the braceros' preferences for foods other than those served at mess halls, and to their desire for "medical attention." Any abuses relating to the day-to-day operations of the program, the article continued, came mainly from hired help; that is, the foremen became the sacrificial lambs (most were Mexican immigrants or second generation themselves). No wonder, exclaimed the author, that the "bracero program is our best example of the 'good neighbor' policy in action." Without a doubt, he added, the program "helps to promote increased goodwill and understanding between peoples of the two countries."[75] One should not assume that the writer spoke from personal experience alone. Senator J. William Fulbright, chair of the Senate Foreign Relations Committee, felt similarly about the benefits wrought by the bracero program for both countries. At a congressional hearing he advised:

> This is an important program to Mexico. It is her second most important source of American dollars. Mexico is one of our best customers and in 1960 our exports to that country were $807 billion compared to imports of $433 billion. Our continued favorable balance of trade with Mexico indicates the importance to American business of maintaining this program.
>
> Aside from the economic importance of this program to Mexico, there are also important intangible benefits which accrue to both that country and ours. The program has been very effective in improving understanding between the peoples of our countries.[76]

However, Fulbright failed to mention that, for Mexico, the program had a significant downside. For example, U.S. cotton growers were in no mood to allow Mexican producers (who were funded by U.S. banks) to freely compete, and from time to time they dumped cotton on the international market—meaning Mexico. Ironically, it was bracero labor that produced the cotton dumped on Mexico; in addition, bracero labor was utilized to produce surpluses for export and to compete with foreign producers rather than shore up slacks in inventories.[77]

The Americanization of Indentured Labor

Photographs sketching the bracero experience accompanied each of the issues of the *California Farm Labor Report* discussed above. The men were invariably pictured as smiling, well dressed, and cared for, living in comfortable surroundings. A typical photo showed men about to board a bus to begin their return trip to Mexico. Its caption read: "These braceros have completed their work contracts.... They have already sent home thousands of dollars ... and take with them new knowledge, new standards of living, health, new clothes, tools, presents, and other purchases."[78] Numerous photos in other issues displayed a similar effort to demonstrate the "before and after" images of the men. Upon their arrival, they wore peasant-like dress; upon their departure, they sported typical American clothing. That the experience changed the men for the better, that it Americanized them, was implied not only in the photos discussed here but in the overall literature as well.

Several affirmations of the program underscored the "uplift" that working in the United States guaranteed for Mexico. One author portrayed Mexicans as a sort of clay ready to be molded into proper human beings, a depiction that resonated with imperialist images of colonized subjects. "For the most part," he wrote, "they are abjectly impoverished, abysmally ignorant, wholly primitive spiritually and morally."[79] In *Mexican Life,* an English-language journal published in Mexico, the defense of the bracero program called to mind conventional European justifications for colonialism. Braceros were said to be uneducated minions from an "inferior environment," which they had left to enter "another that is at a higher stage of development." The bracero experience, a kind of educational odyssey, brought the less fortunate to a higher level of society for reformation. In the process of working in the United States, each bracero "improves himself enormously." The effects on braceros were nothing short of revolutionary:

They replace their sandals with shoes.... [T]hey are obliged, whether they like it or not, to change their material lives for the better. Their food includes meat, milk, bread, as well as tortillas when they can get them; many of them wear wool suits. They have beds instead of mats to sleep on, plus furniture, no matter how simple, and in many cases running water, toilet, radio and other conveniences. They go to the doctor and consume modern medicines. They learn to plant, cultivate, and harvest with modern techniques, and become familiar with various industries and the use of efficient tools and machinery.[80]

Under the United States' tutelage, braceros and therefore Mexico itself were placed on the path to membership in modern civilization.

As the reader can see, not only economic refugees from the Mexican countryside were undergoing progressive change; implicitly Mexico, too, was on the road to modernization. Several authors made it a point to demonstrate that the bracero program went hand in hand with U.S. plans for the economic development of the underdeveloped world. A 1952 Department of State *Bulletin,* for example, considered Mexico's accommodating attitude toward the export of surplus labor and foreign-financed modernization to be a sign of positive interaction between the two governments, whereby "the rewards are great and the benefits are mutual."[81]

One observer noted, in an article ironically titled "Braceros Farm for Mexico," that in the states of Sinaloa, Sonora, and Baja California the returning braceros were making their mark on the economic development of the regions. Success stories were told as if these were the general consequence for all returned men. The account of Pablo Ramos, appearing in the Pan American Union's *Americas,* was typical of the take on U.S.-Mexico relations and the bracero program. It related that Ramos returned to Mexico with new knowledge of "diversified farming," and that with government aid he had purchased 360 acres of undeveloped land, a wheel tractor, a thresher in addition to a Chevrolet pickup truck, and "an assortment of other farm implements." The story was not about Pablo Ramos alone, however. It also connected the success of the bracero experience with the economic development policies designed in Washington and implemented by the Mexican government.[82]

Surrounding Ramos's cotton farm were a variety of U.S. corporate interests providing chemicals, fertilizers, pesticides, machinery, and transportation. In fact, the railroad, dam, electrification, irrigation, and highway construction projects in the area were made possible with sizable loans from several U.S. banks, including the Export Import

Bank, which invested $260,000,000 in highways, railways, electrification, and more. Meanwhile, the International Bank for Reconstruction and Development invested $90,000,000 for dams, electrification, and railroads and the World Bank assisted in the construction of irrigation facilities.[83]

One author described this economic tie (under the heading "Economic Development Program") as one in which the United States has served as the "chief source of foreign capital for Mexico," a virtual open door "that has welcomed the entrance of capital from abroad."[84] The support for this policy among the people of Mexico, alleged the author, comes from an "urge to emulate the United States and its experience." A message reiterated in the literature defending the bracero program advised that Mexico's eventual Americanization resulted both from the transformation of Mexican men undergoing the bracero experience and from programs for economic development, within which returned braceros settled into and assumed leading positions.

Conclusion

One might interpret the celebratory mood of the wartime bracero program as an aspect of the struggle against fascism. However, once the war ended and the original justification for the program dissolved, the arguments for continuing the program amounted to nothing less than wholesale lying to the public. There was never a shred of evidence supporting the contention that the bracero program supplemented a diminished labor supply, contributed to the economic development of Mexico, or led to a radical alteration of the work and living conditions of the returned braceros. Growers never acknowledged their systematic exploitation of the braceros, nor did they promote anything other than an idealized image of the program to the public. In fact, the bracero program failed to change the status of Mexico's subject relationship with the United States; if anything, it exemplified the United States' economic domination. Mexico remained a supplier of labor power and an importer of foreign capital, a condition persisting to this day.

Notes

1. Robert C. Jones, *Mexican War Workers in the United States*, Washington, D.C.: Pan American Union, 1945, p. 40.

2. Marco Alamazan, "The Mexicans Keep 'Em Rolling," *The Inter-American,* vol. 4, no. 10 (October 1945): 22.

3. Carey McWilliams, Director, State of California, Division of Immigration and Housing, to Nelson A. Rockefeller, Coordinator, OIAA, October 15, 1941. National Archives. Department of State Files, Office of Inter-American Affairs.

4. "Memorandum for the Files" (November 17, 1942); "Second Inter-Agency Meeting on Problems of Spanish Speaking Peoples" (December 11, 1942); Joseph E. Weckler, Assistant to the Director, Division of Inter-American Activities, to Mr. Charles Olsen, Office of War Information (April 19, 1943). National Archives. State Department Files. Office of Inter-American Affairs.

5. Carey McWilliams, "They Saved the Crops," *The Inter-American,* vol. 2 (August 1943): 14.

6. Jose Garduño, "Cantando Llegaron de Mexico," *La Opinion* (October 18, 1942).

7. Anne Roller Issler, "Good Neighbors Lend a Hand," *Survey Graphic,* vol. 32, no. 10 (October 1943): 392.

8. Garduño, "Cantando Llegaron de Mexico."

9. "Braceros Mexicanos," *La Opinion* (March 25, 1942).

10. Quoted in "Es Elogiado el Esfuerzo de Los Braceros Mexicanos," *La Opinion* (October 28, 1943).

11. Quoted in "Elogio Para el Esfuerzo de los Braceros," *La Opinion* (December 29, 1943).

12. Dorothy M. Tercero, "Workers from Mexico," *Bulletin of the Pan American Union,* vol. 78 (September 1944): 504.

13. Helen Jean Nolan, "On the Home Front," *The Inter-American,* vol. 4 (July, 1945): 37.

14. Issler, "Good Neighbors Lend a Hand," 391.

15. "Los Obreros Mexicanos, Agasajados," *La Opinion* (November 26, 1942).

16. Issler, "Good Neighbors Lend a Hand," 390.

17. Tercero, "Workers from Mexico," 505.

18. "Celebraran el 5 de Mayo Los Braceros," *La Opinion* (May 4, 1945).

19. "Braceros," *Americas,* vol. 1, no. 1 (March, 1949): 17.

20. *California Annual Farm Labor Report.* State of California. Department of Employment, Farm Placement Service, 1949: 29.

21. Quoted in "Elogio a Los Braceros Mexicanos," *La Opinion* (June 16, 1943).

22. Almazan, "The Mexicans Keep 'Em Rolling," 21.

23. Issler, "Good Neighbors Lend a Hand," 390.

24. Almazan, "The Mexicans Keep 'Em Rolling," 22.

25. Tercero, "Workers from Mexico," 503–504.

26. See for example Issler, "Good Neighbors Lend a Hand;" Tercero, "Workers from Mexico," *Bulletin of the Pan American Union;* and "Regresan a Mexico Otros 201 Braceros," *La Opinion* (January 3, 1946). The latter article quoted a railroad company official who stated "I believe firmly that the movement [of braceros] contributed well to the understanding of the two neighboring countries."

27. Cecilia Razovsky Davidson, "Mexican Laborers Imported into the United States," *Interpreter Releases,* vol. 20, no. 38 (October 18, 1943): 300; see also Albert Maisel, "The Mexicans Among Us," *Reader's Digest,* vol. 68 (March 1956): 184.

28. Carey McWilliams, "They Saved the Crops," p. 12.

29. Marco A. Almazan, "The Mexicans Keep 'Em Rolling," *The Inter-American,* p. 23.

30. "Mexicans on the Job," *Business Week* (January 1944): 82.

31. Carey McWilliams, "They Saved the Crops," p. 14.

32. Dorothy M. Tercero, "Workers from Mexico," p. 503.

33. "Mexicans Assist," *Business Week* (October 1944): 54.

34. Carey McWilliams, "They Saved The Crops," *The Inter-American,* vol. 2 (August 1943): 14.

35. Garduño, "Cantando Llegaron de Mexico," *La Opinion* (October 18, 1942).

36. *La Opinion* (October 14, 1942).

37. William E. Best, "Ayuda de los Braceros en Estados Unidos," *La Opinion* (May 29, 1945).

38. Anne Roller Issler, "Good Neighbor Lends a Hand," p. 394.

39. Marco Almazan, "The Mexicans Keep 'em Rolling," p. 24.

40. "Braceros Mexicanos," *La Opinion* (March 25, 1942).

41. "Las Ganancias de los Braceros," *La Opinion* (October 15, 1944).

42. "El Exodo de Braceros es Conveniente," *La Opinion* (August 24, 1947).

43. Dorothy M. Tercero, "Workers From Mexico," *Bulletin of the Pan American Union,* p. 506.

44. Grace McIlrath Ellis, "A Barrier Traversed," *The Rotarian,* vol. 81 (August 1952): 31.

45. "Se Forman Largas Colas de Braceros," *La Opinion* (May 15, 1946).

46. "5 Braceros Mexicanos Muertos en un Accidente," *La Opinion* (January 4, 1946).

47. "Mal Trato a los Braceros Mexicanos de Oxnard," *La Opinion* (January 10, 1947).

48. Ernesto Galarza, "Program for Action," *Common Ground,* vol. 10, no. 4 (November 1949): 30–31. Galarza and others felt that the transfer of the administration of the Bracero Program for the Farm Security Administration to the Department of Labor undercut the protections afforded braceros and left the door open for grower control of the Program. Carey McWilliams, for example, contended that while the protections were not 100 percent they were nonetheless "substantial." However, he also feared that turning the Program to the Department of Labor by way of PL 45 would nullify protections and hand oversight to the growers, which it did. He feared that a post-FSA managed Bracero Program would be a revival of "the old discredited system of private labor contractors." He was right. (McWilliams, "They Saved the Crops").

49. Ernesto Galarza, "They Work for Pennies," *The American Federationist,* vol. 59 (April 1952): 11.

50. Carey McWilliams, "Migrants: Inquiry of Inquest?" *The Nation,* vol. 171 (September 30, 1950): 286.

51. Eleanor Hadley, "Critical Analysis of the Wetback Problem," *Law and Contemporary Problems,* vol. 21 (Spring 1956): 356; see also George O. Coalson, "Mexican Contract Labor in American Agriculture," *Southwestern Social Science,* vol. 33 (September 1952): 236–237.

52. "And Now Braceros," *Americas,* vol. 90 (March 6, 1954): 587; see also James F. Rooney, "The Effects of Imported Mexican Farm Labor in a California County," *American Journal of Economics and Sociology,* vol. 20 (October 1961).

53. Ernesto Galarza, *Strangers in the Fields,* Washington, D.C.: Joint United States–Mexico Trade Union Committee: 1956, p. 80.

54. Arnold Mayer, "The Grapes of Wrath, Vintage 1961," *The Reporter* (February 2, 1961): 34. The author went on to state "The [bracero] effect on farm labor income has been disastrous. Wages for field labor in most of Texas have stayed at the same level for nearly a decade—about fifty cents an hour."

55. Joseph P. Lyford, "An Army of Ill-Will Ambassadors," *The New Republic,* vol. 136 (March 1957): 19.

56. Richard H. Hancock, *The Role of the Bracero in the Economic and Cultural Dynamic of Mexico,* Stanford, California: Hispanic American Society, 1959, p. 15.

57. Edward C. McDonagh, "Attitudes Toward Ethnic Farm Workers in the Coachella Valley," *Sociology and Social Research,* vol. 40 (September 1955): 15.

58. Cy La Tour and Thomas Gorman, "They Help Feed America," *Today's Health,* vol. 35 (October 1957).

59. La Tour and Gorman, "They Help Feed America," 26.

60. Ibid., p. 27.

61. "A New Deal for the Mexican Worker," *Look,* vol. 23 (September 29, 1959): 56.

62. Fred Eldridge, "Helping Hands From Mexico," *Saturday Evening Post* (August 10, 1957): 63.

63. State of California, Department of Employment. "Mexican Nationals in California," Sacramento: State of California Printing Office (November 2, 1959).

64. Robert R. Cunningham, "North and South of the Border," *America,* vol. 97, no. 2 (August 17, 1957): 502.

65. Laura Randall, "Labour Migration and Mexican Economic Development," *Social and Economic Studies,* vol. 12, no. 1 (March 1962): 76.

66. "Congressional Record," *New Republic,* vol. 136 (April 8, 1957): 5.

67. "New Pact on Braceros?" *Senior Scholastic,* vol. 74 (April 17, 1959): 27–28.

68. State of California, Department of Employment, Farm Placement Service, *California Annual Farm Labor Report* (May 15, 1954), p. 30.

69. State of California, Department of Employment, Farm Placement Service, *California Annual Farm Labor Report* (May 15, 1956), p. 78.

70. State of California, Department of Employment, Farm Placement Service, *California Annual Farm Labor Report* (June, 1957), p. 66.

71. *Why Braceros,* a film produced by the California Council of Growers, 1959. The California Council of Growers also produced booklets, such as "Some Facts About Braceros" advising the public in dry bureaucratic language of their views on the Bracero Program. In the publication mentioned the Council painted the Program in positive terms asserting that all provisions of the contract were rigorously observed. (Council of California Growers, "Some Facts About Braceros," Los Angeles: Council of California Growers (April 1963).

72. State of California, Department of Labor Farm Placement Service, *Annual Farm Labor Report* (June, 1964). Sacramento: State of California Department of Labor, p. 68.

73. U.S. Department of Labor. James P. Mitchell, Secretary. *Farm Labor Fact Book.* Washington, D.C.: U.S. Government Printing Office, 1959, p. 176.

74. Don Taylor, "How Mexico Feels About the Bracero Program," *The California Farmer* (April 20, 1963): 42.

75. Ibid., pp. 43–44.

76. Quoted in T. Richard Spradlin, "Legislation Notes: The Mexican Farm Labor Importation Program—Review and Reform (part II, section 6, Congressional Action), *George Washington Law Review,* vol. 30 (December 1961): 319.

77. Ibid., p. 321. Spradlin quotes a publication of Mexico's Banco de Comercio Exterior: "The situation [imbalances of Mexican foreign trade] is further aggravated by certain cases of open disregard for the vital interests of the Mexican economy, exemplified by the U.S. cotton dumping on the international markets. Mexico does not receive far treatment from her northern neighbor." Spradlin went on to say, "Surely, Mexican cotton producers [who borrowed heavily from U.S. banks], bankers, and government officials are aware that much of the cotton which they complain the United States is dumping of the world market is produced with the labor of Mexican workers." Clearly, the United States protected its own interests even at the risk of hurting Mexican producers and the Mexican economy.

78. State of California, Department of Employment, Farm Placement Service, *California Annual Farm Labor Report* (May 15, 1956), p. 77.

79. Robert C. Cunningham, "North and South of the Border," *Americas,* vol. 97 (August 17, 1957): 501.

80. Carlos Gamio Leon, "Braceros Bring Home New Ways," *Mexican Life,* vol. 10, no. 37 (September 1961): 22.

81. Edward G. Miller, Jr., "Rewards of U.S.-Mexican Cooperation," United States Department of State *Bulletin,* vol. 36 (March 31, 1952): 499–500.

82. Verne A. Baker, "Braceros Farm for Mexico," *Americas,* vol. 5 (September 1953): 30–31.

83. Craig L. Dozier, "Mexico's Transformed Northwest: The Yaqui, Mayo and Fuerte Examples," *Geographical Review,* vol. 53 (October 1963): 558.

84. P. C., "Mexico Today," *The World Today,* vol. 10 (March 1954): 118.

A bracero's home (Nadel Collection, Smithsonian Institution, National Museum of American History)

"I became a bracero because I had few resources and I was of a humble class. My parents were old and I had to do something to give them food and take them to the doctor when they got sick. We lived in an adobe house. The floor was of dirt; the house had no doors. Since my parents could no longer work, at the age of fourteen I decided to become a bracero along with my brother."

—Jose Maria Gonzalez

Men walking to a recruiting center; a grave on the roadside is that of a would-be bracero who died on the way (Nadel Collection, Smithsonian Institution, National Museum of American History)

"The needs were so great that many died on the way but that didn't stop the struggle to come to the United States where there was work."

—Conrado Cardenas

Waiting outside the Mexico City soccer stadium, site of the recruiting center (Courtesy Howard Rosenberg)

"It was very difficult at the recruiting station because we came from long distances and when we got there we suffered a lot, such as not having a place to sleep and food to eat when we ran out of money. Getting a contract brought a lot of suffering. Many had no money to last a month or fifteen days, and they suffered very much. Those who had the resources got off okay. But if they came without enough money then they were sure to suffer."

—Jose Maria Gonzalez

Recruiting center in northern Mexico (Nadel Collection, Smithsonian Institution, National Museum of American History)

"At the recruiting center, we waited about fifteen days for a contract. We slept while waiting in line. We wouldn't go rent a room because we would lose our place in the line. If one got out, another would sneak in."

—Celedonio Perez

Recruiting center in northern Mexico (Nadel Collection, Smithsonian Institution, National Museum of American History)

"At the Empalme recruiting station one had to wait a long time. Waiting lasted from eight to twenty days. The last time I was contracted I waited twenty-two days and didn't eat for three days. My companions also didn't eat. Once in 1959 some people asked me when I had last eaten and when I told them they gave me food."

—Jose Hernandez Diaz

Hand inspection at a recruiting center (Nadel Collection, Smithsonian Institution, National Museum of American History)

"They would check to see who had good hands; who was agile. You know, some had a bad hand, possibly broken at one time and they would look closely at your arms. … Those who had no calluses were not contracted; supposedly they were not good workers."

—Jose Maria Gonzalez

Department of Labor inspector at a recruiting center (Nadel Collection, Smithsonian Institution, National Museum of American History)

"Our stay at the recruiting center was more difficult than trying to get there because we stayed there in the big crowd of people and the contractors were very strict. They selected you as if you were an animal. Depending on the rancher and his requirements, they chose you on the basis of your capacity to work: tomato, onion, chili, potato, and all those things; they wanted a certain capacity in the men for each kind of work. If the work was on the tracks, they selected men of a certain type. If the work required a ladder, then they chose another type of man, depending on their needs."

—Sotero O. Cervantes

Health inspection at a recruiting center (Nadel Collection, Smithsonian Institution, National Museum of American History)

"[The process of becoming a bracero] was difficult in the sense that we had to undergo examinations; it was hard to undergo a general checkup and it was embarrassing; one had to forget not having clothes on. One had to undergo the exam no matter what, because they didn't want infected people under any circumstances; they only wanted healthy people in good condition for work."

—Rafael Luna Anaya

Sprayed with lindane at a border recruiting center (Nadel Collection, Smithsonian Institution, National Museum of American History)

"We had a lot of trouble at the border recruiting center; well, problems for us because we were not accustomed to that kind of treatment nor did we know the rules of the United States. It is probable that they were operating according to the law but for us it was very different. We suffered humiliations; they fumigated us like animals. Perhaps that was according to their law but we felt humiliated, but we were obligated; we had to accept it for our families. Still these things were very hard for us."

—Sotero O. Cervantes

Mexican workers are assigned to pick oranges and lemons near Anaheim, Orange County.

Arriving at Anaheim, California (California Annual Farm Labor Report)

Braceros laboring in a California lettuce field (Nadel Collection, Smithsonian Institution, National Museum of American History)

"In the lettuce there were no fixed days or hours. Whenever a packinghouse order came in, they needed us to work even though it might be raining because if the packinghouse wanted it we had to deliver. Normally, we would work six days but things were often disordered. At the moment the packinghouse placed an order then we had to go to work. They would get us up at 3 in the morning and take us to the field and if the lettuce had ice covering it, then we had to wait for the ice to melt, which meant we'd have to wait maybe 'til 10 in the morning before we could begin working."

—Martin Perez Serrato

Walking to the camp at the end of a day's work (Nadel Collection, Smithsonian Institution, National Museum of American History)

Washing up in a tent camp site (Nadel Collection, Smithsonian Institution, National Museum of American History)

"When we got back to camp, we'd wash up before we went to eat. In the tomatoes, you get really dirty, like a dog, so you'd want to go in there clean, with your clothes changed."

—Rigoberto Garcia Perez

Web work camp housing (Nadel Collection, Smithsonian Institution, National Museum of American History)

"We slept in big bunkhouses. It was like being in the army. Each person had their own bed, one on top of the other, with a mattress, blanket, and so on. They'd tell us to keep the place clean, to make our beds when we got up. We woke up when they sounded a horn or turned on the lights. We'd make our beds and go to the bathroom, eat breakfast, and they'd give us our lunch."

—Rigoberto Garcia Perez

Barrack housing for braceros (Nadel Collection, Smithsonian Institution, National Museum of American History)

Barrack housing for braceros (Nadel Collection, Smithsonian Institution, National Museum of American History)

"My experience as a bracero was very bad. I had to work hard and they treated you like they would a slave. We could not even leave the camp where we lived."

—Conrado Cardenas

Bracero camp eating hall (Nadel Collection, Smithsonian Institution, National Museum of American History)

"At mealtime, if we didn't come quickly and line up when the bell sounded, we wouldn't get a meal. We had to run, line up so that we could eat."

—Bernabe Linares Ramirez

Payday for braceros at a northern California camp (Nadel Collection, Smithsonian Institution, National Museum of American History)

"When we come here, we think that we may be lucky and return to Mexico with a few hundred dollars American. But most of us are only able to make enough to sustain our families while we are away. Our families are so large, you know. And we are not allowed to stay here long enough to make enough money to do the things that we had planned. I know many braceros who have been to your country many times, but I do not know any of them who have been able to make enough money, or keep it long enough to do what they had planned."

—A former bracero (quoted in Anderson, *Harvest of Loneliness*)

Going home (California Annual Farm Labor Report)

"It was humiliating. They rented us. They took advantage of our labor, and when they no longer had use for us, then they sent us back."

—Manuel Herrera (quoted in "Antiguos Braceros Se Oponen al Plan de Bush," *La Opinion*, January 14, 2004)

Chapter 5

Economic Power Versus Academic Freedom: The Case of Henry P. Anderson and the University of California

PROTECTING THE IMAGE OF THE BRACERO PROGRAM emerged as a primary objective of the officials charged with managing the program. Obviously, this positive spin hid the reality experienced by braceros; but those who sided with the braceros and critiqued the bracero program became subject to the state's power to silence. Such a fate befell a young graduate student and scholar named Henry Anderson. In 1957, few beyond the School of Public Health at the University of California at Berkeley (UC Berkeley) knew of Anderson, the author of a National Institute of Health grant administered by his mentor Edward S. Rogers within the School of Public Health. At age 29, he had earned a seat at the research table (and a graduate student wage) at a university renowned as a world-class institution and was enjoying a career that many graduate students merely dream of. In particular, Anderson planned to study health practices and their modifications among braceros.

Armed with two master's degrees, in Public Health and Sociology, Anderson engaged in his sociological studies using a meticulous survey methodology that explored the linkages between health practices and culture. In his investigation of braceros he asked one basic question: To what extent and why do these temporary immigrants change their cultural health practices when entering a new cultural environment? Equipped with this rigorous methodology he anticipated interviewing

2,500 braceros—initially, as they entered the United States and, later, as they repatriated.

However, Anderson learned more than he bargained for, concluding from firsthand observation that the bracero labor migration system, one of the largest mass movements of labor in history, shared much in common with colonized labor in British South Africa, that in some ways "was worse than slavery," and had become saturated with corruption. Such a conceptualization of state-managed migration infuriated owners and top management. Agribusiness officials, together with state bureaucrats charged with administering the bracero program, set in motion the machinery for implementing the abrupt halt to Anderson's research project by the University of California.

These officials and bureaucrats took great umbrage with Anderson's personal perspectives on the bracero program and sent memoranda to the university administration detailing Anderson's transgressions. Subsequently, Berkeley Chancellor Glenn Seaborg, in consultation with University President Clark Kerr, halted Anderson's research without due process, causing Anderson to resign his position on June 30, 1959, and leave the university. Only 1,149 braceros were interviewed before the university closed his project. Although the administration allowed Anderson to write a complete study, they subsequently demanded all of the data he had amassed and ordered that he may not, under any circumstances, publish his findings. All copies of the completed report were confiscated and destroyed on the Berkeley campus. As compensation, he was given the opportunity to pen an "expurgated" version of that report, which was distributed to a limited number of "competent" readers but not formally published.

Early in his once-bright career Anderson discovered that the University of California was not an independent institution, a walled preserve where all viewpoints find equality of expression. He experienced firsthand a power originating beyond the university that presided over the conduct of research, even at this institution heralded as a world-class leader in the production of knowledge. Anderson quickly learned who defined the parameters of academic freedom in a society dominated by large-scale capital. The main issue that brought an end to this young scholar's research was his personal interpretation of the bracero program, which contrasted sharply with the image broadcast nationally and internationally by Washington officials, and especially by the economic sector dependent on bracero labor. The unfolding drama of Henry Anderson's dismissal offers a window through which we can view the tightly woven interconnection of economics and politics within the state, the power wielded by the state apparatus, and the use of that power.

Agribusiness and the University of California

Such a large and vitally important undertaking as agriculture requires a wide array of ancillary systems. Available credit, sufficient irrigation, accessible railroads and highways, practical problem-solving research, as well as a favorable political climate, are indispensable for the optimal realization of production goals. Agricultural interests never allow the state's political apparatus to exist independently; on the contrary, they exert pressure in determining public policy that affects the agricultural sector and its branches. In the time period under discussion here, this sector sought to guide research that served its interests through securing a dominant presence within the School of Agriculture at UC Berkeley. As one observer reported,

> California's "most vital industry" owes a good share of its vitality to the Division of Agricultural Sciences of the University of California. As the farm evolved into big business or agribusiness, the University's College of Agriculture also emerged from its humble beginnings in a corner of a basement to become a gigantic complex of schools, field stations, and extension services.[1]

The university originated as a land-grant institution bound by its contract to serve the economic interests of the state and, as the prime economic sector, agriculture weighed heavily upon it. Not surprisingly, the first college established within the university would be the College of Agriculture. Undoubtedly, the "business of agriculture became the business of the University."[2]

The university's research mission generated the founding of Experimental Stations for conducting agricultural experiments in the field; eventually that research was carried to the growers via the Extension Service, also managed by the university, in collaboration with growers and county authorities. Among the functions of the Extension Service, one proved vitally important: promotion of "labor efficiency." Ultimately, the educational programs launched by the Extension Service evolved into countywide organizations of farmers, becoming known as Farm Bureaus.[3]

Over time, as agriculture expanded dramatically in the early years of the twentieth century and concentrated in the hands of corporate enterprises, the ties binding the university to agriculture expanded and deepened. Having promoted the development of Farm Bureaus on a local level, the Extension Service, at the behest of the San Joaquin County Farm Bureau, then took the initiative to form a statewide organization. The Agricultural Extension Service sent out statewide announcements to the county chapters, inviting their participation. In 1919 the California Farm Bureau Federation was inaugurated and immediately emerged as the "most powerful single political and economic organization in the State."[4] Interestingly, the meeting establishing the statewide Farm Bureau was held at the College of Agriculture on the Berkeley campus. The Bureau eventually assumed a powerful place within university policymaking—in part, through the efforts of one major donor. The largesse of Amadeo P. Giannini, the founder of the Bank of America and an investor in the state's agriculture, made possible the development and expansion of the university's program in agricultural economics in 1928. Giannini's $1,500,000 gift established the Giannini Foundation for Agricultural Economics, an integral component of the College of Agriculture and the facility chosen to house the California Farm Bureau headquarters. As the bracero program entered into its fourth year, University President Robert Gordon Sproul candidly elucidated that relationship: "The interests of the College of Agriculture and the Farm Bureau are common interests."[5]

It is in this context that applied research linked intimately with the leading organization representing agriculture would take precedence in the University of California, particularly in the School of Agriculture. Free and unfettered theoretical research took a backseat. Indeed, just before the Great Depression ended, President Sproul proudly announced that the College of Agriculture had served as the "silent partner of the agricultural industry of California." To be sure, the vocal partner would be agribusiness, and key administrators ensured university cooperation with the agricultural industry. Claude B. Hutchinson, the first director of the Giannini Foundation and, later, dean of the Agricultural College, would be described approvingly as "the hired man, so to say, of more than 150,000 California farms" in an article praising Hutchinson for his leadership.[6] Rendering a political relationship between the college and agriculture in such a fashion illuminated a truth captured in a college report on university-farmer collaboration: The association is "a continuous two-way communication between farmers and the University on farmers' needs and problems and University solutions."[7] The report did not exaggerate. Dean Hutchinson himself served on the statewide Advisory Committee on Farm Placement, which continuously reviewed the need for seasonal farm workers and searched for means to effectively allocate labor from region to region.[8]

Such favorable leverage benefiting agriculture inevitably influenced the direction of research undertaken by the state's leading public institution, particularly within the College of Agriculture, which dealt with matters related to harvest labor as well as to the bracero program. In short, the state's offices served as a pathway through which agriculture realized its interests—one of which was to maintain existing relations with harvest labor and preserve access to its seasonal labor supply. Indeed, College of Agriculture publications never critiqued the bracero program and always sought to place the program within the needs of the industry. In 1954, for example, an Experimental Station–sponsored study on domestic and imported workers expressed the view that "[t]he major contribution of the Mexican National farm labor program has been its role of reducing uncertainty of labor supply."[9] The same argument in favor of the bracero program also appeared regularly.

In the early 1960s, when the bracero program came under severe criticism from social reformers and the possibility of termination loomed, UC Berkeley, at the behest of agribusiness, submitted its own report to the State Board of Agriculture defending the program's continuation.[10] That report, titled "Seasonal Labor in California Agriculture," bore the approval of Daniel Aldrich, who was dean of the Agricultural College (and soon to be chancellor at the newly founded University of California at Irvine). It concluded: "The Mexican contract (bracero) labor source is an important one to California agriculture, both in terms of the manpower it contributes and also in terms of the insurance against uncertainty of labor supply."[11]

The Anderson Study

By the mid-1950s many thousands men, recruited and processed by the Mexican government at the request of U.S. federal authorities, had been transported across the border to work in agriculture, primarily in corporate-owned agribusinesses in Texas and California. During the twenty-two-year life of the labor importation program, 7.5 million labor contracts were signed, involving an estimated 450,000 men who had been imported to labor for periods ranging from six weeks to eighteen months. Thousands of them became virtual "professionals," returning for several stints as harvest laborers. Huge numbers of men entering and leaving the United States annually prompted Anderson to define a critical feature of the bracero program. "The importation of braceros as a commodity," he observed, "has become one of this country's principal exercises in foreign trade."[12]

During an era when few knew about the bracero program outside of official circles, and when even fewer cared about the welfare of the imported laborers, it fell to Henry Anderson, a scholarly graduate interested in a career in academia, to pursue a study of the health customs and practices of these hundreds of thousands of men. He described the four elements of his research objectives as follows:

> (1) Descriptive: the health status of a particular cultural group, and the influences affecting such health status; (2) Methodological: delineation of this clustering of health attitudes, customs, and influences in replicable, quantifiable terms; (3) Theoretical: "Do Mexicans undergo culture change as a result of their coming to a new country, and, if so, in what ways, and how fast?" (4) Practical: are there any areas of objective or subjective health needs which are unmet, and, if so, how might they be filled more effectively?[13]

Under the supervision of his graduate advisor, Anderson authored an ambitious grant proposal and sent it to the National Institutes of Health (NIH) in 1956. Shortly thereafter, Anderson received welcome news: The study group had evaluated the proposal with high marks and granted the handsome sum of $15,525. He then applied for and received a seed grant from the Haynes Foundation, and soon initiated a pilot research project to engage archival research and interview government officials charged with administering the bracero program. At a relatively young age, Anderson had thus achieved a successful standing in the UC Berkeley School of Public Health, in charge of a study on bracero health and cultural practices in California under the supervision of his graduate mentor, Dr. Edward Rogers. During the very year that he received the grant, approximately 450,000 contracts were signed (an unknown number of braceros signed several contracts), sending several hundred thousand Mexican men to work across the nation, with a third ending up in California; fortunately, no dearth of subjects would undermine the study. Everything seemed in order; Anderson pre-tested the questionnaire (which he revised eighteen times) at Stockton (having hired Dolores Huerta, a schoolteacher who would later work closely with Cesar Chavez and the farm workers union), and subsequently Anderson hoped to begin interviewing in the central state of Michoacan, Mexico, a leading bracero-sending region.

Unfortunately for Anderson, and perhaps as a hint of things to come, the Mexican government flatly denied him permission to conduct research in Michoacan. Henceforth, his interviewing would be conducted at El Centro, the final processing station known as the "Reception Center" for braceros moving north and the stepping-off point for braceros entering California's great agricultural valleys. Prospective braceros had already undergone at least two inspections before arriving in El Centro; still more procedures remained for determining the admissibility of the arriving men. In the early stages of research Anderson sought to broaden his knowledge of braceros by visiting the border "Reception Center" at Calexico. Here Anderson received his first taste of the bracero system. After introductions with the Center's head administrator, an "escort" guided him through the selection process. Personal observations revealed the bracero program that had been successfully hidden from the general public, and from Anderson as well.

His first stop was the "bullpen," the lower level enclosure where perhaps as many as three thousand men would be quartered at a time during the harvest season, waiting to be called up for an extended examination. As they walked through the "bullpen," the "strutting little peacock," as Anderson described his guide, identified the qualities that defined "the ideal bracero." The guide pointed at individual men and evaluated their potential to be a useful bracero. Those deemed expendable were described one at a time: this one too tall, he is too "cocky," that one a "loafer," another "lazy and irresponsible," he's a "smart aleck," this one a "ladykiller" and not "peon" enough. On the other hand the "right man," according to the guide, was "built right. He's a farm worker, you can tell that ... he hasn't any big ideas. He's got the right attitude. He's humble, not fresh or cocky. He's an Indian type, probably from Jalisco or Guanajuato." That experience exposed Anderson to a program that he, until then, was largely ignorant of; his learning curve went straight up. He would write in his diary

> These "cocky," "lazy," "lying," "loafers," "smart alecks," and "ladykillers" were, in fact, with very few exceptions, the meek, ill-clad peasantry of Mexico, bowed by the centuries of peonage. To realize that this insufferable little bully—or, for that matter, anyone else—had almost literally the power of life or death over them, and that they had no choice but to submit—all of this made me ill. I could think of nothing so much as the slave markets as I imagine they existed a hundred years ago in Baltimore, or Charleston, or New Orleans. . . . I don't believe I had ever an epiphany in my life before. I had one now. The bracero system was wicked. It was wicked for my country to be involved in it . . ."[14]

Despite his personal feelings, Anderson decided he would have no other option than to engage his research and leave opinions aside. During the harvest seasons up to 2,000 men a day were processed at El Centro. Each man underwent careful scrutiny; those deemed appropriate for seasonal labor, once they were officially declared braceros, proceeded to a specific grower's representative and were bused to their living quarters and work sites. This bustling, if surreal, human drama offered Anderson a treasure trove of possible interviewees. The incoming men he designated as the "control group." Later, as their work contracts expired, the same men—now the "experimental group"—were to be interviewed as they returned to Mexico. The fieldwork progressed smoothly for a year and a half; progress reports were periodically issued, and the several papers presented at the meetings of the U.S.-Mexico Border Health Association were well received. Anderson's request for an extension in order to complete the interviews and statistical compiling was granted by the NIH a year into the research.

It was at El Centro that Anderson would first be exposed to the real world of the bracero program, a massive social panorama that few Americans knew existed. What he saw, and how he interpreted what he saw, would eventually supply the material evidence that ended his career as a social scientist and changed his life. In his words, "my ignorance about the farm labor in general and the bracero program in particular gradually gave way to a series of fairly definite impressions and conclusions, founded upon first-hand sights, sounds, and smells in the field."[15]

An Invitation to Contribute to Social Awareness

After a year and a half in the field, without any suggestion of difficulties, the American Friends Service Committee (AFSC) in Tulare, California, invited Anderson to submit a personal statement about the bracero program for discussion at a meeting of the AFSC Farm Labor Project. Also invited to the meeting were bracero program administrators and growers who employed bracero labor—two groups who obviously felt positively regarding bracero labor. Anderson, however, could not attend and mailed his personal statement written, as he recalled, with the belief that he had "as a citizen ... not only the right to express myself, but an obligation to inform other citizens of the facts which most of them had never had the opportunity to observe for themselves."[16] He titled his submission "Social Justice and Foreign Contract Labor: A Statement of Opinion and Conscience," with the caveat that it was not intended for distribution but if the AFSC decided to distribute the paper it should do so with his name deleted. Such a request indicated that Anderson knew his statement presented severe, albeit carefully considered, criticisms based on firsthand observations against a powerful political machinery.

He sent the statement and continued to conduct his very successful research project. By then he had presented papers at several professional meetings, and more were certainly on the horizon. The seemingly innocuous meeting of the American Friends Service Committee in May 1958 and the presentation of his statement had set the stage for his eventual ouster from UC Berkeley. But it was his honest opinions, not his research, that would cause his dismissal—and what he said of the bracero program explains the "why" of what would eventually occur.

For ten pages Anderson severely critiqued the bracero program and its bureaucratic apparatus, citing the bribery of men in Mexico hoping to become braceros, braceros living in overcrowded and squalid quarters, insufficient health care, wages below contract stipulation, braceros cheated out of wages, company store–like gouging, braceros bribing U.S. officials for the "privilege" of becoming braceros, and the bracero program itself pushing local labor into unemployment lines but not before lowering wages across the board. Paragraph after paragraph detailed a vast system of corruption and unfettered exploitation of labor:

I have seen many bracero camps in which the men were furnished meals costing the employer less than 50 cents per man per day, including supplies, equipment, utilities, and labor. These braceros were uniformly charged $1.75 a day, and were allowed no choice but to take their meals on these terms.

I have seen bracero camps in which the bunkhouses, beds, showers, and privies were totally unfit for human, even animal use.

I have talked with braceros who were permitted to go to town only once every 15 days, and on those occasions the foreman charged them $2 to ride on the truck.

I have talked to braceros who were peremptorily shipped back to Mexico for asking to see a doctor or asking for an accounting of their wages.[17]

All of these conditions and more Anderson witnessed firsthand or recorded during his interviews with the men.

The powers-that-be had heard many of these complaints before, but they generally responded that such conditions were not widespread and, where such infractions existed, correctives were quickly taken. Public-relations efforts intended to stifle complaints like those Anderson catalogued found expression in local media outlets, including television, newspapers, radio, official state journals, and films sponsored by grower associations.[18] However, Anderson contended that not much oversight existed and that, consequently, protections written into the bracero agreements were largely ignored, allowing growers to take few precautions in their exploitation of braceros. He concluded that

injustice is built into the present system, and no amount of patching and tinkering will make of it a just system.... I [do not believe] that through any amount of amendment the bracero program can be made consonant with the best aspirations and promise of either Mexico or the United States. I am convinced that the bracero program—indeed, foreign contract farm labor programs in general ... in whatever form and guise, will by their very nature wreak harm upon the lives of the persons directly and indirectly involved and upon human rights which our Constitution still holds to be self-evident and inalienable. I am convinced that foreign labor programs must be extirpated root and branch, and that temporizing with them is as immoral as the programs themselves.[19]

All that Anderson requested of those who listened to the reading of his statement at the Tulare meeting was that they examine the record. "Let the important questions be aired!" he implored. Anderson assumed, naively perhaps, that once the "important questions" had been presented, society's conscience would demand a thorough review of the bracero program and its eventual demise. The words "I am confident of the outcome" closed his statement. But the actual outcome was more surprising than he could ever have imagined.

Clearly the statement Anderson had submitted was a hard-hitting condemnation of the entire bracero program, but he expected his unsigned statement to stay within the confines of the meeting and the AFSC executive board. In fact, without his permission, the statement *with his name affixed* was distributed at the meeting and sent out to AFSC offices nationally and abroad. It eventually reached California growers dependent upon bracero labor and state administrators charged with managing and policing the program, who then conveyed it to the national center of power, Washington, D.C. In the opinion of very influential parties, Henry Anderson, the public health investigator, was a potential troublemaker who deserved to be removed from an institution that could well be offering him a venue to publicly expose the bracero program.

During the course of the conflict Anderson learned more than he bargained for—indeed, far more about the relationship of the academy to political and economic power than his study alone would ever have taught him. The corruption that enveloped the bracero program spread to UC Berkeley like a dark cloud. The vast power in the hands of corporate agriculture, and the exercise of that power, provided a lesson that Anderson would not soon forget. The process that swirled about him—the clumsy, ham-handed arguments for his dismissal without benefit of hearing—resembled a classic Kafka trial.

Economic Power and State Administrators

Two years after he began his research, Anderson received what would be the first of several letters and phone calls from California state and federal officials in charge of administering the bracero program, accusing him of making reckless and unfounded accusations and demanding a retraction or evidence of charges. The drumbeat roiled for the next several months, putting Anderson on the defensive. He was justifiably concerned that his career in academia would be destroyed and that the public would be denied an assessment of his research findings. Reviewing this portion of the Anderson affair brings into sharp relief the interconnections between the exercise of economic power and the meaning of academic freedom.

In early July 1958, a flurry of memos among state officials called attention to the statement Anderson had sent to the AFSC. On July 10, Edwin F. Hayes, the chief of the California Farm Placement Service—an agency with close ties to the California Farm Bureau (which occupied an office on the Berkeley campus) and the University of California School of Agriculture—wrote a memorandum to Glenn Brockway, regional director of the U.S. Department of Labor Bureau of Employment Security (BES) in San Francisco. The regional BES acted as a special agency charged with overseeing and managing the bracero program on a district level. Hayes, who owned a farm and held a personal interest in the case, enclosed two copies of Anderson's statement, with an added detail: "I understand that Mr. Anderson is at the University of California in Berkeley in the Department of Mental or Medical Research or some sort of department of that type." He went on to direct Brockway's attention to "many allegations and accusations," said that Anderson had never filed formal complaints, and finished by suggesting that the Farm Bureau be informed.[20]

Brockway then joined the chain-letter campaign and sent a letter to Walter Francis, manager of the El Centro Reception Center (the site of Anderson's fieldwork), with a copy of "Social Justice and Foreign Contract Labor." "We are certain," began the memo, "you will be interested in reading the attached statement." Brockway continued:

> [W]e understand [Anderson] has spent considerable time at the Reception Center, interviewing braceros relative to health problems. For your information, we propose to try to contact Mr. Anderson as we are quite disturbed by some of the allegations made in his statement.... [Y]ou may want to discuss with him some of the charges he has made.[21]

The name Henry Anderson was now on the radar screen of officials across the state and fast becoming the target of formal charges.

On July 18, H. W. Stewart, the director of the California Department of Employment, the second state agency charged with administering and policing the bracero program, penned an angry letter to

Anderson. He called attention to the statement written by Anderson for the AFSC meeting and referred to one specific charge in the statement. Anderson claimed—and rightly so, given that substantial evidence had borne out his charges—that local labor seeking work is arbitrarily forced out of the labor market by the importation of braceros, a clear violation of the bracero agreements. Stewart then went on to say that the "policy of this Department is to provide priority of job opportunities to available domestic farm labor." He hammered away at Anderson, charging that he had failed to refer the allegations to proper authorities for correction (this being a policy enforced by the Department of Employment):

> I would assume that any responsible person preparing an article relating to social justice would have been equally concerned that he apprise those whom he charges with dereliction of duty in order that they may be given the opportunity to review the material and to take corrective action if necessary. This you have failed to do.[22]

Anderson responded that he never made "charges" or accused individuals of "dereliction of duty." "I do not believe," he wrote, "any such language will be found in my memorandum." Moreover, he pointed out that his intention was not to "call into question the administration or administrators ... of the program" but, rather, to direct attention to a program that "was inherently unworkable."[23] The administration of the program, he continued, is a "task so vast, so unwieldy, so full of internal contradictions and conflicts that miscarriages are inevitable."

The wheels of justice, as defined by bracero program administrators, now moved in a new direction. On July 17 Anderson and Louie Tagaban, Anderson's research assistant conducting interviews at El Centro Reception Center, decided to cross the border and venture to the Empalme bracero recruiting center in the northern Mexican state of Sonora (operated by U.S. officials for the purposes of selecting men from west-central Mexico). Anderson stayed only two days and left Tagaban to interview men who had not yet undergone the screening process. The day after Anderson departed, a frightened Tagaban decided it better to leave the premises. He wrote Anderson that U.S. authorities had accused him of seeking out information about bribes from potential braceros. His notes and papers were taken from him, and the interviewing abruptly stopped. Although his papers were returned and he was allowed to continue after an explanation that he was not interested in bribery, he was constantly watched. Not unexpectedly, a distressed Tagaban returned to El Centro seeking refuge, and continued interviewing.[24] Little did Anderson know at the time that the accusation of researching to uncover bribery would come up later and be added to the list of charges against him.

On July 24 Brockway continued his mission and independently assumed the responsibility of informing Washington. Robert Goodwin, director of the U.S. Department of Labor Bureau of Employment Security, received Anderson's statement along with a brief review of the latter's earlier request for information from the BES relative to his research. Brockway also included previous letters to Anderson from the California Department of Employment (H. W. Stewart) and from the BES office (H. D. Huxley, discussed below). The letter informed Goodwin that the matter had been discussed with the district director of the Immigration and Naturalization Service and the regional director of the Department of Health, Education, and Welfare—the agency overseeing the National Institute of Health. Brockway closed with "Both are pursuing the charges made against their respective agencies."[25] Although Anderson never charged either agency of any malfeasance, it is clear that associates were being invited to join the efforts to silence Anderson.

On the same date that Brockway sent his memo with attachments to Goodwin, H. D. Huxley, the deputy regional director of Bureau of Employment Security, sharply rebuked Anderson in an official letter.[26] (Interestingly, Huxley copied Brockway, who included it in the materials sent the same day to Goodwin, demonstrating the cooperation among the officials.) Huxley knew of Anderson's research, since the latter had requested from Huxley's office statistical information regarding the bracero program. In his letter, Huxley immediately demanded to know why he, Anderson, had not mentioned the "allegations" to his staff at that time. Huxley added: "We are asking you now to designate a time and place to suit your convenience, at which you will present evidence and information which will make it possible for us to investigate the allegations." He then listed two "charges" that appeared in Anderson's statement and required corroboration. The first of these related to bribery of officials working for the U.S. Immigration and Naturalization Service, the Public Health Service, and the Department of Labor. The second referred to the use of braceros to work at the homes of U.S. Department of Labor employees.

Anderson responded to Huxley that he had not personally observed instances of bribery or of braceros working in the homes of government officials, but that braceros had offered such information during the course of their interviews (as was expressed in his statement). And furthermore, repeating what he had said earlier to Stewart: "Far from preferring charges against the culpability of any individual or group, it was the burden of my remarks that the personnel associated with the Mexican National program have been put into an unenviable position of having to work with a program which is by its nature unworkable." Anderson also pointed out that he himself had made no charges—that his statement was an ethical one rather than a legal one, in the sense that he had expressed his own opinion of the bracero program as a citizen, and that he had the right to freely express these opinions. He closed by saying that he was not an "off-duty … watchdog over the minutiae of the bracero program," and that with a little amount of time "it would seem that persons on your staff, who are trained and paid for this type of work, should be able to unearth without too much difficulty … all sorts of illustrative cases that I've mentioned."[27]

Anderson took a stand in opposition to these attacks faintly concealed behind bureaucratic rhetoric exercised by officials hoisting the banner of government privilege. He then sent the letters he'd written to Stewart and Huxley to Robert Goodwin, director of the Bureau of Employment Security in Washington, D.C., and requested a copy of his circulated statement in order to analyze whether any changes had been made without his knowledge. He asked for the copy because, in his words, "Your Pacific Coast representatives have been unusually attentive to me in the past week, and have put a great many questions based upon their reading of my memorandum."[28]

By then, Anderson's statement given to the American Friends Service Committee had reached "all offices of the Bureau of Employment Security, all reception centers, all migratory stations, all Farm Placement Service offices, all farm labor associations within the state."[29] He now had reason to question whether UC Berkeley would see fit to dismiss his project; his premonitions had proved true in that on or around July 24 university officials "demanded … an explanation" of Anderson's conduct apparently related to his statement. But, as Anderson wrote to Father Thomas McCullough, his close friend, mentor, and colleague, as well as spiritual minister to braceros in the

Stockton area, he would "never back down on the things I wrote in my memorandum."[30]

The case against Anderson, far from uncoordinated, continued. From San Francisco Glenn Brockway sent a packet of materials to Goodwin four days after receiving Anderson's letter. In the packet were copies of communications from Anderson to Brockway, Stewart, and Huxley. But more was in order. Brockway advised Goodwin that he had discussed the matter with the district director of the Immigration and Naturalization Service, and both agreed that Anderson's letters fell far short of a complete "retraction of the unsupported charges." Brockway continued:

> [A]ccordingly [the district director] has requested an immigration officer in Southern California confer with Mr. Anderson with a view of obtaining a complete and unequivocal retraction of all the charges. If he is unsuccessful … we propose to bring the matter up to the attention of the officials of the University of California by whom Mr. Anderson is employed on a special project, and request that he review the situation and take whatever action is necessary.[31]

Brockway further pointed out that H. W. Stewart (director of the California Department of Employment) "is agreeable in joining us in any further action that suggests itself," and that the regional director of the Department of Health, Education, and Welfare had inquired of the Washington office "as to any action they may have taken in this case." The demand that Anderson provide evidence had evolved into a demand that he retract all allegations, termed "charges" by his antagonists. In a sharp turn of events, charges would now be brought against Anderson.

Clearly the tide was moving toward a coordinated cornering of Anderson and a coerced retraction, at the very least. Yet, the complaints leveled from San Francisco to Washington were not that he had made "unsubstantiated charges" but that he had made allegations in sharp contradiction to the protections embedded in the Bracero Agreements and, even more important, had said that corruption was rampant. Furthermore, public-relations efforts to protect the bracero program by denying that wholesale contract violations existed were potentially undermined by Anderson's statement.[32] Not unexpectedly, the charges moved beyond threatening letters to concrete repercussions.

By the end of July, Anderson had received three anonymous phone calls as well as a call from an official of the Los Angeles office of the

Department of Labor. Another anonymous individual, who identified himself only as an "investigator," questioned him at his residence. Each referred to his "charges" and raised the same allegations that appeared in the Brockway, Goodwin, Huxley, and Stewart letters. Finally, on July 29 Louie Tagaban advised Anderson that, although he was still at the El Centro Reception Center, he no longer "moved about freely as I used to." The assistant manager of the Center, according to Tagaban, "is angry because I am still here" in part because Tagaban refused the Center manager's job offer at a considerable raise over what he earned as a research assistant. To top it off, Tagaban was told that he "might have a new boss soon."[33] Clearly the authorities wanted more than a retraction; they wanted Anderson removed.

In response to Anderson's letter of July 22, H. W. Stewart, director of the State Department of Employment, used terms more threatening than any said previously: "You have completely ignored my request," and "your article is not balanced." Then he raised the bar: "[U]nless I receive specific information in support of these statements in order that I may further investigate them I must assume that they are not accurate and press for a more thorough disposition of the matter."[34] At that point Anderson sought legal advice and was told that no possible charges could be brought against him and that Stewart was probably bluffing. Anderson felt reassured and continued his work. His ease was short-lived.

UC Berkeley Takes Charge

In mid-August or thereabouts, Anderson was ordered to report to Berkeley. Anderson's graduate mentor, Edward Rogers, informed him that "high sources outside" the university recommended that the price of keeping his position was a thorough retraction of the "charges." (Rogers conveniently ignored the power that corporate farming interests, particularly the Farm Bureau, held on campus). Furthermore, the retraction must make it clear "that they [charges] were neither specific charges nor sweeping generalizations and that ... information was for the most part indirect and hearsay."[35] A defiant Anderson ignored Roger's request and refused to comply.

A month later, on September 8, Chancellor Seaborg informed the School of Public Health that Anderson's study was to cease immediately.

Shortly afterward, Anderson's research mentor advised him that he "could 'write up' the data already in hand" but that all interviewing must stop at once. Furthermore, he was notified that a guard at the El Centro Reception Center would arrest him if he set foot on the premises and that this decision came directly from Robert Goodwin in the Department of Labor.[36] Anderson inquired whether the university intended to comply with the Labor Department's order and the reply was chilling. Anderson wrote of this moment: "They wrote back and said not only were they going along with the Department's order, but were forbidding me to conduct any more research ... and were notifying the Department of Labor accordingly."[37]

At no point was Anderson given the right of due process or even the opportunity to appeal or to discover the nature of the charges and justification for the university's decision. UC Berkeley declared Anderson expendable, but the decision to halt the project was not the university's alone. In fact, it originated with officials administering the bracero program. The university merely served as a conduit, although it publicly presented a far different line of authority in the decision-making process. President Clark Kerr acknowledged that the matter came across his desk and pointed out, disingenuously, that his verdict was based solely on the conclusion that Anderson had deviated from the terms of the NIH grant. Further, Kerr contended that the university acted independently, free from "any pressure" in its decision to release Anderson. That Anderson had been offered the opportunity to record his findings and submit them to his committee was considered sufficient.[38] At that point Kerr felt that the matter required no further discussion.

Several years later Anderson discovered that an official with the Farm Bureau, an agency housed in the Giannini building on the Berkeley campus, had spoken about Anderson with UC Berkeley Vice-President Harry Wellman, also a professor of Agricultural Economics working at the Giannini Foundation. Wellman and the *Farm Bureau* enjoyed a warm professional relationship, and the Anderson affair would not change that. The message that reached the administration went something like this: "It won't be long before you'll be going to the legislature again, asking for an appropriation to run the university. It would be very embarrassing if some rural senator were to ask why you kept on your payroll this fellow who's been running around making these reckless accusations." Wellman knew that his friends in

the corporate farm sector considered the university a friendly institution and that keeping Anderson would endanger a long-standing
working relationship. Under such circumstances Anderson seemed as
disposable as the braceros he had studied, exemplifying what might
occur to others were they to buck the "old boys' club." Beneath the
actions taken to eliminate Anderson was a commitment on the part
of bracero users, the Farm Bureau and government officials to secure
the bracero program and protect it from criticism.

Along with the order that he immediately halt all research and
dismiss his research assistant Louie Tagaban, now that the "project
was ... at an end," came the option of writing up his findings, which
offered an opportunity to bring closure to the half-completed project
he had begun so promisingly several years before. And so he commenced the writing phase of his research project. The university,
however, freely imposed parameters on what Anderson could report
in his final written document. In particular, the members of his
committee demanded that he restrict his writing to "purely technical aspects"—namely, the "attitudes of the braceros toward medical
care and health practices."[39] Though intent on finishing his project,
Anderson underwent a most disillusioning experience, forcing him
to review and revise his long-term career plans. In a letter to Father
Thomas McCullough, he described the toll taken on him after several
months of state and university harassment:

> [T]he thing that has really taken the heart out of me is the reaction
> of a great, proud State university, which has shown itself obviously
> more interested in avoiding controversy than in pursuing either truth
> or justice.... I couldn't live with myself if I were to continue with an
> academic career, after what has happened.

In a letter to his friend and fellow activist Ernesto Galarza, Anderson
characterized the University of California as one in which an "atmosphere
of such hypocrisy and intellectual dry rot" prevailed.[40] Anderson's long-
range plans—a book on the bracero program leading to a doctorate and
a research career in a major university—were now cast in doubt. The
academy, that much-celebrated generator of pure knowledge, appeared
to be nothing more than a puppet controlled by powerful economic
interests represented by such agencies as the California Farm Bureau.

Anderson's immediate goal, the termination of the bracero program, remained more important than ever, and he immediately

devoted his energies to assist Galarza in that endeavor. But the matter of the research report submitted to his faculty committee also remained.

The Final Research Report

For a year and a half Anderson labored (including clandestine interviewing) to complete a lengthy manuscript summarizing his findings. Finally, a preliminary 750-page draft was produced, titled "The Bracero Program in California: With Particular Reference to Health Status, Attitudes and Practices." He described it, and rightly so, as a "formidable compendium of historical materials, verbatim quotes from interviews, statistical tables, extracts from Congressional hearings ... woven together into a single skein." Anderson mimeographed copies for members of his advisory committee, who evaluated the work. As expected, they judged it to be "dangerously controversial," "too political," "shoddy research," "too far from the subject of health," "too contentious," "out of bounds," and so on. With the exception of an economist with expertise in Mexican immigrant labor, Dr. Paul S. Taylor, who deemed it excellent, the committee "wrote it off as being without redeeming social merit."[41] Anderson recalled that the chair of the committee was quite frank in expressing the reasons for his downbeat assessment: "He said that he had no intention of going through any more pressure from the Farm Bureau, over an issue that was not of his choosing, and which he didn't consider that important." Clark Kerr's assessment matched that of the committee. He wrote several years later that

> [u]pon completion of the study, Mr. Anderson submitted a preliminary report to Dr. Rogers and the committee. Dr. Rogers and the committee were agreed that the preliminary report contained a considerable section devoted to Mr. Anderson's observations and opinions on the political and economic power structure involved in the bracero program. The material was not relevant to the basic study, especially in terms of the NIH grant.[42]

In 1958, in a meeting asked for by Anderson, Kerr maintained that he had made this decision largely because the report "ought to have been more factual."[43] Soon thereafter, even though at the outset of the research a book publication was expected to ensue, Anderson was ordered to immediately turn in all copies sent to reviewers, plus the 100 or so that he had made with the intention of distributing them to interested parties. In a show of "heart," the committee agreed that he could keep one copy for personal use, but this was marked "confidential" with the names of the advisory committee inked out. The School of Public Health officials chose to destroy the copies in their possession, lest they become evidence against the university; those still in Anderson's hands were recalled and later burned in an incinerator in Earl Warren Hall on the Berkeley campus. Not content with book burning, the university also demanded all of the interview transcripts, photographs, and other materials that Anderson had collected during the course of his research. What became of these materials is not known; later inquiries to the school went unanswered. An NIH-funded study of bracero health practices also came to an end.

Under the guise of academic freedom, the University of California allowed Anderson the privilege of writing a shorter version of his larger manuscript, with the warning that he should avoid "politics." Further, this version was limited in distribution to "an audience of responsible persons," meaning those officials charged with managing the bracero program. The university never published the censored version, which was completed in 1961 and comprised 326 typed pages, although Anderson kept a copy for himself. Thereafter, he was excluded from any further academic endeavors, in no uncertain terms. His opinion of the university would never again be the same. Of this he wrote:

> If one obscure fledgling scholar can be crushed in this manner, is any scholar, however eminent, truly free? If one monograph can be burned at the University of California, is any monograph really safe? And if bona fide freedom of inquiry and expression are not safe in a university which styles itself one of the greatest in the world—is there any place where they are safe?[44]

Scholarship Beyond the University

After his dismissal, and while completing his large study, Anderson joined efforts to organize a farm labor union, working for the Agricultural Workers Organizing Committee in Stockton as its research director. Later he served as chair of the Citizens for Farm Labor in

Berkeley and edited *Farm Labor,* a journal published by that organization. Throughout his years of working with farm workers and observing their efforts to organize a union, he never lost sight of his goal of reproducing the 750-page manuscript that had been burned. He had secretly kept the original stencils, so the hope became a reality. In 1964, with the backing of friends, a limited number of copies, re-titled *Harvest of Loneliness,* were made available—and we are the beneficiaries. It remains the richest repository of the braceros' experiences, expressed in their own words, as well as one of the most informed and damning critiques of the bracero program itself. It also stands alongside the classic works of Ernesto Galarza, with whom he collaborated closely and shared a deep interest in terminating the bracero program.

Whatever else Anderson's work accomplished, it answered one important question posed in his research project: "What happens when the bearers of one culture are moved into another cultural setting? The answer: Nothing when they are not free men."[45] On the other side of the equation Anderson took measure of the men and women who administered the bracero program and who in turn were affected by it. It angered him that individuals who believed strongly in the free-enterprise system—powerful growers and their political representatives in the state bureaucracy—should create a system that denied freedom to others. Likewise, it angered him that men who believed in academic freedom should so easily kneel before the same system that organizes and administers indentured servitude, defends wholesale violation of legal protections, allows wholesale corruption, and then deliberately obscures that truth.

In the long run, the effort to silence Henry Anderson failed. From 1963 until 1967 he edited *Farm Labor,* a critical investigative journal that published articles from a wide range of contributors. A few years later the book *So Shall Ye Reap,* co-authored with Joan London (daughter of Jack London), provided a serious examination and overview of the dreadful conditions experienced by farm laborers amidst their organized efforts to unionize.[46]

Eventually, interest in developing the field of Chicano Studies resulted in the "discovery" of Anderson's "expurgated" and greatly shortened study *Braceros in California.* In a special series on such studies, Arno Press published the book in 1975, long after the bracero program had ended. UC Berkeley prevented its publication in 1961, but knowledge that such a book existed could not be closeted for long. Regardless of the limitations enforced by the Berkeley administration, *Braceros in California* remains a must-read for anyone interested in studying and learning about the bracero program and for previewing what a "guest worker" program would mean for the men and women who actually become involved as "guests."[47]

University harassment continued long after Anderson had left the hallowed halls of Berkeley. He had begun a monthly radio program on an independent Berkeley station (KPFA) and, in the early 1960s, detailed his experiences with the university during an airing of his program. Shortly afterward, he received a phone call from the University Academic Senate offices requesting his appearance at a committee hearing to deliberate his charges. As he recalls, he was harshly questioned for reasons that he still cannot fathom; but nothing ever came of that informal subpoena. About that episode Anderson wrote: "Kafka Lives! ... For two solid hours I was grilled as though my KPFA remarks were a felonious offense. I tried my best to get the committee turned toward its proper jurisdiction—which, I think, does not include criticism of radio scripts [broadcast] by people who have no connection with the University. I couldn't get them to see that anything untoward had happened to their beloved campus."[48] Obviously, Anderson's candid review of his case several years after the sorry episode inflamed the university to respond antagonistically. The term "Kafkaesque" falls short of adequately describing Anderson's many experiences at UC Berkeley.

Several years after his dismissal, and as the bracero program was about to reach its final year, Anderson looked back on that labor system and summarized its meaning for future generations:

> It is saddening that other men, from another country, to whom pride and dignity are very important—these, really, are all that they have left—should permit themselves to fall into thrall to a system which humiliates them mercilessly. It is saddening that men, caught in the toils of such a system, are estranged from all those things which ought to give their lives sense and dimension. Within the bracero system, men are estranged from their families, their homeland, their culture; they are estranged from their fellow workers on the land, from the land itself, and the harvests which grow upon it. Above all, the men are estranged from themselves, from what they would like to be, and from what they are capable of becoming.[49]

Anderson never allowed bitterness to overcome his desire to see justice prevail. He remains a fervent supporter of farm labor, has presented several papers on the bracero program at professional meetings, and, like many former braceros themselves, actively opposes all forms of bracero programs that today go by the sanitized name of "guest worker" programs. We must never forget, however, that the Anderson case reveals the dangers inherent in the open-door policy that allows powerful economic interests to shape the direction of research in academia.[50] In today's university environment, heavily influenced by the neoliberal mantra, critical independent thinkers sometimes become expendable; worse, they become the enemy.

Notes

1. John K. Flynn, *A Century of Service to Agriculture*, Pasadena, Calif.: American Friends Service Committee, 1967, p. 1; see also Ernesto Galarza, *Farm Workers and Agri-business in California, 1947–1960*, Notre Dame: University of Notre Dame Press, 1977, pp. 90–93.

2. Ibid., p. 19.

3. Ibid., p. 16.

4. Ibid.

5. "University President Discusses Work of College of Agriculture and Its Value to the Farmers," *California Agriculture*, vol. 1, no. 1 (December 1946): 1–2.

6. John E. Pickett, "Hired Man of 150,000 Farms," *California Magazine of the Pacific*, vol. 29, no. 4 (April 1939).

7. *University-Farmer Cooperation in California: The Extent of Assistance Received by the Division of Agricultural Sciences from the Farmers*, Berkeley: University of California Office of Agricultural Publications, 1958, p. 6.

8. "State Advisory Committee on Farm Placement Service," *California Annual Farm Labor Report*, Sacramento: California State Department of Employment, 1949, p. 1.

9. Varden Fuller, John W. Mamer, and George L. Viles, "Domestic and Imported Workers in the Harvest Labor Market," Berkeley: University of California Agricultural Experiment Station, 1956, p. 6.

10. "U.C. Report Submitted to the State Board of Agriculture Confirms Grower Harvest Losses," Council of California Growers' *Newsletter* (January 31, 1966): 1.

11. University of California, Division of Agricultural Sciences, "Seasonal Labor in California Agriculture," Berkeley: University of California Division of Agricultural Sciences, 1963, p. viii.

12. Henry Anderson, "Social Justice and Foreign Contract Labor: A Statement of Opinion and Conscience," typed manuscript, Department of Special Collections, Stanford University Libraries, 1958, p. 10.

13. Henry Anderson, *Harvest of Loneliness: An Inquiry into a Social Problem*, Berkeley: Citizens for Farm Labor, 1964, p. 1; see also Henry Anderson, "Fields of Bondage:

The Mexican Contract Labor System in Industrialized Agriculture," mimeographed typescript (1963), pp. 69–70"

14. Henry P. Anderson, Personal Diary, February 20, 1958.

15. Anderson, *Harvest of Loneliness*, p. 2.

16. Ibid.

17. Anderson, "Social Justice and Foreign Contract Labor: A Statement of Opinion and Conscience," p. 2–3.

18. See, for example, *American Vegetable Grower;* State of California Department of Labor, *Annual Farm Labor Report;* U.S. Department of State *Bulletin;* U.S. Employment Service *Employment Security Review;* and the film *Why Braceros?* produced by the Council of California Growers (1956).

19. Anderson, "Social Justice and Foreign Contract Labor: A Statement of Opinion and Conscience," p. 10–11.

20. Edwin F. Hayes to Mr. Glenn E. Brockway, July 10, 1958. (All letters subsequently cited are also from Mr. Anderson's personal collection.)

21. Glenn E. Brockway to Walter Francis, July 18, 1958.

22. H. W. Stewart to Henry Anderson, July 18, 1958.

23. Henry Anderson to H. W. Stewart, July 22, 1958.

24. Louie M. Tagaban to Henry Anderson, July 20, 1958.

25. Glenn E. Brockway to Mr. Goodwin, July 24, 1958.

26. H. D. Huxley to Henry Anderson, July 24, 1958.

27. Henry Anderson to H. D. Huxley, July 25, 1958.

28. Henry Anderson to Robert Goodwin, July 25, 1958.

29. Henry Anderson to Reverend Thomas McCullough, July 24, 1958.

30. Henry Anderson to Reverend Thomas McCullough, July 24, 1958. Anderson described Father McCullough as "a local Catholic priest whose ... job is ministering to the spiritual wishes and needs of braceros in the Stockton area. He is immensely vigorous and likeable young man, and quite remarkable in his grasp of the way things spiritual are bound up with things social. I asked him [Father McCullough] what specific problems of well-being he thought I should focus upon, and without hesitation he gave me ... the most arresting (reply) I have yet received. It was this: the bracero program is, in effect, a program for dissolving Mexican homes." (Anderson, Personal Diary, January 5, 1957).

31. Glenn E. Brockway to Robert Goodwin, July 29, 1958.

32. Ernesto Galarza considered the BES reaction predictable. He wrote to Anderson: "[W]hat they have been trying to do is to (a) seal all possible sources on present operations information; (b) discredit all public criticism of themselves; and (c) make haste to reform sufficiently so that when the showdown comes they will be in a better position to hold on to the program" (Ernesto Galarza to Henry Pope Anderson, November 11, 1958).

33. Louie M. Tagaban to Henry Anderson, July 29, 1958.

34. H. W. Stewart to Henry Anderson, July 30, 1958.

35. Henry Anderson to Ernesto Galarza, August 19, 1958.

36. Anderson, *Harvest of Loneliness*, p. 4.

37. Henry Anderson to Reverend Thomas McCullough, November 11, 1958.

38. Ibid.

39. Ibid.

40. Henry Anderson to Ernesto Galarza, August 19, 1958.

41. Anderson, *Harvest of Loneliness,* p. 9.

42. Clark Kerr to Mrs. Daniel N. Hoffman, February 15, 1958.

43. Henry Anderson, "Chronology, 1958–1960," typed manuscript, n.d.

44. Henry Anderson, "Who Will Guard Us From the Guardians?" Unpublished radio transcript (November 13, 1964).

45. Ibid., p. 12.

46. Henry Anderson and Joan London, *So Shall Ye Reap,* New York: Crowell, 1970.

47. Henry Anderson, *The Bracero Program in California,* New York: Arno Press, 1976.

48. From the private diary of Henry Anderson, April 8, 1965.

49. Anderson, *Harvest of Loneliness,* p. 12.

50. Anderson was not the last to fall victim to powerful politics. In the fall of 2003, Ignacio Chapela, assistant professor of ecology in the department of environmental science at UC Berkeley, was denied tenure. An outspoken critic of the relationship of the university to the corporate world—particularly the biotech industry—Chapela's case parallels that of Henry Anderson. Although Chapela received unanimous support for tenure from his departmental colleagues, as well as from the ad hoc review committee established by the Academic Senate review committee, the committee and Chancellor Berdahl overruled the uniformly supportive lower recommendations. Chapela's failing was not that he didn't publish or that his teaching appeared to be below par but, rather, that his research was deemed "too controversial."

The main obstacle proved to be his contentious paper published in *Nature,* in which he reported finding traces of bioengineered corn in Mexican maize. Chapela's finding suggested that maize biodiversity might well be eliminated for all of time. Furthermore, his research contradicted a major contention of biotech firms—namely, that the movement of genetically engineered crops would be minimal and that such plants behaved differently from wild or domesticated versions. No sooner had his paper appeared than discord surfaced, with some attacking the paper and others supporting it. Finally, at the behest of one external reviewer and a public relations campaign mounted by the Bivings Group working for Monsanto, coordinated with an e-mail attack by two fictitious scientists, *Nature* issued a retraction and declared Chapela's paper lacking in merit (Marc Dowie, "Biotech Critics at Risk: Economics Calls the Shots in the Debate," *San Francisco Chronicle,* January 11, 2004). (The editorial board's decision, which silenced Chapela, seemed much like the University of California's decision to burn Anderson's research report at Earl Warren Hall.) Later, scientists at the Instituto Nacional de Ecologia in Mexico reported that they had duplicated one of Chapela's disputed findings; three subsequent investigations sustained Chapela's research ("Dr. Ignacio Chapela on Controversy, Corn and What's Really at Stake in Mexico," *Global Pesticide Campaigner,* vol. 12, no. 2 [August 2002]; see also Hugh Dellos, "Altered Corn Ignites Furor in Mexico," *Chicago Tribune,* May 1, 2004). Unfortunately for Chapela, that research by independent investigators supporting his work failed to influence the chancellor's decision to deny tenure. One reporter affirmed that "largely on the strength of that retraction [in *Nature*], Chapela was … denied tenure at UC Berkeley."

Chapela's case was similar in important respects to Anderson's. For instance, Chapela offered opinions that differed dramatically with assumptions regarding genetic engineering and, moreover, actively opposed the research consortium reached between UC Berkeley and the Swiss biotech firm Novartis. Did UC Berkeley side with the findings of conventional biotech research because of its contract with Novartis? As it turns out, the latter offered $25 million over five years to support this research, which included equipment, new faculty slots, additional support for graduate students, and university "access to Novartis's gene-sequencing technology and DNA database on plant genomics" ("Novartis Revisited: Pro: Bob Buchanan/Con: Dr. Ignacio Chapela," *California Monthly,* vol. 112, no. 4, February 2002). Obviously, then, although Novartis never intended to support research that contravened its entrepreneurial raison d'être, it held a deep interest in research that supported its overall business ventures.

The Chapela case may well serve as an example of the consequences of close ties between powerful industrial enterprises and academia. One of Chapela's departmental colleagues, a faculty veteran with twenty-four years at Berkeley, believed this to be the case. He referred to the tenure decision as "disgraceful" and emphasized that "powerful researchers who benefited from the Novartis deal had made Mr. Chapela a victim of politics" (Sharon Walsh, "The Faculty," *Chronicle of Higher Education* [January 9, 2004]; see also Tom Abate, "Hot Seat May Cool for Berkeley Prof," *San Francisco Chronicle,* August 26, 2002).

Chapter 6

Indentured Labor: A Convention in U.S.–Mexico Relations

SINCE THE FIRST DECADE OF THE TWENTIETH-CENTURY Mexican migration to the United States has ensured a constant integration of Mexican labor within the core of the largest capitalist enterprises in the world. Mexican labor has entered via a variety of auspices, not the least of which is state-managed migrations that have operated on three different occasions from 1909 to 1964 and continually since 1965 under the provisions of the H2-A program incorporated into the 1952 Immigration and Nationality Act. Each policy initiative provided giant agricultural corporations with access to substantial sources of foreign labor. Although Mexican labor supplies a large percentage of farm workers in the United States and seldom has been in short supply, attention to securing that source has occupied leaders in both Mexico and the United States on a regular basis. Recent events bear out this economic bond. Shortly after George W. Bush's election to the presidency, Mexico's President Vicente Fox was invited to Bush's Crawford, Texas, ranch to initiate high-level negotiations over a renewed "guest worker" agreement. After weeks of discussion and wide media coverage, the terrorist 9/11 attack abruptly cut short the meetings. Little more than rhetoric resulted from this celebrated fanfare between the two leaders, and the matter fell from public view for two years.

In the early stages of the 2004 elections (and with an eye toward attracting the Latino vote), the Bush administration took the opportunity to resuscitate the previous proposal, which in effect amounted to yet another tender of state-managed importation of temporary labor. In this instance, Bush proposed "legalizing" (he sometimes used the term "regularizing") the undocumented, which amounted to establishing a "guest worker" status for undocumented immigrants—a proposal that resonated with the "drying out" policy incorporated into the bracero program from 1947 until 1949. The Bush proposal emphasized once again that Mexican immigrants are the primary targets for serving as guest workers in behalf of U.S. capital.

With Bush's pronouncement regarding a new guest worker agreement aimed at undocumented workers, widespread discussion of the "true" nature of the proposal commenced immediately. Perspectives varied from "wait and see" to positive and negative, with no position dominated by a majority. Both the Republican and Democratic parties sparred over winning the Latino vote by offering some form of guest worker program and conditional amnesty proposals. What is evident in the pronouncements from the two camps is that the debate about legalization of undocumented persons tied to a guest worker program was merely in the earliest planning stages.

Perhaps a more fruitful approach to understanding the Bush proposal is to briefly examine the discourse that has taken place regarding establishment of a guest worker program with Mexico. Despite widely ranging responses, and even opposition from Bush's own party and conservative groups, several very important aspects of the Bush proposal have been overlooked. Here I address not only the "nuts and bolts" of the Bush plan but also previous proposals delivered by private citizens, academics, and government officials for enacting legislation concerning the importation of indentured labor from Mexico. We should also keep in mind that Bush's plan broke no new ground but merely resuscitated a long-standing discourse in the history of U.S.-Mexico relations—a discourse very similar to that during the temporary labor program of 1917–1921, the Bracero Agreements of 1942–1964, and the existing H2-A program. As historian Roger Daniels has observed, "George W. Bush's proposal is fully consonant with much of past immigration policy."[1]

Note that proposals have also come from officials of the Mexican government, indicating that migration—particularly guest worker migration—complies with the Mexican elites' domestic policies, though from a different vantage point. Keep in mind that while the U.S. and Mexican versions are basically identical, it is the United States that designs and controls these policies over the long run. When it comes to labor, particularly guest worker policies, there is no such thing as interdependence. Rather, what we're witnessing here is one-way traffic in cheap labor from Mexico to the United States and back. Hardly the stuff of "interdependence."

Pre-Bracero Temporary Contract Worker Proposals

The Davila Proposal (1929)

In a 1929 address before a conference hosted by an organization named the Friends of the Mexicans at a Southern California university campus, José M. Davila, inspector of immigration at the Tijuana, Mexico, border crossing, critiqued legislative efforts to stop Mexican immigration. It vexed him that restrictions based on "national origins" were a real possibility. Instead he offered a solution to the perennial unemployment and dire poverty affecting a large sector of the Mexican immigrant population, which in his opinion posed a legitimate argument, as far as the restrictionists were concerned, for curbing Mexican immigration.[2] Davila argued that Mexican poverty and reliance on public assistance during periods of unemployment resulted not from any specific character defect (although he admitted that some Mexican immigrants lacked "the spirit of thrift" and failed to "look into the future") but, rather, from the manner in which specific economic branches utilized Mexican labor. In place of public charity, he proposed public and private policies that ensured year-round employment. To this end he recommended a method for teasing out "more working days in the year by taking advantage of his [the Mexican's] migratory qualities." He then proceeded to flesh out his proposed state-sanctioned and -regulated system for rationalizing the use of Mexican labor: "Transport and shift him away from those sections of the country where the season is closed and work is scarce, to places where the season begins and there is demand for workmen."[3]

In addition to this method of mass mobilization of Mexican seasonal labor (and only Mexican labor) from region to region, Davila suggested a payroll deduction system aimed at creating a compulsory savings plan so as to "encourage thrift" and thereby further reduce the numbers on relief roles. Finally, he asserted that following implementation of such a labor policy, the demands for restrictions on Mexican immigration would be quieted and an open door to Mexican migration would be ensured, thereby maintaining a "safety valve" during Mexico's economic crises.

While Davila's recommendation did not quite constitute a guest worker proposal, it did encompass several of the basic terms contained in subsequent contract labor policies. First, it provided that the state intervene and manage an operation to move resident Mexican immigrant labor from work site to work site on the basis of confirmed labor shortages in specific locales. Second, it tied the worker to a specific employer or type of employment for the duration of the work period; as such, it constituted a limited form of indenture for temporarily resident immigrant workers. Finally, Davila's proposal strongly recommended a "compulsory" savings plan designed to alter the alleged wasteful spending habits of the worker—one that could be accomplished only through some form of obligatory wage deduction. These items are strikingly similar to the practices included in the bracero program, which would follow thirteen years later. They also resemble measures, such as matching a "willing" employer with an existing work force, that are markedly similar to those in the Bush proposal that would follow seventy-five years later.

The Santibanez Proposal (1930)

A year after Davila offered his proposal, Enrique Santibanez, the Mexican consul stationed at San Antonio, Texas, published a book containing a series of essays on Mexican immigration that were originally published in article form in the Spanish-language press.[4] What is certain is that the consul was not acting on an individual basis; rather, he was advising his fellow countrymen of their homeland government's position on a number of concerns affecting the expatriate community. In so doing, Santibanez carefully articulated the Mexican government's position on immigration policy and related issues. In classic diplomatic fashion, the book eschewed polemics and discussed the main features of U.S. immigration policies, the growth of the Mexican population, the types of labor restricted to Mexican immigrants, regional variations in labor and community, and racial prejudice, among other themes. However, his principal essay and the final inclusion, titled "How the [Mexican] Immigration Problem Can Be Resolved," offered his most important views on Mexican migration. In his opinion the much-discussed "Mexican immigration problem" affected Mexico to a far greater degree than it affected the United States, and this observation formed the crux of his deliberations.

In his government's opinion, widespread unemployment in Mexico forces an emigration that cannot be controlled. While Mexico may *in the future* require an available labor supply at home, that time has not yet come; consequently, a rational migration policy that meets the requirements of both nations needs to be implemented. Santibanez asked the reader to keep in mind that the Mexican unskilled laborer is in great demand in the cotton and beet fields in the United States rather than in Mexico. In addition, given that many Americans want to see Mexican immigration restricted, his proposal (really his government's) promised a solution that "harmonized the interests of the two nations." Considering that the United States has a far greater need for seasonal labor than for year-round workers, Santibanez proposed that the United States and Mexico enter into an accord that enabled

> large labor contracting offices [to] be established in Laredo, El Paso and Nogales under the supervision of officials of both countries where the worker and the empresario can enter into a labor contract; upon its expiration the worker would be returned to his home in Mexico.
> An identification card would be issued and the worker advised that punishments would be meted in one or the other country if he violated the contract provisions.[5]

Santibanez finished by declaring his "fervent desire that the two republics live and work in harmony." In his estimation, his proposal offered a "win-win" situation: unemployed Mexican people, employers of Mexican laborers, and immigration restrictionists all benefited. The Depression silenced further discussion about a contract labor program, but a program similar in several respects to Santibanez's made its appearance twelve years later and remained in place for twenty-two years.

Post-Bracero Guest Worker Proposals

California Governor Brown's Proposal (1965)

The next stage for contract labor proposals followed the termination of the bracero program in 1964. The Mexican government never agreed to end the program, but liberal critics and labor unions successfully led an assault against it. One significant attempt at overturning the program's termination was led by the Democratic governor of California, Edmund G. "Pat" Brown, who unsuccessfully lobbied to have the program continue while it underwent a five-year "phase-out." Brown's decision to lobby for an extension, which amounted to a thinly veiled request for a continuation of the bracero program by other means, was based in large part on a 1961 report authored by a state senate Fact Finding Committee. The Committee predicted that the program's termination would "be devastating to vast segments of this State's agriculture, and irreparably damaging to California's economy as a whole."[6] Even though a subsequent report by UC Berkeley suggested that other means such as mechanization and a rational employment system[7] could secure a harvest labor force (which the growers disagreed would occur), the governor lobbied the Department of Labor to enable the 1952 immigration act (Public Law 414), which allowed the importation of temporary labor under the H2-A provision, to "provide for Mexican laborers for California growers over a five-year period."

In assuaging the organized opposition to the bracero program, led in part by the Catholic Church, Brown's proposal also aimed at improving the wage, housing, and working conditions of domestic farm laborers. Growers were very active in soliciting support for another bracero program; nevertheless, they opposed any housing or wage guarantees for labor. Like the Santibanez proposal a quarter of a century before, Brown's plan attempted to please both sides of the issue. With an active anti-bracero lobby voicing its opposition, Secretary of Labor Willard Wirtz turned down Brown's five-year phase-out proposal, a decision that pleased the anti-bracero constituency.

Undeterred, Brown offered yet another proposal to Washington, this time calling for "arrangements ... with the Mexican government to insure prompt processing of Mexican workers into California if their services become necessary within the next month." Brown argued that "[a]ll of the evidence indicates that in the very near future it will be necessary for our Department of Employment to certify to the need for a substantial number of foreign workers to work in our California crops." He then sent a lobbying crew to the Department of Labor to convince Secretary Willard Wirtz of the state's predicament.[8] The Department of Labor responded that it would "make no arrangements with the Republic of Mexico ... until such time as the need for additional workers was demonstrated." Rather than shutting the door to temporary labor, the Department of Labor left open a window of opportunity for a future bracero program; the timing, however, was not yet quite right.

The Mexican government, too, opposed the bracero program's termination, taking the position that when and if this outcome became necessary, it should occur gradually rather than abruptly. More important, the government found that the bracero program served as a means to control "illegal migration" and therefore worked in the interests of both countries. Finally, contrary to critics of the program, it believed that the bracero program protected the rights of all workers and in no way prejudiced the rights of domestic workers. In the Mexican government's view, illegals and not braceros were the underlying cause of the worsening conditions affecting domestic agricultural workers, which the opposition to the bracero program ignored. The official Note delivered to the State Department expressing Mexico's interest in maintaining the bracero program stated, "It was precisely the presence of the 'wetbacks' in the fields . . . that created a situation undesirable from every standpoint."[9] Mexico joined the vocal chorus in the United States that abhorred the "wetback" invasion and in the process quietly lobbied for an extension of the program. As one Texas representative put it, "Officials do not shout from the housetops what they think about it, but they recognize it [the bracero program] as a tremendous boon to the country."[10] Far from being indifferent, the Mexican government was concerned about losing the export of 200,000 unemployed rural citizens and their remittances, a source of funds second only to tourism. These worries proved illusory, however, as Mexico's unemployed continued to fill the migratory pathways that extended across the border. The tide of undocumented immigrants rose to record levels and filled the farm worker breach left after the termination of the bracero program.

Mexican President Echeverria's Proposal (1974)

Several years after California's Governor Brown proposed a five-year extension, the president of Mexico, Luis Echeverria, declared "with much fanfare" his support for a new bracero program. In his 1974 State of the Union address he affirmed that his administration had attempted to enter into negotiations for a renewed bracero agreement in order to stem the tide of undocumented migration caused by the program's termination. In the post-bracero years, Immigration and Naturalization Service (INS) arrests increased alarmingly from approximately 90,000 in 1963 to 300,000 in 1969–1970.[11] However, in 1975 Echeverria changed course and, even after signing a temporary-worker accord with Canada, announced that Mexico now rejected "the idea of a new migrant agreement" on the basis that "such agreements have never succeeded in preventing undocumented migration in the past."[12] Echeverria appeared to dramatically alter course; however, since he had just signed what amounted to a bracero agreement with Canada, we can assume that the door remained open to future bracero agreements with the United States.

In regard to both Mexico and the United States, the opposition to a renewed bracero program proved the exception rather than the rule. As we shall see, Echeverria's critique of bracero programs deviated from the positions taken by Mexico and the United States. After a quarter-century of unrelenting emigration—legal, contracted, and illegal—both Mexico and the United States were in no position to permanently jettison a type of labor program that for over two decades had successfully served the labor requirements of agribusiness. Echeverria's sudden dismissal of a temporary-worker agreement was a temporary distraction, with no long-term consequences. U.S. and Mexican presidents issued at least four more proposals since Echeverria's sudden departure from the long-held policy: In the early 1980s, the Reagan administration proposed a trial bracero program; in the late 1980s, President Salinas de Gortari announced his administration's support for a revived bracero program; later, the Clinton administration discussed the possibility of a bracero program; and recently, the Bush administration and members of the Democratic Party have offered a number of proposals under the "guest worker" rubric. Taken together, these demonstrate that a temporary contract labor program is seldom far from the negotiation table.

With the influx of undocumented immigrants after the termination of the Bracero Agreements, a public outcry erupted over the seemingly uncontrolled entrance of Mexican immigrants. Legislation aimed at harnessing and controlling the U.S.-Mexico border triggered a long period of debate and discussion over the most effective means of immigration regulation. In 1977 the Carter administration proposed a measure that nine years later would be the basis for the Immigration Reform and Control Act (IRCA), which legalized the U.S. presence of some Reform undocumented immigrants (under certain residency restrictions) and included employer sanctions for knowingly hiring undocumented workers—sanctions that are rarely enforced. While immigration reform was being heatedly debated, and several years before the IRCA was passed, the Reagan administration entered the fray with its own immigration plan—one that advocated employer sanctions but went beyond the Carter proposal in calling for a guest worker program. The Reagan proposal was one of several guest worker plans to be put forward in the 1980s, and guest workers immediately became central to a debate about controlling "illegal aliens."

Below we examine several official and nonofficial proposals to import Mexican labor on a temporary basis.

The Wayne Cornelius Guest Worker Proposal (1981)

Nearly simultaneous with the Reagan administration's unveiling of a new "guest worker" program, Wayne Cornelius, director of the Program of United States–Mexican Studies at the University of California, San Diego, offered another proposal based on his sociological investigations. Cornelius, who later became an advocate for free trade, asserted that although it is the desire of immigration legislation to control undocumented migration, this aim cannot be accomplished under existing immigration policies. Even if the ceiling on legal immigration from Mexico were quadrupled, he argued, bureaucratic entanglements as well as the financial costs facing aspiring migrants virtually excluded any possibility of successfully regulating Mexican illegal immigration. He then laid out his plan to import labor on "temporary worker visas permitting up to six months ... of employment in the United States per year, for a total of five years."[13] Each aspirant would have to apply at a U.S. consulate and compete with other aspirants on a "first come first serve" basis for a set quota of positions determined by "fluctuations in the U.S. demand for foreign labor,"[14] and each temporary laborer would be required to return to Mexico for six months before reapplying and, if selected, would need to acquire another visa.

Each worker held the right to work for any employer who was willing to hire him for the six-month period. Standard wages, work conditions, and benefits were to be honored; workers could enter with their dependents in tow (although they were not eligible for welfare benefits); and they could join a labor union. In addition, temporary visa holders could apply for permanent legal residence "subject to existing quotas." Cornelius proposed a first-year ceiling of 750,000 and recommended that the program be limited to Mexican workers, since, among other things, "Mexican workers are more accustomed to periods of short-term employment" and are apt to use their permanent legal status to periodically return to Mexico, much like guest workers. Such a system would ensure continued "cordial relations with Mexico" in addition to resolving the seemingly unsolvable problem of "the flow of undocumented aliens." Like several of the previous proposals, Cornelius's promised a win-win situation. Much like Santibanez in 1930, Cornelius believed that all would benefit: the guest workers, who would be employed on the short-term basis they preferred; the employers, who would retain access to a dependable supply of workers; the United States, which would gain control of its borders and "markedly" reduce illegal immigration; and finally Mexico, which would profit from the employment of its poverty-stricken masses. Moreover, if enacted into policy, this version of a guest worker program would eliminate all of the negative conditions associated with the 1942–1964 bracero program.

The Cross and Sandos Proposal (1981)

Simultaneous with the presentation of the Cornelius proposal, two university researchers published a volume on Mexican economic development and migration to the United States at the Institute of Government Studies at UC Berkeley.[15] Their proposal for "A Five-Year Program to Admit Migrants" occupied only three pages but appeared to be the most important aspect of the publication. In keeping with the tradition among authors of guest worker proposals, this proposal was aimed both at meeting employer needs and at resolving the continual unemployment problem in Mexico. According to the policy formulators, the program would admit male and female eighteen-year-olds without quota restrictions to work for one year under visas renewable for up to five years. These temporary laborers would be able to work for the employer of their choice and travel freely. Their selection would be determined by a literacy test, a health test, and proof of age. If accepted, applicants were required to pay a $30 fee to cover processing costs and, upon entry, to deposit $300, which would be "reclaimed with interest" upon their return to Mexico.[16]

Again, as with nearly all indentured worker programs and guest worker proposals, a deduction would be taken to ensure departure. All rights and privileges applied to working people in the United States would be applicable to guest workers. Interestingly, the proposal also intended to diminish the overall number of undocumented immigrants; as Harry Cross and James Sandos put it, the program would "greatly increase Border Patrol capability ... while strongly encouraging entry into the United States through legal channels" and furthermore "would have the intended benefit of removing from the migrant the stigma of illegality."[17] However, it is difficult to fathom how those persons likely to migrate could ever come up with $330 to cover the costs of attaining "legal" status for one year. Such a proposal would not only winnow potential migrants down to just a handful of relatively well-off people but also lead to continued undocumented migration.

Cross and Sandos concluded that in the long term the United States and Mexico needed to jointly plan an economic policy that took into consideration their existing linkages, particularly migration. Such a policy would be "designed to help Mexico meet some of its employment goals."[18] It stands to reason that emigration as a means to overcome Mexico's perennial lack of sufficient employment would be included in a binational economic strategy; less expected, however, was the incorporation of the existing migration pattern into this proposal. In short, a temporary-worker program for workers from Mexico would serve to institutionalize an ongoing migration, not to end it. A program to import temporary workers would simultaneously provide a method to curtail the existing migration of large numbers of undocumented immigrants. Yet sectors of the economy dependent on these immigrants would be assured that their labor supply would not be negatively affected.

The Reagan Proposal (1981)

In the summer of 1981 the Reagan administration joined the ongoing discussion over whether or not to enact a "guest worker" program. The *New York Times* described the policy proposed by Reagan as a mechanism to "outlaw the employment of illegal aliens ... [and] fine employers for violations and suggesting an experimental program admitting 'guest workers.'"[19] In addition, a legalization process would allow undocumented immigrants to gain legal status after a ten-year waiting period. However, like the Mexican government's opposition to ending the bracero program, Reagan's proposal was put forward as part of the general agenda of controlling undocumented migration. Under the Reagan proposal, guest workers would "work at jobs for which domestic labor is in short supply" (one more convention among guest worker proposals) and limited to only 50,000 workers per year.[20] Only single workers, and presumably male ones, would be admitted, and they would be ineligible for welfare benefits such as unemployment insurance, food stamps, federally assisted housing, and the like. However, the measure allowing workers to be free to change employers moved Wayne Cornelius to describe the Reagan plan as a "vast improvement" over the former bracero program even though, according to Cornelius, the limitation of 50,000 "guests" per year would fail to effectively "reduce illegal entries."[21] As we now know, few in Washington, D.C., were convinced of a need for a new guest worker agreement, and although a sweeping immigration bill was passed in 1986 that included legalization and employer sanctions (which have rarely been enforced), no guest worker accord came of Reagan's proposal.

Current Guest Worker Proposals

The Bush-Fox Guest Worker Proposal: I (2001)

In early January 2001, only a few months after George W. Bush had been elected, newspaper headlines rang out over a "new era" of U.S.-Mexico relations and promises to clear away the lingering problem of undocumented migration. As part of the overall effort to cooperate with the Bush administration and negotiate with Mexico, a high-level but small bipartisan contingent of U.S. senators traveled to Mexico to initiate discussions "over the more contentious issues along the border." Of course, immigration was at the top of the list. According to news reports, the meeting augured a first step toward "outlining a preliminary proposal for a guest worker program."[22] For ninety minutes the five senators—four republicans and one democrat—discussed immigration with Mexican President Vicente Fox, former Coca-Cola executive and governor of the State of Guanajuato. The group "showered praise" on Fox, and Senator Phil Gramm (R-Texas), the leader of the entourage (and an expert conservative economist), suggested that both nations were on the verge of "[getting] the ability to stop illegal immigration" and getting control of the border.[23] The essence of this border control appeared in a measure for importing temporary workers using the existing H2-A program, which allowed the importation of around 43,000 temporary workers from Mexico and the Caribbean. To be sure, Fox was most collaborative over the matter of establishing a guest worker agreement and lobbied with the citizenry in Mexico to gather support for such an agreement. Meanwhile, in the United States "increasing support among both Republicans and Democrats for measures that would increase the numbers of Mexicans granted temporary work visas each year" seemed to predict that an eventual agreement was in the offing.[24]

Senator Gramm also introduced legislation in the Senate to "legalize" undocumented Mexican immigrants working in the United States and thereby transform them into a form of "guest workers." However, an undocumented person wishing to become a "guest worker" would have the right only to apply for guest worker status and, if selected, would be obliged to return to Mexico within a year. Gramm's proposal included a provision for importing temporary workers who would work under similar terms—namely, an obligatory savings account and return within a year. Year-round guest workers brought from Mexico could reapply for renewed permits for up to three consecutive years before having to return to Mexico for at least one year. And seasonal workers under guest worker visas would be eligible for an indefinite number of permits. The obligatory savings account was designed to motivate repatriation. Based on a 10 percent paycheck deduction, this account could be tapped into only upon one's return to Mexico. As Gramm put it, "you get your money when you return."[25] Workers under the "guest worker" program might work in service, agriculture, construction, or jobs in which undocumented immigrants already work. Ultimately, the senators touring Mexico seemed to be of one mind for developing such a worker agreement with Mexico.

Americans witnessed an upsurge of publicity as this matter swelled the media, including research institutes. The Carnegie Endowment for International Peace, together with the Autonomous Technological Institute in Mexico, published a policy statement arguing that any "comprehensive new strategy should match Mexico's surplus of young workers with U.S. industry's shortage of unskilled labor." One member of the Mexican team put it rather bluntly: "Mexico has lots of young people willing to work, and the U.S. population is aging."[26] The question of the undocumented hovered at or near the surface; as one binational panelist stated, "this is a window of opportunity" for both nations to solve the undocumented immigration problem as well as for the United States to procure Mexican labor under excellent conditions.

Two months after the senators' meeting with Fox, Presidents Bush and Fox began a round of talks on a range of issues, not the least of which was immigration, at Fox's Mexican ranch. Bush made clear that among the issues that his administration wished to discuss seriously, free trade was equal to, if not above, guest workers on the negotiating hierarchy. However, the media attached themselves to a single issue: immigration. Amid much fanfare and media attention, "high-ranking officials" from both nations were "assigned to address both nations' concerns."[27] In preliminary meetings, Bush and Fox poured effusive praise on each other. Bush described his counterpart as "the kind of man you can look in the eye and you know he's shooting straight with you." Fox returned, "I want you to understand that we consider you a friend of the Mexican people and a friend of mine."[28] A casual shirtsleeve, cowboy hat, and boot atmosphere in a country-club setting seemed to characterize the various sites selected to quarter Bush and his family. Bush's wish to establish "a safe and orderly migration" policy—that is, a guest worker program—remained at the forefront of the talks. Condoleezza Rice, Bush's national security advisor, accompanied Bush and observed that the two presidents "share the same goals." Indeed, headlines across the nation included the phrases "New Partners," "New Realities," and "New Era," leading to the impression that whatever stage the negotiations were in, it was "new." This became the media's keyword regarding the Fox-Bush meetings.

The Senate Foreign Relations Committee, under the chairmanship of Jesse Helms, accompanied the Bush team at the negotiating table and held private talks with Fox. Some found Helms's support for an immigration bill to be rather puzzling; but as Ginger Thompson pointed out, Helms represented North Carolina, a state where agricultural interests were "among the most vocal advocates for expanding guest worker programs."[29] Obviously, the economist in Helms had warmed to the idea of more Mexican immigrants in North Carolina, even as temporary workers. One report offered a reason for the guest worker support, stating that "North Carolina's economy has grown beyond textiles and tobacco, and is attracting new workers—primarily Mexican workers, so many that the Mexican government has opened a new consulate office there."[30] And it wasn't just Senator Helms who looked forward to importing temporary labor. Senator Charles Hagle asserted that, in his home state of Nebraska, "economic development in some districts is a direct result of having workers from Mexico coming to work."[31]

Meanwhile, Fox proposed a minimum of 250,000 temporary workers as well as an amnesty provision of the undocumented now working and residing in the United States. His proposal envisioned the existing H2-A program under the 1952 Immigration and Nationality Act, which enabled agricultural interests to import temporary labor if a labor shortage could be demonstrated. At the time of the Fox-Bush meetings the provision capped annual recruitment at about 43,000; Fox wanted to enlarge H2-A to 250,000. In addition, a conditional amnesty for undocumented immigrants appeared to be a part of the Fox plan. In July, Fox began a tour to pitch his plan, arguing that "we want more than maquiladora factories." However, in the United States amnesty received a cool reception among the general populace, whereas guest workers appeared to have the support of employers already dependent on Mexican labor. Prominent among the backers of the measure was the Essential Worker Immigration Coalition (EWIC); formed in 1999 and composed of "an array of influential organizations" that included the U.S. Chamber of Commerce, it actively lobbied for an eventual agreement. The EWIC counted among its members the National Association of Chain Drug Stores, the American Health Care Association, the American Hotel and Lodging Association, the National Council of Chain Restaurants, the National Restaurant Association, and the National Retail Federation.[32] Like many of his colleagues in California, a vegetable grower expressed strong support for guest worker agreement, noting that "this measure cannot be passed too soon."[33] Accordingly, an aide to a Democratic senator noted, "Everybody has been clamoring for some kind of legalization program because they can't find sufficient, low-skilled workers to fill jobs."[34]

In the United States, newspaper and television coverage generally proffered the Bush administration position on controlled, state-managed migration. Journalists broadcast that the proposed policy discussions had the broad support of the Mexican and North American population. One headline reading "U.S. Warms to Idea of More Guest Workers" seemed to reflect the general tenor of the coverage. After the meetings were completed and officials on both sides had departed, Senators Biden and Helms issued a joint statement declaring that the times "produced a political environment ripe for genuine progress."[35] Without doubt, a "new era" of U.S.-Mexico relations *had* commenced; but more work was needed before a bilateral migration policy could be enacted. Such work would have to wait: The September 11 terrorist attack on the World Trade Center moved any novel partnership with Mexico to the margins, where it resided for the better part of two years.

The Bush-Fox negotiations over a renewed bracero program prompted discussion among some academics who imagined a new and bright day for Mexican migration by way of a guest worker agreement. Shortly after the initial euphoria over a renewed guest worker program had died down, one of the major figures in migration studies, Douglas Massey, along with several of his contemporaries, authored a work arguing that the flow of undocumented workers in the post-bracero years, 1964–1986, amounted to a "piece of well-ordered machinery" and a "benign labor process" thrown into disarray by policies such as the Immigration Reform and Control Act of 1986 and the Clinton administration's Operation Gatekeeper. As a means of restoring the one-time "natural" flow of surplus Mexican labor into the United States, Massey and his co-authors recommend a renewed bracero program that would repeat several of the recommendations made in the Bush proposal, such as "regularizing" undocumented migrants. In particular, Massey and his colleagues argue that a new guest worker program would promise reduced illegal migration and the restoration of a stable, normal, and legal migratory flow to the United States.[36]

As many previous advocates of renewing a guest worker program would assert, the real problem is the flow of undocumented—and to rationalize this flow, a system of controlling labor through a state-managed system is highly recommended.[37] In keeping with theoretical convention, U.S.-Mexico economic relations are defined as mutually beneficial and "interdependent," and NAFTA, the current manifestation of that celebrated interdependence, is of incalculable benefit to Mexico in the long run. Until this benefit moves Mexico into developed-nation status, migration will be a necessary part of its social and economic process. Such being the case, a new bracero program needs be institutionalized.

The Bush Guest Worker Proposal: II (2004)

Previous to 9/11, former Coca-Cola executive Vicente Fox and oil magnate George W. Bush evoked images of a strong, friendly working relationship. Both neoliberal stalwarts seemed on a path of creating some form of guest worker agreement; Mexico asked for the "whole enchilada," which included amnesty for undocumented immigrants as well as a guest worker program. Then–Foreign Minister Jorge Castañeda repeatedly promised Latino audiences across the United States that as part of the immigration reform package, amnesty was non-negotiable; as he stated on numerous occasions, "it is the whole enchilada or nothing." Then came the terrorist attack, which put the guest worker discussions on the far back burner; there it remained for two years, although every now and then a report signaled that the guest worker interest had not died out entirely. Indeed, in mid-November 2002, a visit to Mexico by a Washington delegation led by Secretary Colin Powell again raised the possibility of a guest worker agreement; shortly after Powell's visit, Fox renewed the call for a new guest worker agreement, urging the two nations to "take up our negotiations again with a newfound energy."[38]

A year went by before headlines read "U.S. and Mexico Pledge to Revive Immigration Drive." And indeed, the discussions were finally on the table again, simultaneous with the news that Peace Corps volunteers were now welcome in Mexico; one month later Bush unveiled a broad design for a new guest worker agreement. On Christmas Eve 2003, Bush proposed a temporary labor program that included both undocumented workers now living in the United States and potential guest laborers living in foreign countries. Bush unabashedly described his immigration proposal as one that "promote[s] compassion" and "serves the American economy and reflects the American dream." However, in contrast to the pre-9/11 discussions and contrary to Fox's expectations, the Bush immigration proposal left Mexico out of the deliberations. The United States unilaterally proposed a guest worker program, aimed primarily at Mexican undocumented immigrants now working in the United States and, to a lesser extent, at potential workers from Mexico. Mexico rediscovered that the United States determines the ingredients of the "whole enchilada."

The Bush guest worker proposal concentrates, first, on incorporating as guest workers the millions of undocumented immigrants living and working in the United States. Its aim is to control illegal immigrants now working by bringing them into a state-administered guest worker program while simultaneously securing the border. Under the proposal it is unlikely that labor from Mexico will be imported in significant numbers (except possibly in agriculture), given the presence of millions of potential guest workers now available in urban areas. If laborers from abroad are imported, they will be used to supplement the existing supply of undocumented farm workers in states like California where agriculture is geared toward labor-intensive crops. As Bush said during the final presidential debate at Arizona State University on October 14, 2004, his proposal focuses on undocumented workers. "I believe," he stated, "there ought to be a temporary-worker card that allows a willing worker and a willing employer to mate up, as long as there's not an American willing to do the job.... It makes sure that people coming across the border are humanely treated, that they're not kept in the shadows of our society."[39]

Second, the new guest worker program will be open to both women and men. Unlike the old bracero program, which admitted only men, Bush's proposal—which refers to those "who want to work and to fulfill their duties as a husband or wife, a son and daughter"—makes clear that women are eligible as well. (The phrase "husband or wife" refers logically to undocumented immigrants working in the United States with families rather than to potential guest workers from abroad who would more likely emigrate as individuals.) Since hotels, resorts, convalescent care centers, janitorial crews, and professional housekeeping services, among other enterprises, regularly employ men *and* women, and since in some sectors women predominate while in others men comprise the labor force, expanding the guest worker eligibility to include both sexes makes sense. We can expect that one social consequence of the guest worker program will be the further stabilization of gender relations now existing on the lower-paid rungs of the economy.

Third, central to the Bush proposal and perhaps even more important than the matter of guest workers is the matter of bank accounts and remittances. The proposal goes beyond guest workers alone in that a bank account automatically opens for all guest workers and a portion of their pay is placed into a tax-free account that is accessible upon their return to their home country. (Granted, this theme was very familiar in previous proposals.) In conjunction with these guest worker accounts, plans have been made to channel into savings accounts the remittances of Latin American immigrants, particularly Mexican immigrants. (These remittances have reached record levels and their totals are still climbing). U.S. banking and financial institutions will be the main beneficiaries, as these will increase their volume of business for banking services. But the story doesn't end there: These funds will be coupled with neoliberal economic policies such as NAFTA that now dominate state policies in Mexico.

Finally, amnesty occupies no place in the Bush proposal. Guest workers are promised a conditional three-year contract, a tax-free savings bank account (based on paycheck deductions) coupled with an ATM card with which to send remittances to family members in Mexico, and nothing else.

Many observers deem the proposal to be a means of resolving the problem of illegal immigration and bringing the problems faced by illegal workers to national attention for resolution. Not all, however, are convinced by such motives. "Was it an election year tease to attract Latino voters?" asked some; others discarded the agreement as half-baked, without much chance of passing through Congress. Still others, California Democratic Congresswomen Loretta Sanchez among them, consider the proposal to be a first step toward an effective and just solution to the problems encountered by the millions of undocumented immigrants working across the United States. In a similar vein, AFL-CIO president John Sweeney cautioned that the United States needed to "reform, not expand, temporary worker programs."[40] And there were those, such as future presidential candidate Senator John F. Kerry (a strong supporter of NAFTA and Free Trade for the Americas), who criticized the proposal as a potential invitation to exploitation. Kerry ultimately, as presidential candidate, expressed support, stating, "We need a guest worker program, but if it's all we have, it's not going to solve the problem." Spokespersons for the Kerry-Edwards 2004 campaign underscored Kerry's support for guest worker programs; according to David Bacon, they contended that "Senator Kerry does not believe that we can abolish guest worker programs altogether," and that Kerry "will establish a secure channel for a limited number of temporary workers to come."[41] Kerry supports the so-called AgJOBS bill, negotiated between the United Farm Workers Union and growers; essentially a version of the existing H2-A guest worker program, it has been expanded to allow foreign workers to work under ten-month contracts, with a route to legalization. The measure would anchor farm labor more securely by preventing early exits from seeking work outside of agriculture. If they "worked a certain number of days of farm work [i.e., 90 days] each year for five years ... they could earn an immigrant status under bills pending [in 2000] in Congress."[42] Meanwhile, others, such as Patrick Buchanan, have argued that a guest worker program tied to legalization does nothing more than reward lawbreakers.

Mexican immigrants, the crux of Bush's proposal, seemed unimpressed with Bush's plan and either took a wait-and-see approach or dismissed the proposal as nonsense. Among the most vociferous critics of this proposal were former braceros who had experienced the bracero program first hand and who rejected the proposal outright as a guaranteed repetition of a labor system that has been compared to a form of slavery. Ex-braceros, the most consistent critics of guest worker agreements, were also the first to take a firm stand against the guest worker agreement proposed during the pre-9/11 discussions between Fox and Bush.[43]

However, as in the case of the bracero program, the most ardent supporters of the Bush proposal are the very employers who have come to depend on Mexican labor, both illegal and legal. Hotel chains, resorts, restaurants, and especially agribusiness expressed strong support for the Bush measure. In agriculture, 80 percent of all farm workers are hired by just 10 percent of all farming outfits, which comprise most of the large-scale enterprises already heavily subsidized.[44] Even before Bush made his announcements, agribusiness interests were pushing a guest worker program. According to two agronomists at the University of California, Davis, agribusiness lobbied long before Bush's election for a new bracero program, even though no shortage of labor existed. They wrote:

> California growers are intensifying their push for a guest-worker program at the new millennium. They cite INS claims that border and internal law enforcement of immigration laws will eventually succeed

in reducing the flow of workers across the border, as well as the reluctance of U.S. citizens to work in the fields. It is likely that in the next 25 years we will witness new experiments with federal guest-worker programs for agriculture.[45]

Not surprisingly, one California tomato grower called the Bush plan "a Christmas present." Others similarly chimed in; a representative of the U.S. Chamber of Commerce labeled the initiative "momentous."[46] The president of the California Restaurant Association praised the Bush plan, saying that "we are very enthusiastic" and that "it will allow industries like ours to legally find and hire workers."[47]

After some initial indecisiveness, Fox enthusiastically accepted the 2004 proposal, claiming, "This is a very important step forward."[48] He gleefully declared that Bush's proposal would protect guest workers' "labor rights and their human rights" and concluded, "This is what we want."[49] Mexico had no other choice than to accept the offer. By all appearances, Fox and Bush stood "shoulder to shoulder" on a measure that, if ratified in Congress, would ensure continued Mexican migration (albeit state managed, as in the case of the 1917–1921 contract labor program, the 1942–1964 bracero program, and the H2-A program) as well as the further integration of undocumented Mexican labor within the confines of U.S. corporate capital. If enacted, and Fox plans to lobby in Washington for its passage, the proposal guarantees one more chapter in the century-long history of Mexican labor migration. Of that there can be no doubt.

According to the proposal outlined by Bush, workers will be placed in agricultural, service, and other industries that can demonstrate a labor shortage unmet by domestic legal workers. (The bracero program, too, required employers to demonstrate a labor shortage; however, requests for braceros were seldom verified or denied.) Guest workers are to be paid the "prevailing wage" (another similarity with the former bracero program, which guaranteed braceros a prevailing wage—though, of course, bracero employers made up their own "prevailing wage") and are to be given the same labor protections offered to domestic labor (the bracero agreements stipulated more rights than workers in the United States enjoyed, yet the exploitation of braceros has been compared to slavery). However, in contrast to the bracero agreements, the current proposal offers the possibility of acquiring legal status with qualifications and no guarantee of outright legalization. In fact, contrary to the contention of some critics, the Bush proposal is neither outright amnesty nor anything resembling amnesty; clearly, the proposal was not intended to grant amnesty. Procedurally, *employed* undocumented workers must voluntarily sign on to a labor contract of up to three years under the sponsorship of an employer, with the possibility of a second renewal and no more.

During the course of the contract, the guest worker may apply for a green card, which allows the holder to assume legal immigrant status. However, for all intents and purposes, an undocumented worker who becomes a guest worker is placed in line with all other applicants for a green card, with no guarantee at the end of the three- or six-year contract (or as many years as the final proposal states) that legal status will be accorded. The possibility remains that the person may be deported at any time before or after termination of the guest worker status. Yet, over the course of the contract, which does not obligate the employer to retain the guest worker for any length of time, the guest worker must demonstrate a good record confirming that he or she deserves to remain in the United States. The proposal does hold out incentives for guest workers to voluntarily return to their homeland. In particular, it includes a tax-free savings account that can be cashed out upon the guest worker's return—in essence, becoming a "bonus" that promotes the workers' desire for repatriation. (Braceros were also extended a "bonus," from 1942 to 1949 in the form of 10 percent of their wages retained to be paid upon their return to Mexico; but many braceros never received this withheld wage. It went instead into the coffers of banks or politicos.)

Bush's proposal also includes an electronic employment registry system, a procedure whereby each potential guest worker living abroad is matched with a "willing employer" who determines his or her entry into the guest worker program. In all likelihood, imported guest workers will be shipped to agriculture, where the greatest need for seasonal labor exists. In contrast to undocumented immigrants who choose to enroll in the program, agricultural guest workers will probably be largely male. All other qualifications apply, including prevailing wages and the existence of labor shortages. Here we see one more similarity with the old bracero program. In both the Bush and the bracero programs, the existing employment patterns of Mexican labor in the United States provide the context for guest worker employment. However, it appears that working undocumented immigrants—that is, those now living and working in the United States—will receive the greatest attention.

Clearly, the meat of the proposal is its focus on these 8–12 million undocumented immigrants (a number that fluctuates depending on the study), 60 percent of whom are Mexican and the targets of the guest worker proposal. Controlling this population appears to be the main objective of the Bush proposal. They are asked to "out" themselves and to enter into an entirely new legal status, one that offers the possibility of a three- or six-year temporary work period but nothing beyond. In this sense, the Bush proposal differs only slightly from the reform proposed by then–Senator Phil Gramm in 2001, whereby work permits would be issued for one year, after which the worker is required to leave. In the Bush proposal (and all other "guest worker" plans), an undocumented person who comes forward becomes a "rented worker," under the direct power of the state for determining the worker's fate.

This proposal certainly does appear to be one method to control immigration, and it is alleged to have the power of an Operation Wetback and Operation Gatekeeper. On the one hand, it is touted as a means of bringing in the required unskilled and semi-skilled labor and, as such, promises to stabilize labor within economic sectors already dependent on immigrant labor. However, there is no evidence that such a proposal will stop the ingress of undocumented workers. One thing is for sure: Each guest worker's future as an employee will be tied to a specific employer, even though in theory the guest worker may change employers. However, the tendency will be for workers to shrink from seeking alternative employments, given their unfamiliarity with the employers, their lack of knowledge of available employment opportunities, and their lack of transportation. If, for example, a worker is sent to North Carolina to work on a tobacco farm or to Arkansas to work in a chicken processing plant, their chances of becoming familiar with available employment in the area are slim. In all probability, then, most workers will work out their contract with the same employer as long as work is available. Ultimately, the beneficiaries are the employers of Mexican labor who are interested in access to and stabilization of the workforce they have depended upon for decades.

The Matter of Remittances

Although the question of temporary labor is an important one, one overriding factor remains to be discussed. The continually increasing flows of remittances sent by immigrants to their native lands—in this case, Mexico—is central to any guest worker bill. Neither the architects of the Bush proposal nor their staunch collaborators, the members of the Fox administration, have overlooked this matter. An estimated $14.5 billion in remittances were sent last year to relatives, friends, and family—an amount that surpasses income from all other sources, including direct foreign investment, oil, and tourism. And it is certain that guest workers (who in the main will be recruited from among the undocumented) will continue the tradition of sending remittances to support relatives left behind. Remittances are not only the backbone of the Mexican economy but also provide basic needs for 18 percent of the adults in the population; indeed, if their dependents are also taken into consideration, we find that one-quarter of Mexico's population relies on remittances. Not only will the guest worker's labor be under state control, but there are plans to steer the guest workers' remittances into banking and other financial institutions as well. The only unknown for the guest worker is legal status at the termination of the contract.

At the same time that Bush's guest worker plan was being proposed, a number of reports were urging that particular attention be paid to the opportunities offered by remittances, which remain underutilized. In particular, both the PEW Hispanic Center and the Inter-American Dialogue published findings that examined the gap between the amount of remittances sent home and the inefficient manner in which the monies were used. The two entities recommended a three-pronged approach to a more productive use of remittances—namely, the integration of these monies into government-administered economic and social programs.

First, to increase the size of the remittance figures they recommended lowering the fees charged for sending remittances and urged that governments lobby all institutions involved in sending remittances to lower fees. It is expected that lower fees will lead to a rise in the volume of remittances, simultaneously increasing the revenue for the sending institutions. Second, in a related move they recommended steering remittances, likened to a "fuel pump," into banking and financial institutions, thereby establishing a substantial new market for savings accounts and borrowers (i.e., enlarging the customer pool for banks). The majority of remittances, in excess of 55 percent, are sent and received outside of the banking system, and women head nearly half of the families receiving remittances.[50] Consequently, most remittances are kept at home and used for cash purchases, sidestepping any intermediary. It is this private use of money that is the target for change. As one official for the U.S. Bank remarked, remittances supply "an opportunity to turn the un-banked into a consumer of the bank."[51] Thus, guest worker remittances will not only become a means of survival for families at home but can also provide an opportunity for enlarging banking business. Citibank, Wells Fargo, and the Bank of America recently revised their customer services to expand the scope of checking and savings accounts by linking them with remittances. The *Wall Street Journal* accurately described the objective of these banks: "Remittances are also a way to get Latinos in the door and sell them more sophisticated and bigger-ticket services."[52] The implication is that with the tying of Mexican immigrant community into the bank account system, the customer base, including borrowers, will enlarge along with the profit margins.

Third, according to the Inter-American Dialogue, through "banking the unbanked," the "developmental horizons of the nations and communities" are expanded, jobs are created, and pressure to migrate declines.[53] In other words, remittances have the raw power to stimulate economic development. These three recommendations are expected to result in an increase in the amount of remittances; an increase in business and, therefore, in profits for banks; and greater availability of funds for investing in a failed model for economic development. We should note that the proponents for NAFTA also promised national economic security, but such was never delivered; instead, Mexico's economy has been on a steep downward slide since 1994. Given the ensuing impoverishment of Mexico and the rise of undocumented migration and settlement in the United States, the same people who were driven from their homeland soon emerged as denizens of the poorest sectors of the United States. Now they are being asked to step in and resolve the dire consequences of free trade in Mexico. But nothing is new here. At the Summit of the Americas held in Quebec in 2001, at a time when Mexico was already reeling from widespread poverty and unemployment, the joint summit declaration labeled remittances "a source of developmental capital" and called on governments to plan accordingly. The Mexican government, ever at the service of the neoliberal model, actively cooperates with banks in managing these remittance flows. According to Mexico's undersecretary for foreign affairs, Enrique Berruga, "the bankers come to us" and the *matricula* [personal ID] is "very good news for the American banking industry in that all the money that was under the mattress is now in their arteries and their financial systems."[54]

Upon the direction of the Office of Foreign Relations, consulates do their part in the "remittance reform" agenda by issuing *matriculas* for those without immigrant documents. The whole point behind the *matriculas* was to pave the way for undocumented expatriates—the pool of future "guest workers" in the Bush plan—to open bank accounts.[55] Of course, banks and the Mexican government well understood that these ID cards would be honored as official documents for the purpose of opening a bank account that, in turn, would be the medium for sending remittances. As do its competitors, Citibank takes full advantage of the *matriculas* by regularly sending representatives to consulate offices on scheduled registration days to hawk bank accounts to the *matriculados* among the Mexican immigrants. But Citibank has an advantage: It owns Banamex, one of the largest banks in Mexico, with which it partners in the remittance business.

By all accounts, the banking business is booming in the immigrant market. In the first six months of 2002, Wells Fargo, the first to accept the *matricula,* opened an estimated 30,000 accounts on the basis of the ID.[56] Not surprisingly, bank accounts opened by virtue of the consular document played a large part in raising the remittance level to a record $14.5 billion in 2003, up from around $8 billion just a few years before.[57] Through steering remittances into banks and other financial institutions, the funds of working people in the United States will take up some, but not much, of the slack of a failed economic model that has forced thousands to flee their homeland. Using remittances under the aegis of free trade and NAFTA forces the sender of remittances to become an unwitting partner in supporting policies that condition migration to the United States. Meanwhile, the U.S. banking industry's coffers will expand significantly.

The Mexican government also has other methods of diverting a substantial amount of monies from the expatriate community into government-administered "economic development" programs. The developmental model Fox has in mind is none other than the neoliberal free-trade model that has been applied in Mexico since the mid-1980s. While the United States and Mexico were discussing a possible guest worker agreement prior to 9/11, Mexico was busy soliciting "investors," affectionately termed *padrinos* (godfathers), among the migrant community to "invest in communities that send the majority of migrants." In certain cases, the Mexican government would match the *padrinos'* contribution. According to the Mexican government, such investment is needed for solving the problem of unemployment in the sending villages. The former head of the Mexicans Living Abroad office, Juan Hernandez, envisioned projects that included schools, hospitals, and roads in ninety poverty-stricken and immigrant sending "micro regions." One expatriate who eventually came to own a clothing distribution company in New York became a *padrino* by investing in a clothing assembly plant in San Salvador el Seco, his former hometown. He is now lauded as an ideal example of the Fox program.[58] Whether owned by small investors or by major corporations, maquiladoras have never made a dent in underdevelopment in any country where they have been installed. The entire Mexican northern border area is filled with assembly plants surrounded by working-class shack towns mired in poverty. Over a million people now work in assembly plants across Mexico, and the poverty rate remains unchecked, affecting 60 percent of the population.

Clearly, while the Bush guest worker agreement may have accomplished nothing more than election-year rhetoric, the matter of remittances is an ongoing project.

Conclusion

After several years of discussion Bush revived the guest worker proposal in his 2005 State of the Union Address stating, "It is time for an immigration policy that permits temporary guest workers to fill jobs Americans won't take ..." The details of the guest worker proposal remain to be elaborated and finalized after deliberation by Congress. The complexity of organizing the undocumented into guest workers seems at first blush overwhelming. Millions work in the informal economy as day laborers, nannies, home seamstresses, gardeners and other off-the-record jobs. These have little opportunity if any under the Bush proposal to become guest workers. Will the guest worker agreement bring in women to work as nannies? Housekeepers? Hotel maids? Seamstresses? If yes to each, the proposal will secure one more existing social relation. No one has commented on the inclusion of women who may be hired to work in agriculture. Will women be hired from abroad to work in agriculture and if so, will these women be housed by growers? Will growers house men? If guest workers are housed the oldest tradition in Chicano labor history, the company town, will be revived. If an undocumented worker refuses to out himself/herself, what risks do they run? Will employers continue to employ them while others in their work force chose the guest worker path? Observers note that there will be a great many obstacles to the Bush Proposal becoming law before and even after elections, and Bush seemed to lack the will to hammer out an agreement that he demonstrated two years previous. Upon his election the questions remain.

With so many questions whirling about, critics abound. Many journal reports suggest that Bush mounted an election strategy meant to engage the Latino vote. Others point out that the operation of such a program would be a bureaucratic nightmare, far too enormous in scope to be handled efficiently. Many, but certainly not all Democrats oppose the proposal and a number of reasons pepper their positions. Some believe that guest workers will lower wages, that domestic labor is available, or that workers will fall under the control of employers. (However, since the target of the Bush proposal is the existing pool of undocumented, the Democratic critique stands wide of the mark given that existing workers will probably earn the same as guest workers.) Some democrats believe that while the Bush proposal is a first step, it does not go far enough and stops short of offering access to amnesty. On the other hand, some Republicans accuse the Bush plan as nothing more than a veiled amnesty, which they generally oppose; yet others on the conservative side agree that the proposal is a first step to solve the dilemma of the undocumented working across the United States. On the Mexican side the Bush proposal has received glowing government support and Fox has indicated that his administration will lobby in Congress for the passage of such a bill.

Since the immigration question was brought to the fore, which seems to be the one thing that all find positive, there is no indication of a final legislative result. Nonetheless, proposals and discussion steam forward. One jointly sponsored bill put forward by Senator John McCain (R-Arizona) and Senator Edward M. Kennedy (D-Massachusetts) implements the main attributes of the Bush proposal incorporating the Bush refrain "linking willing workers with willing employers." For one, the McCain-Kennedy bill would allow foreigners as well as undocumented workers to become guest workers. However, new contract workers would pay a hefty $500 processing fee, a background review and a health exam and demonstrate that an employer is waiting for him or her. On the other hand, undocumented workers would be obligated to pay a total of $2000 in fines to work legally for three years renewable for another three years; after six years of laboring as a guest worker he/she could earn a green card and legalization. Before receiving a permanent residency card the guest worker must demonstrate that he/she paid taxes, is proficient in English, pass a medical exam and finally "undergo a stringent criminal background check." Traditional employers of undocumented workers as well as some unions embraced the proposed bill without reservation.[59] The final outcome of the bill is far from certain given the number of Republicans who prefer a "work and return program" and refer to the proposed bill as a virtual amnesty.

However few in Congress, the media, or the public raise the connection between the serious economic problems of Mexico resulting from its historical economic relationship with the United States and migration, legal and illegal. A nearly invisible minority declared, and rightly so, that there is no possible solution for Mexican migration apart from the economic independence and development of Mexico. Consequently, it is argued, if the Bush guest worker proposal is an attempt to resolve the thorny issue of Mexican illegal immigration (which it is), it is bound to fail.[60] A poll taken of a cross-section of Mexico's adults show that nearly one of every five is considering migrating to the United States.[61] Without dramatic improvement in Mexico's long-standing and woeful economic situation, exacerbated by the North American Free Trade Agreement, Mexicans will carry forward a century of migration.

One thing for sure, Bush opened a contentious debate that appears at this writing more of a cacophony than a considered discussion over specific issues. If Congress eventually passes some form of a guest worker measure, we can be sure that many of the exploitative conditions that were once foisted upon braceros will befall the guest workers. Indeed, undocumented workers already face the lowest wages, poorest working conditions, extended working hours, few benefits, and substandard living conditions that add up to the worst forms of poverty in the United States.[62]

Status as a guest worker holds no promises to change those conditions that have greeted Mexican immigrants for generations; instead these conditions will remain firmly institutionalized. An undocumented immigrant who becomes a guest worker will remain in the same social and economic position as previously; the job, pay, work conditions confers to the guest worker, and nothing will change. Perhaps the Canadian guest worker experience sheds light on what an American guest worker program will look like. In 2001 nearly 17,000 guest workers labored as temporary laborers in Canada (7,300 from Mexico and 12,000 were expected in 2002), a program that is mistakenly referred to as a "model" of its kind.[63] As in the Bush proposal the Canadian system requires that before a guest worker can be hired no Canadian is available to work. Workers are selected on the basis of experience in agricultural work, much like the old Bracero Program, and if selected must pay his way to Canada. The typical workweek in the Leamington, Ontario, area is six and a half days. Again, as in the Bracero Program it is the responsibility of the consulates to insure that the rights of the workers per the agreement are observed. Workers complaints are typically ignored. According to the *San Diego Union-Tribune,*

> Isolated complaints of harsh treatment and poor living conditions have surfaced over the years. This spring, 100 workers gathered at a Leamington (Ontario) church parking lot to complain that they were forced to spray pesticides without protection, live in overcrowded buildings with leaking sewage and put in long hours without overtime pay.[64]

There were several more complaints of more serious nature. Practices reminiscent of the Bracero Program were widespread; one worker alleged, "workers' final checks and refunds, totaling millions, were never forwarded from Canada." More, there are indications that workers are jumping their contracts, that is, entering the "illegal" immigrant stream, just as occurred in the Bracero system. A study by the Guadalajara CIESAS Institute "found that 15 percent ... fail to return home each year. For those who participate five years or more, the figure climbs to 50 percent."[65] One observer active in support work with the laborers noted "workers are completely vulnerable" so that employers enjoy an "intimidating power" to select a guest worker out of the program. A labor leader active with the United Food and Commercial Worker union referred to the program as "slavery," and that the workers "want to speak out but didn't want to get sent back." And that is precisely why many braceros endured the slave-like conditions: they needed the work and if they spoke out they ran the risk of being labeled a "trouble-maker." It is not administrative oversight of the program that is the problem; it is in the nature of guest worker programs, they inherently create a labor supply vulnerable to the power of the state and the employer. Nonetheless, the Fox administration seeks and expansion of the temporary worker program with Canada, meaning that Mexican labor is increasingly expendable.[66]

With or without a guest worker agreement, undocumented migration will continue to flow into the United States providing an unending supply of labor for service, agriculture, construction, and related fields. What is not clear is whether any sort of amnesty, such as the conditional amnesty for approximately 500,000 farm workers spoken of by the leaders of the Democratic Party will be forthcoming. Historically, both parties have supported at one time or another some form of guest worker program (and both are staunch "free traders") and if conditions are right both wings will come together in the future with a general plan for reviving a guest worker agreement with Mexico. Meanwhile, undocumented workers will fill the bill as they have for most of the twentieth century and contrary to Bush administration statements, this will be the case whether a guest worker program is enacted or not. For as most studies have shown, guest worker programs have never stifled undocumented migration, rather they have stimulated it.[67]

Although the new guest worker proposal under discussion in 2004 attends primarily to undocumented immigrants now holding jobs, the old guest worker programs and proposals worked nearly exclusively with importing workers, and only male workers on a strictly temporary basis. Nevertheless, we find the previous guest worker programs, provide historical precedents for demonstrating how a guest worker program for Mexican labor would likely play out. And contrary to the hopes of some, there is never such a thing as a "good" guest worker program. All share one thing in common: an efficient utilization of the cheapest labor available to work on a temporary basis. Or as Senator Gramm put it, "you come, you work, you accrue the benefits of working, and then you go home."[68]

Notes

1. Roger Daniels, "An Old New Immigration Policy, Flaws and All," *Chronicle of Higher Education,* February 6, 2004.

2. José M. Davila, "The Mexican Migration Problem," *Pan Pacific Progress,* vol. 10 (January 1929).

3. Ibid., p. 25.

4. Enrique Santibanez, *Ensayo Acerca de la Immigracion Mexicana en los Estados Unidos,* San Antonio, Texas: Clegg Co., 1930.

5. Ibid., p. 105.

6. State of California Assembly Committee on Agriculture, "The Bracero Program and Its Aftermath: An Historical Summary," California Legislative Assembly, Legislative Reference Service (April 1, 1965), p. 6.

7. Davila might have called this system a case of "déjà vu all over again."

8. Ibid., p. 20.

9. "Note from the Mexican Ambassador to the Secretary of State of the United States" (June 21, 1963), quoted in George C. Kiser and Martha Woody Kiser, eds., *Mexican Workers in the United States: Historical and Political Perspectives,* Albuquerque: University of New Mexico Press, 1979, p. 120.

10. James F. Creagan, "Public Law 78: A Tangle of Domestic and International Relations," *Journal of Inter-American Studies,* vol. 7, no. 4 (October 1965): 548.

11. Edwin P. Reubens, "Immigration Problems, Limited-Visa Programs, and other Options," in Peter G. Brown and Henry Shue, eds., *The Border That Joins: Mexican Migrants and U.S. Responsibility,* Totowa, N.J.: Rowman and Littlefield, 1983, p. 191.

12. Manuel Garcia y Griego, "The Importation of Mexican Contract Laborers to the United States, 1942–1964: Antecedents, Operation and Legacy," in Peter G. Brown and Henry Shue, eds., *The Border That Joins: Mexican Migrants and U.S. Responsibility,* p. 78.

13. Wayne Cornelius, "Legalizing the Flow of Temporary Migrant Workers from Mexico: A Policy Proposal," Working Papers in U.S.-Mexican Studies 7, Program in United States–Mexican Studies, University of California, San Diego (1981), p. 4.

14. Ibid., p. 8.

15. Harry E. Cross and James A. Sandos, *Across the Border: Rural Development in Mexico and Recent Migration to the United States,* Berkeley: University of California Institute of Governmental Studies, 1981.

16. Ibid., pp. 121–122.

17. Ibid., p. 123.

18. Ibid., p. 123.

19. Robert Pear, "White House Asks for a Law to Bar Jobs for Illegal Aliens," *New York Times,* July 31, 1981.

20. John M. Crewdson, "Plan on Immigration," *New York Times,* July 31, 1981.

21. Wayne Cornelius, "The Reagan Administration's Proposals for a New U.S. Immigration Policy: An Assessment of Potential Affects," *International Migration Review,* vol. 15 (December 1981), p. 774.

22. "Candor on Cross-Border Labor," *Los Angeles Times,* January 22, 2001.

23. "New U.S.-Mexico Relations Pledged," *New York Times,* January 10, 2001.

24. Ginger Thompson, "U.S. and Mexico to Open Talks on Freer Migration for Workers," *New York Times,* February 16, 2001.

25. Tara Copp, "Gramm Initiates Bill for Hispanic Workers," *Orange County Register,* January 23, 2001.

26. James F. Smith, "U.S.-Mexico Migration Plan Urged," *Los Angeles Times,* February 15, 2001.

27. Thompson, "U.S. and Mexico to Open Talks on Freer Migration for Workers."

28. Edwin Chen and James F. Smith, "Bush and Fox Broach Issue of Migration," *Los Angeles Times,* February 17, 2001.

29. Ginger Thompson, "Senators Led by Helms Meet with Mexican Leader," *New York Times,* April 17, 2001.

30. Alfredo Corchado and Ricardo Sandoval, "U.S. Senate Panel's Visit to Mexico Marks New Era for Neighbors," *Dallas Morning News,* April 16, 2001.

31. Chris Kraul, "Mexico Visit by Helms Reflects New Realities," *Los Angeles Times,* April 18, 2001.

32. David Bacon, "Both Bush, Kerry Endorse a Return to the Braceros," *Pacific News Service* (Wire Service), October 21, 2004.

33. Dena Dunis, "Bill Aims to Ease Farm Labor Troubles," *Orange County Register,* September 24, 2002.

34. Greg Miller and Patrick J. McDonnell, "New Amnesty for Migrants Possible," *Los Angeles Times,* July 16, 2001.

35. Jesse Helms and Joseph Biden, Jr., "Unique Visit to Mexico Builds Trust in Its Wake," *Los Angeles Times,* May 1, 2001.

36. Douglas Massey, Jorge Durand, and Nolan J. Malone, *Beyond Smoke and Mirrors: Mexican Migration in an Era of Economic Integration,* New York: Russell Sage Foundation, 2002.

37. Massey and his colleagues write: "Although clandestine migration cannot be eliminated, reasonable steps should be taken to minimize the number of people living and working in undocumented status through a combination of regularization programs, temporary work visas, and moderate border and immigration enforcement" (Massey et al., *Beyond Smoke and Mirrors: Mexican Migration in an Era of Economic Integration,* p. 155).

38. "Mexico Chief Presses Bush on Immigration," *Washington Post,* November 27, 2002.

39. Dena Bunis, "No Easy Answers," *Orange County Register,* October 20, 2004.

40. John J. Sweeney, "Statement by AFL-CIO President John J. Sweeney on President Bush's Principles for Immigration Reform," AFL-CIO newsletter, January 8, 2004. at http://www.aflcio.org/issuespolitics/immigration/ns01072004.cfm/RenderForPrint=1

41. Bacon, "Both Bush, Kerry Endorse a Return to the Braceros"; Bunis, "No Easy Answers."

42. Philip L. Martin and J. Edward Taylor, "For California Farmworkers, Future Holds Little Prospect for Change," *California Agriculture,* vol. 54, no. 1 (January-February 2000): 24; see also Philip Martin, "Guest Workers: New Solution, New Problem?" *Pew Hispanic Center Study* (March 21, 2002). Interestingly, the AgJOBS bill was negotiated between the United Farmworkers Union and growers, indicating that employers of farm labor find the bill much to their liking. According to David Bacon, "[U]nions even agreed to expansion of already-existing guest worker programs." However, Republicans have thwarted the bill mainly because of the route to legalization contained within the bill, even though it would effect a more secure agricultural labor force over time. Any bill with legalization prescriptions meets Republican objections, which means that both the Republican and Democratic parties agree on one thing: Guest worker programs are useful means of securing labor (David Bacon, "Collision Coming Over Farm Worker Legalization," article e-mailed to author, July 10, 2004).

43. Lucero Amador, "Rechazan Un Nuevo Programa 'Bracero,'" *La Opinion,* July 18, 2001.

44. Kathleen Reynolds and George Kouros, "Farmworkers: An Overview of Health, Safety and Wage Issues," *Borderlines,* vol. 6, no. 8 (October 1998): 2.

45. J. Edward Taylor and Philip L. Martin, "Central Valley Evolving into Patchwork of Poverty and Prosperity," *California Agriculture,* vol. 54, no. 1 (January-February 2000: 32.

46. Janet Hook, "Plan Packs Political Bonuses for the President," *Los Angeles Times,* January 8, 2004.

47. James B. Kelleher et al., "Bush Plan's Effect Likely Minimal," *Orange County Register,* January 8, 2004; Warren Vieth, "Economists See Benefits to Bush's Plan," *Los Angeles Times,* January 8, 2004.

48. G. Robert Hillman and Afredo Corchado, "Fox Backs Bush's Immigration Plan," *Dallas Morning News,* January 13, 2004.

49. Richard Boudreaux and Maura Reynolds, "Fox Backs Bush's Reforms," *Los Angeles Times,* January 13, 2004.

50. Alexandra Spieldoch, "NAFTA Through a Gender Lens: What "Free Trade" Pacts Mean for Women," *CounterPunch,* December 30, 2004.

51. Eduardo Porter and Kathryn Kranhold, "Latinos Urged to Buy into Banking," *Wall Street Journal,* October 26, 2003.

52. Ibid. Also note an editorial in the *Los Angeles Times* (January 31, 2005) that describes a banking campaign designed to lure Latino customers by promoting low fees for money transfers abroad: "Bank of America, following in the footsteps of Citigroup and Wells Fargo, now realizes that one of the best ways to gain market share in the important Latino market is by allowing people to essentially share accounts across borders. Deposit your paycheck here, and your relatives back home can withdraw funds with an ATM account." Another southern California newspaper's headline tells much the same story: "Bank of America Is Latest to Trim Fee for Wiring Cash to Mexico, Service Is Free to Customers with Accounts as Bank Tries to Bring in More Customers" (*Orange County Register,* January 28, 2005).

53. "All in the Family: Latin America's Most Important International Financial Flow," Report of the Inter-American Dialogue Task Force on Remittances. Washington, D.C.: Inter-American Dialogue, January 2004. p. 9.

54. Graham Gori, "A Card Allows U.S. Banks to Aid Mexican Immigrants," *New York Times,* July 6, 2002.

55. Dudley Althaus, "Opinion Split on Result of Fox's Visit to U.S.," *Houston Chronicle,* November 9, 2003.

56. Gori, "A Card Allows U.S. Banks to Aid Mexican Immigrants."

57. Richard Boudreaux, "Fox's Efforts to Aid Migrants Garner Praise, U.S. Criticism," *Los Angeles Times,* November 7, 2003.

58. John Rice, "Mexico Government Looks for Business Godfathers in the United States," *San Diego Union-Tribune,* July 6, 2001.

59. Johanna Nueman, "Joint Bill Would Revamp Immigrant Worker Rules," *Los Angeles Times,* May 13, 2005; and Dena Bunis, Sweeping Immigration Bill Added to Debate," *Orange County Register,* May 13, 2005.

60. I base this conclusion on a presentation at the 2000 Southwest Labor Studies conference in Los Angeles given by Kitty Calavita, a professor at the University of California, Irvine, who is a noted specialist on migration. She contends—and rightly so, I believe—that Mexican migration will never abate until Mexico undergoes a radical

economic development. Unfortunately, there are no signs that such a development will occur.

61. "Remittance Senders and Receivers: Tracking the Transnational Channels," Washington, DC: Pew Hispanic Center (November 24, 2003).

62. See Mike Anton and Jennifer Mena, "Hard Living, Santa Ana Style," *Los Angeles Times,* September 5, 2004. According to studies released by the Nelson Rockefeller Institute of Government, the city of Santa Ana, California, received a "hardship index" indicating greater hardship than in all other cities in the nation. One-fourth of the city's population of 338,000 is estimated to be undocumented. According to the article's authors, in Santa Ana "it's common to find apartments crammed with six, eight, 10 people to a room and where sleeping on someone's living room floor can run you $150 a month." These are the conditions facing undocumented workers that will be secured via a guest worker agreement. See also Sylvia Moreno, "Shantytowns Migrate Far North of the Border in Texas," *Washington Post,* August 2, 2004. One Texas state representative stated: "You've got people living in these Third World conditions.... It is a serious problem in urban counties.... People move out there because it's too expensive to live in the city, into areas that are not regulated." Across the Texas border areas, *colonias* are formed of "shacks made of scrap metal or dilapidated trailers. The spring rains bring massive flooding ... and with that contamination, disease and disruption of life." Undoubtedly, a large number of the inhabitants are undocumented.

63. See Manuel Garcia y Griego, "Mexico and U.S. Guest Worker Proposals in 2000," available online at www.cirsinc.org/fte/Chapters2.pdf:33.

64. Diane Lindquist, "Abuses Cited in Model Canada Guest-Worker Agreement," *San Diego Union Tribune,* July 2, 2001.

65. Ibid.

66. "Fox Aims to Expand Migration Program with Canada," *Orange County Register,* October 22, 2004.

67. Philip Martin, "There Is Nothing More Permanent Than Temporary Foreign Workers," Center for Immigration Studies *Backgrounder* (April 2001). Martin, a professor of agricultural and resource economics at the University of California, Davis, writes: "Guest worker programs tend to increase legal and illegal immigration" (p. 1). See also Barbara A. Driscoll, *The Tracks North: Railroad Bracero Program of World War II,* Austin: Center for Mexican American Studies, University of Texas, 1999. Driscoll writes: "The railroad program ... was not without serious consequences for Mexico. The most notorious concerned internal migration to recruitment centers in the U.S.-Mexico border, as well as undocumented migration to the United States.... [T]he bracero program not only failed as a strategy to control labor movements within Mexico but exacerbated them" (p. 171).

68. Dena Sunis, "Hispanics Draw Line on Work Plan," *Orange County Register,* March 9, 2001; and Tara Copp, "Gramm Initiates Bill for Hispanic Workers," *Orange County Register,* January 23, 2001.

Chapter 7

The Hispanic Challenge? Or the Imperialist Challenge?

Shortly after George W. Bush reintroduced his guest worker proposal in December 2003, Harvard University professor Samuel P. Huntington published a detailed article on the historical and contemporary influences that Hispanics have on the United States. Critics immediately took aim, retorting that Huntington's fears of an emerging linguistic and cultural separatism constructed by Hispanics are unfounded and that, in the main, Mexican immigration simply represents the latest chapter in U.S. immigration history. The critics added that Mexican immigrants, like their European predecessors, are experiencing the "American Dream." However, as will be argued below, Huntington decried continued migration and focused attention on some very real and important social conditions evolving within Hispanic communities; meanwhile, his critics celebrate that same migration and ignore the social conditions discussed by Huntington. Not one critic mentioned the bracero program or the Bush guest worker proposal in their response to Huntington. We can thus extrapolate that these variations within a century of Mexican migration are in step with, say, Italian immigration. Again, the "one size fits all" model for explaining Mexican migration was raised in defense of a century of immigration, which has now spread to include Latin America. In keeping with tradition in American political culture, U.S. imperialism is excluded from explanations of Mexican immigration and of the historical experience of the Mexican ethnic minority.

It's important that we review the "flap" over the Huntington piece, because it exemplifies the conventions used to explain Mexican migration and its experience as an ethnic minority in the United States. To this analysis we now turn.

Introduction

From London to Mexico City and Washington to Los Angeles, Samuel Huntington's article "The Hispanic Challenge," which appeared in *Foreign Policy* in 2004, was treated to a storm of criticism, supported by only a handful of readers. The controversial piece, based on the then-soon-to-be-published book *Who Are We? Challenges to American National Identity,* created an immediate sensation. The voluminous criticisms of the article clearly overshadowed the few responses to the book, which apparently attracted less attention.[1] The article (and the book) had an important message to convey: Hispanics, particularly Mexicans, threaten to overturn the cultural legacy, the Anglo Protestant creed, the root of America's political and cultural identity, and practices handed down to the present from the colonial era. However, the strongest criticisms thus far (the overwhelming majority focusing on the article) have issued from Latinos, members of the population targeted by Huntington as part of the general "Challenge." Those responses to the article are the subject of the present analysis. In seemingly organized fashion, a variety of Latino leaders stepped forward, including Raul Yzaguirre, president of the Mexican American Legal Defense and Education Fund (which received its initial funding from the Ford Foundation); Gregory Rodriguez, senior fellow at the New America Foundation; Roberto Suro, director of the PEW Hispanic Center; and Marcelo Suarez-Orozco, co-director of the Harvard Immigration Project.

Granted, non-Latino colleagues also joined the assault; these included highly respected intellectuals from diverse political perspectives such as Roger Daniels at the University of Cincinnati, Gary Orfield at Harvard, Daniel T. Griswold at the Cato Institute, and Wayne Cornelius at the University of California, San Diego. From Mexico, the well-known novelist Carlos Fuentes and former Foreign Minister Jorge Castañeda added their critical assessments. And from Great Britain, authors whose work appeared in the *Economist* opinion pages and a *Guardian* article made clear their objections to Huntington's bleak forecast of the future of America's founding creed. His supporters were few and far between; perhaps the most influential of them was Pat Buchanan, who, while backing Huntington's thesis, also displayed a depressing assessment regarding the potential to turn back the rising Hispanic challenge.

Were Huntington merely looking for attention, he could not have asked for more; but his views were roundly condemned. Indeed, critical newspaper editorials and opinion pieces appeared in the *Los Angeles Times,* the *Washington Post,* the *New York Times,* and Mexico City's *Excelsior.* Nonetheless, Huntington contended that his arguments were misinterpreted and misunderstood, and that his detractors stopped well short of a "serious, informed, and reasoned exchange."[2] There is an element of truth in Huntington's retort that deserves attention. And there is more to Huntington's thesis than he allowed to be known in his much-critiqued piece; this needs to be addressed as well. First, I will examine the latter.

The Unwritten Stuff of the Hispanic Challenge

There are two elements in Huntington's argument that were not elaborated in his famous article but are expressed in earlier statements and should be examined thoroughly in order to distill the deeper concerns underlying "The Hispanic Challenge." One is his desire to maintain the existing global geopolitical distribution of power under the mantel of what he terms "Western civilization." The second pertains to the need to put America's house in order—that is, to assimilate Latinos into Western culture such that challenges to the dominance of Western civilization can be successfully thwarted. Let us examine the first of these.

In a 1997 televised Online NewsHour interview, David Gergen, editor-at-large for the *U.S. News and World Report,* invited Huntington to discuss his book *The Clash of Civilizations and the Remaking of World Order.* In reflecting on the work and its themes, Huntington took a broad cultural brush to the global political landscape, dividing the world into eight cultural encampments, which more or less corresponded to the current distribution of economic and military power in the world.[3] The dominant encampment, representing Western civilization, is composed of the United States and its close ally, Western Europe; next in line are Japan, Russia, and China; and then there is the Third World, represented by the African, Indian, Middle Eastern, and Latin American civilizations. Each represents an identifiable, coherent, discrete, and dynamic civilization.

Upon closer scrutiny we find that Huntington not only urges the maintenance of the current power map and the containment of the major challengers to Western domination originating from China and Islamic nations; he also looks back upon the 1920s as the "golden age" of Western civilization when most of the globe was under Western domination. In response to Gergen's question regarding Huntington's assertion of a decline of Western power relative "to that of other civilizations," Huntington reminisced on the golden years of imperial domination:

> [T]he peak of western power occurred early in the century, in say the 1920s by some indices. In 1920, the West ruled huge amounts of the world. Over half of the world's territory and half of the world's population were directly ruled by western governments. Well, that's no longer the case.... [T]he overall western power is gradually fading. It will take time, and certainly the West will remain the dominant civilization into the next century, but the decline is continuing.

Huntington goes on to say that at the cusp of the twenty-first century the eight civilizations are in a potentially adversarial mode, and the objective of Western civilization (i.e., the United States and Western Europe) is to maintain its dominance. Huntington warns that the most important objective as far as U.S. foreign policy is concerned is to "[p]romote the unity of the West." He then clarifies that such unity should manifest "not just in military and economic terms but in moral terms and in commitment to western values." The two civilizations that pose an imminent threat to Western civilization are Islam (i.e., the Middle East) and China. An alleged overpopulation of Islamic peoples and the "economic dynamism" of China create the greatest potential for conflicts that challenge Western civilization.

Noting that the heady days of European imperialism cannot be restored, Huntington argues for the maintenance of current relations of economic and political power. But Huntington, who served on the National Security Council as coordinator of security planning in the late 1970s, is not alone in wishing to maintain Western dominance; others have made the same argument. For example, as Stephen Peter Rosen put it in a recent *Harvard Magazine* article, "[O]ur goal is ... maintaining our imperial position and maintaining an imperial order."[4] And syndicated columnist Ben Wattenberg expanded the scope of U.S. imperialism: "We are No. 1 in a way no other nation in history has ever been before: militarily, geo-politically, scientifically, linguistically, demographically, educationally, culturally—and globally.... [O]ur primary goal should be to stay first."[5]

What is most evident from Huntington's musings on Western civilization is his allegiance to an imperialist world order that enjoyed its heyday in the early twentieth century but is in danger of momentous decline. However, as in the 1920s, the United States and Western Europe remain the dominant players on the world power map, followed by Japan, Russia, and (in a peaceful mode, one hopes), China. Hence, a stable division of the world among the imperial powers, each dominant in its particular sphere, is the goal pursued by Huntington. The lesser lights—Africa, India, Middle East, Latin America—all remain under the sway of the imperial powers. Thus, with the West in power, order in the global house is secured, much to the satisfaction of the United States and its European allies.

Second, given the global division of civilizations, the United States must have its own house in order if its global agenda is to succeed. If a domestic "clash of civilizations" were to occur, the global interests and objectives of the Western powers would be jeopardized. Based on Huntington's analysis in "The Hispanic Challenge," the greatest potential for creating internal divisions emerges from the Latino population. Huntington argues, in a detached and a rather "matter of fact" manner, that Mexican immigrants, within the larger Latin American immigrant population, are unique in the annals of immigration history and are presenting the United States with a growing major political problem. Huntington bases his assessment on six factors: 1) contiguity of the two nations, one rich the other poor; 2) the high volume of immigration; 3) the high numbers of illegal immigrants; 4) the high concentrations of Mexicans in limited zones; 5) the persistence of immigration particularly in recent decades; and finally, 6) the contention that the old Mexican territory now in the United States is still considered by many Mexicans to be part of the greater Mexican nation.[6]

These six factors lead inevitably to bilingualism—the retention of the Spanish language alongside English and Latin American culture (note: not Western civilization)—among the immigrants. The latter consequently pose long-term threats to the preservation of the political culture—that is, the Anglo Protestant creed of the United States, the heart of Western civilization.

Huntington, however, follows a well-worn sociological path. He implicitly defines Western civilization in a manner that resonates in fundamental ways with the theoretical maxims of the famed sociologist

Max Weber for explaining the origins of bourgeois societies. Like Weber, Huntington upholds the importance of cultural values founded upon the Protestant ethic, which in turn fostered the "necessary kinds of behavior" for a "systematic rational emphasis on growth," hence modernization. For Huntington, the United States and Western Europe, the holders of Western civilization, are prime examples of the Protestant ethic and the rise of a "rational system"—that is, the capitalist order.

In "The Hispanic Challenge," however, Huntington refocuses the Protestant ethic to become the *Anglo* Protestant ethic in order to reconcile it with the cultural expression of Western civilization in the United States. Hence, in the United States, the Anglo Protestant ethic is a variation on the theme of Western civilization. We assume that in France it is expressed as the French Protestant ethic, in Germany as the German Protestant ethic, and so on throughout Western Europe. On the other hand, there is no Protestant ethic governing overall behavior patterns in Latin America, which remains ensconced within a culture that inspires nondevelopmental behaviors and, consequently, a history of national underdevelopment and continental backwardness.[7]

According to Huntington, the Anglo Protestant creed, anchored during the colonial era, developed and moved on into the present, surviving only as long as English remained the lone common language. In short, it derived its strength from English as the United States' language. All immigrant groups (previous to Mexican and other Latin American immigrants) transferred to the English language and abandoned their national languages shortly after arriving, thereby integrating into the social fabric of the United States. American institutions successfully socialized immigrants to the dominant cultural system. The fact that immigrants historically assimilated the English language allowed fundamental economic, social, and political institutions to function and progress in a more or less orderly fashion.

Such is not the case with Mexican immigrants, according to Huntington. Not only are Mexicans retaining Spanish alongside English, but they also maintain a culture that is "profoundly different" from one that has historically undergirded American institutions. In contrast to the culture of the English-speaking majority, Mexican culture allegedly promotes a self-generating, separate cultural identity and value system that leads to excessive educational dropouts, limited occupational opportunities, poverty, and related social problems. It is these details upon which critics focus their attention and unfortunately disregard the viability of the six factors upon which Huntington based much of his assessment. In addition, Huntington's imperialist objectives, and the play of those objectives in the domestic arena, attracted absolutely no interest from his critics. Presumably, Huntington fears that in addition to weakening the strength of Western civilization and its local expression, the American Creed, Hispanics will not acknowledge, embrace, or support Western civilization in the face of its multiple challengers. An examination of the criticisms and their validity is therefore required.

The Critics and Their Criticism

Latino authors as well as non-Latinos have criticized Huntington's article severely on the basis of contentions that are allegedly far from the reality that most Latinos experience. One of their arguments is that Latin Americans share ideals consistent with the "American Dream"—that Latino culture values education, success, ambition, self-reliance, and, indeed, all of the other American values enshrined in the Anglo Protestant creed. Furthermore, like all previous immigrants coming to America's shores, Latinos are assimilating: They are dropping Spanish and acquiring English and thus pose no political or cultural barrier to the maintenance of the status quo, and are a positive force in America, helping to realize its fundamental objectives.[8] As Raul Yzaguirre puts it, "The principal goals that Latinos (immigrants and natives alike) articulate are the essence of the 'American Dream.' Hispanic priorities are education, homeownership, health, and economic security." Roberto Suro echoes Yzaguirre in saying: "Many indicators confirm that linguistic assimilation is proceeding faster today among Latinos than it did during the golden past that Huntington extols." Similarly, Wayne Cornelius (who had previously advocated a guest worker program) writes that "these latter-day migrants are far more assimilated than their predecessors, even before beginning the journey."[9]

In short, Huntington is accused of resuscitating historic anti-Mexican racism, and of artificially constructing a "Hispanic Challenge." Noticeably absent from the critical reviews is any mention of the six factors that Huntington contends are at the basis of the Hispanic

Challenge. Virtually all of the critics apply a "one size fits all" approach, maintaining that Mexican immigrants are just one more immigrant group in a long history of immigration to the United States. The varied forms that Mexican migration has taken—indentured, legal, illegal, H2-A temporary labor—have gathered little notice. And among all the criticisms analyzed here, only one addresses the then-current discussion over the new guest worker program.

Among the critics, only Jorge Castañeda acknowledges the efficacy of any of the six basic contentions that buttressed the analysis of an alleged Hispanic Challenge.[10] Castañeda points out that the continuity, scale, regional concentration, and preservation of Spanish are a reality, but like the other critics he claims that assimilation is nonetheless proceeding apace. Understandably, the critics focused on Huntington's trashing of Latino culture, but it is singularly unfortunate that all except Castaneda disregarded the issue of Mexican migration. Furthermore, none discussed the causes of migration and their disastrous affects upon Mexico, particularly since the implementation of NAFTA. Lastly, segregated settlement patterns, the continuation of the tradition of "Mexican work" and the "Mexican wage," and the reality that immigrants *are* undergoing cultural retention seemed not to matter either. However, Castañeda, a former Mexican foreign secretary and proponent of a guest worker program (who later decided to become a candidate for the Mexican presidency), repeated his recommendation for a renewed guest worker program as a solution to unremitting Mexican migration. Ultimately, then, the pertinent evidence cited by Huntington in arguing his case has been dismissed without a hearing.

It is vitally important to question the thesis that Mexicans behave "just like all other immigrants," as Huntington's critics insist, and to question whether Huntington's analysis is purely racially generated. Here I wish to point out that, despite the obvious fallacy of the argument that Mexican culture (and Latin American culture more generally) fails to value education, several of Huntington's points relative to Mexican immigrants are on target, two are wide of the mark, and each in turn needs to be examined closely.

What About the Cuban Connection?

In addition to the six conditions discussed above, Huntington's assertion about the existence of an undifferentiated Latino mass, which his critics agreed is the case, deserves critical review. Huntington points to the Miami Cuban immigrant community to demonstrate one example of nonassimilating Latinos. However, his superficial "combining" of the Miami Cuban émigrés with Mexican immigrants has unfortunately been accepted by his critics. Huntington not only merges two entirely distinct immigrant peoples but also conflates Cuban political émigrés and former supporters, if not members, of the Mafia-ridden Batista regime with all other Latinos. Is Huntington on target in suggesting that Mexicans are just another version of Cubans (and vice versa) and that both are resisting assimilation and forming their own culturally and economically discrete communities and regions? Are poverty-stricken Mexicans "reconquering" the Southwest and wealthy Cubans taking over Miami, constructing in the process a mutual end to the "American Dream"? Are Mexicans operating from below, and Cubans from above, a cultural vise—as Huntington contends?[11] In fact, the differences between these two groups must not be overlooked. Miami's Cubans hold economic and political power in addition to wielding staunch conservative support for the very foreign policy objectives that Huntington seeks. By a ratio of 4 to 1 Cubans vote the Republican rather than Democratic ticket and, by all measures, have realized the mythical "American Dream." By contrast, Mexican immigrants are for the most part at the bottom of the class order and hold little political power, although they lean toward supporting the Democratic Party.

Historically, Mexican immigrants were uprooted and pushed into migration as an army of labor by the effects of foreign capital and, more recently, by NAFTA (see below); they represent the human side of the destruction of Mexico's economic sovereignty, constitute a ready supply of cheap labor for U.S. capital, and exhibit little interest in returning to their homeland. Cubans, on the other hand, left to escape a revolution that overthrew the U.S.-backed Batista dictatorship and actively sought to depose the Castro regime and reconquer their homeland. Perhaps the only connection between the two immigrant peoples is that they both speak Spanish; beyond that, there is little shared history.

The Six Factors Making for a New Immigrant Experience

An argument can be made that Huntington's six factors, unheard of in the annals of U.S. immigrant history, make Mexican migration an entirely unique social phenomenon; yet this argument received no attention from his critics. And like many of his detractors, Huntington has simply gotten the explanation for migration wrong (and has overreacted on the subject of irredentism). But let's look now at what Huntington got right.

It is absolutely important to point out that the United States and Mexico are the only First and Third World countries to share a border. (Note that this contiguity also contributes to the long-term unequal economic relationship between the two countries, as addressed earlier and further discussed below.) In addition, unlike other cases of immigration, Mexican immigration has been long term, in process for over a century. Finally, the elevated volume of Mexican immigration, particularly over the past thirty years, together with increasing Latin American immigration, has led to high concentrations of immigrants, particularly in Southwestern rural and urban centers of the United States. Each of these factors has contributed to the uniqueness of Mexican immigrants in U.S. immigration history.

The volume and unremitting nature of this migration has slowly pushed second- and third-generation Latinos to the margins; in the process, it has also reconstructed the generational composition of the Mexican community, which now resembles the population pattern of the 1920s when immigrants predominated. Recent figures reflect the rising importance of the immigrant population within the ethnic Mexican population. Between 1960 and 2000 the Mexican-born population grew from about 500,000 to over 9 million. In 1970 around 17 percent of the Mexican Latino community were immigrants; today that figure is over 40 percent and still climbing.[12] Large numbers of Mexican immigrants populate many California cities marked by poverty and segregation; among them are rural towns like Guadalupe, Madera, Shandon, Reedley, Parlier, and Selma and urban centers like Oxnard (66 percent Latino), Santa Ana (76 percent), El Monte (72 percent), and East Los Angeles (98 percent).[13] One of the five poorest cities in the state, Parlier, serves as an example of the concentration of Mexican immigrants in the rural Southwest. In 1990 Latinos comprised 95 percent of the population; nearly seven of every ten farmworkers were immigrants. Each year the population increases by 4 percent or more due to immigration from Mexico. Not surprisingly, 90 percent of all of California's 800,000 farm workers are immigrants, 60 percent earn incomes below the poverty line, and the vast majority "crowd into small rural towns, creating a new concentrated poverty there."[14] The figures on segregation are rising across the United States, such that in 1990 Latinos resided in moderate or worse levels of segregation in six metropolitan centers; ten years later that figure had risen to eleven. The figures for farmworkers are even higher; approximately 15 percent of Latinos are farm laborers, comprising nearly eight of every ten farmworkers across the United States.[15] With that concentration comes a cultural retrenchment or, as one UCLA professor of law put it, a "desire to maintain a link with Latin culture."[16]

Politics Compared. With continuously increasing immigration over the past twenty to thirty years, the proportion of first to second and third generations has greatly altered the cultural configuration of the population. This generational imbalance within the Mexican population is significant, and we must pay attention to it as an evolving condition. Looking back on the political history of the Chicano community, we see that its politics is closely linked with the national political agenda. For example, school desegregation, liberal educational reform, equal employment opportunities, labor unions, and police community relations made up the core of that population's political agenda, particularly during the 1940–1970 period. The 1960s Chicano civil rights movement provides a prime example of national political engagement—in this case, over issues dealing with educational reform and equalization of educational opportunities. But note that over the course of that movement, immigrants for the most part did not take leadership positions; instead, members of the second- and third-generation, who were largely assimilated, were its leaders. Many activists (possibly most) could not speak Spanish or spoke it hesitatingly; more important, the goals and objectives of the movement were of a piece with national civil rights agendas and political methods such as sit-ins, marches, and the like.[17] Film documentaries on Chicano political struggles in the pre-1980s era underline the integration of activists into the national body politic. Such documentaries as the four-part series *Chicano! A History of the Mexican American Civil Rights Movement* and *Los Mineros* manifest the convergence of political themes associated with the second and third generations with national political issues. However, this political balance would soon change. Two emerging patterns within the Latino population—political interests and language retention/bilingualism—as well as a third factor—remittances, which have been around for decades but recently have grown into very significant proportions—demonstrate this distinction.

A brief examination of remittances shows the growing linkage between immigration and the communities of origin. This linkage promotes political and cultural connections with the Mexican localities that they left to enter the migratory trail. One more measure of rising migration is the amount of remittances sent. Currently, about 10 million people send money to Latin America, providing "extra cash and a livelihood for an estimated 80 million people."[18] And in 2003 an estimated $14.5 billion was sent to relatives, friends, and family in Mexico, an amount that surpasses income from all other sources including direct investment, oil, and tourism. As noted in Chapter 6, a full one-quarter of the Mexican population is dependent to some degree on remittances. In addition, as part of a plan for privatizing the social safety net, the Mexican government has offered to match funds for public works projects in sending communities. With the government's offering of this cooperative effort, many immigrants now want to have a hand in how that money is spent and to actively involve themselves in organized collection and use of remittances.

Next, let us examine the political interests of the rising immigrant population, which appear to differ in significant ways from those of the second and third generation. Recent trends indicate that Latino immigrants tend to relate to the politics of their home countries—Mexico, Guatemala, El Salvador, Puerto Rico, and so on—over the politics of the nation where they have taken up permanent residence. Indeed, Mexican immigrants provide an excellent example of retention in interest in home-country politics. Mexican state governors regularly make trips to visit their states' expatriate communities, and the matter of whether immigrants will have the right to vote and participate as candidates in Mexican elections has become a major topic of discussion. As one immigrant put it, "I cannot forget the place. When we lived there, we worked the land. We say the land got in us and we can't get it out.... I think it's great that we can have our concerns heard, particularly since we send money back there."[19] This perspective differed radically from that of the Chicano Civil Rights Movement of the 1960s, which focused on conditions within barrios (i.e., conditions north of the border), experiences that ultimately shaped the era's political agenda.

Recently Michoacan's governor, Lazaro Cardenas Batel, made a visit intended to "strengthen business and political relations" with his fellow Michoacanos in southern California's Orange County. His choice made a lot of sense since Michoacan state has sent a substantial number of immigrants, estimated at 100,000, to live in Orange County. One member of the community noted that "[t]here are so many Michoacanos in Santa Ana [the county seat], it's like another Michoacan here."[20] There are ample reasons for such a comment: 67 percent of the population are noncitizens. A crowd numbering in the hundreds greeted the governor, followed by meetings with individuals and groups.[21] Over 1,000 fellow Michoacanos attended one meeting, pleading special cases for improvements in their hometowns. And an organization, the Federation of Michoacanos in Orange County, is already active in local matters—that is, actively engaged in matters relating to the various hometowns left behind.

This kind of activity is repeated across the United States where Mexican communities are found. For example, expatriates from the state of Zacatecas (who comprise half of the state's population) have formed 240 social clubs said to extend "from Alaska to Maine" and are considered to be the best-organized among the immigrant groups. Among the results of the clubs' lobbying is the establishment of two state legislative seats for emigrants. Activities such as campaigning for city council and state legislative seats in Mexico and the matter of remittances further enjoin local communities with Mexican national politics. During a visit to Garden Grove, California, the Zacatecan state governor urged his state's expatriates to send remittances into special government matching programs. Even though "we are eager to invest," as one former resident of Zacatecas stated, not all feel confident that the government is to be trusted. One organization of Zacatecanos refused to send the $20,000 raised from donations until guarantees on how the money would be spent was forthcoming. As one Zacatecan immigrant put it, "There is no trust."[22]

Elections are bringing immigrants into the political picture—in Mexico. A tomato farmer in Yolo, California, won a seat on the city council in Jerez, Zacatecas, but the election was overturned because residency requirements were not met. In 2004, elections in six Zacatecas towns included candidates from Mexican communities across the United States. On the other hand, two California men and a Texas woman representing the Partido Revolucionario Institucional (PRI), the Partido Revolucionario Democratico (PRD), and the Partido de Accion Nacional (PAN), respectively, are vying for the two legislative seats set aside for the expatriates. The PRI candidate became the first of his party to "earn the oath of his party on U.S. soil" at a ceremony attended by the party's candidate for state governor. An indication of the candidate's explanation for running for office in Mexico can be gleaned from his reflection upon becoming an official aspirant: "This is a historic candidacy. It will begin in the United States, end in Mexico and represent the real binational nature of our state [Zacatecas]."[23] Another activist busy organizing in southern California commented that "I wanted to help Mexicans, Michoacanos, people who had come here like me."[24] Note that he refers to fellow immigrants from his state, not to those born in the United States, indicating a political consciousness that emphasizes fellow immigrants and Mexico. No wonder that ranking party officials are eagerly increasing their presence among expatriate communities.

Mexico's national political parties have established official liaisons with local communities in the United States in an attempt to foster support for each party's political agenda. The PRI, for example, has authorized federal legislator Laura Martinez to work with émigrés. And on the opposite side of the aisle, the PRD employs immigrants from the most populous states to represent that party. (Felipe Aguirre, a resident of Maywood city, represents the PRD in California.)

Meanwhile, the Republican and Democratic parties play the Latino card in order to gain votes. Sometimes they use the "illegal immigrant" threat to gain conservative votes; at other times policy proposals are merely accommodated to the reality that immigrants are a large sector of the American voting public. Several examples serve to demonstrate the overriding significance of the immigrant generation in the politics circulating outside and within Mexican communities. The first concerns the methods employed by the U.S. armed services to gather Latino recruits. Enticements include earning a fast-track to citizenship, a tease that would never occur if the composition of the Latino community conformed to pre-1970 proportions. Military recruiters even prowl high schools with large Latino enrollments to tap into the "Hispanic . . . recruiting market."[25] Privileges like quick citizenship are taken seriously, especially in places like the Texas county where the former head of the U.S. Iraqi occupation, Lieutenant-General Ricardo Sanchez, was raised; it has a population that is 98 percent Latino.

A second example concerns the debate in various states legislatures over whether to grant driver's licenses to undocumented immigrants.

In California, the state legislature's Latino caucus busily crafted and negotiated a bill granting driver's licenses to the estimated 2 million undocumented immigrants there—a bill that Republican Governor Schwarzenegger vetoed. On the matter of the military recruitment fast-track and its inclusion in the proposed Dream Act (which would grant illegal students residential status in higher education) Latino lawmakers have voiced no opposition; on the other hand, conservatives roundly oppose granting licenses to undocumented immigrants. More recently, a debate surged in New York over what kind of license to grant to undocumented immigrants, eliciting tense exchanges over whether to include a ban on driver's licenses in the federal intelligence reform bill that passed recently without a ban on licenses for undocumented immigrants.[26] Both party positions, however, reflect on the increasing immigrant composition of the Mexican community and its extension across the United States.

A third example concerns discussions over a new guest worker program and amnesty proposals relative only to undocumented immigrants that the Bush administration placed on the election-year agenda. Bear in mind that it is the nonimmigrant element of the Mexican Latino community that stands at the forefront of the legalization of undocumented immigrants. The objective in the latter proposal was to curry favor both with Latinos (most of whom are registered Democrats) and with the conservative sectors of the Republican Party. Each political party jockeys for positions around these key issues, playing one-upmanship in the process. As one newspaper headline put it, "Dueling Immigration Ideas Frame a Key Election Issue." The accompanying article went on to say that "[i]n many parts of the country, and especially in swing states such as Florida and New Mexico, both parties are courting immigrant constituencies."[27] Note the phrase "immigrant constituencies."

Language. The language of the Latino community—in homes, commerce, banking, news media, television, radio, music, recreation, churches, school, and even work—often involves a mix of Spanish and English. In many barrios, however, the *lingua franca* is exclusively Spanish; immigrants have no need to learn English in such environments. This scenario is repeated across the Southwest as well as in areas without Mexican immigrant populations of note, including Arkansas, Kansas, Georgia, North Carolina, and Florida. Unlike immigrants from Europe who spoke multiple languages and needed to learn English to communicate across neighborhoods, business districts, and workplaces, the vast majority of Latin American immigrants arrive in the United States speaking just one language. Consequently, the large-scale Latino immigration brings with it a tendency toward linguistic homogeneity over wide areas. Television and radio corporations, interested in the bottom line, have seized the opportunity to emphasize Spanish-language programming and advertising. During the Chicano civil rights era of the 1960s and 1970s, activists sought ways to learn Spanish and promote bilingualism; many even traveled on personal odysseys to Mexico to capture their cultural roots. The opposite situation exists today. At present, Spanish and Mexican culture is preserved within Latino communities in the absence of special educational endeavors to develop bilingualism or a return to their roots. Research demonstrates that bilingualism characterizes 24 percent of the first generation but nearly 50 percent of the second generation and approximately 25 percent of the third generation.[28] Overall, bilingualism is a common cultural pattern within Latino communities.

Public schooling also serves as an arena for the convergence between Latino culture and its practice. Perhaps no other institution better demonstrates the increasing isolation of the Mexican immigrant population. Across the nation, Latino (as well as Black) children are progressively schooled apart from the dominant community. Over the past thirty years, school segregation affecting Latinos has increased, as have the disparities in resources.[29] California schools provide a clear illustration of this condition: Nine school districts in the greater Los Angeles area have a minority student population, mainly Latino, ranging from 52 percent to 100 percent. For example, in the Los Angeles Unified School District 72 percent of the students are Latinos, up from 29 percent in 1981. In the same year, 206 schools across the state were predominantly minority; today that figure stands at 370. At Belmont high school the enrollment is 90 percent Latino, and only half the students speak English fluently. East Los Angeles schools are 90 percent minority—again, primarily Latino. And in the city of Santa Ana, an hour's drive from downtown Los Angeles, 91 percent of the district's 62,000 students are Latino, up from 19 percent in 1981.[30]

One southern California school district rather clearly demonstrates this transition. Two decades ago the district was entirely composed of

White students; now it is divided between schools attended by Whites on one side of a freeway and by Latinos on the other. Two of these schools tell the story especially well: The first is 92.3 percent White, the second is 97.4 percent Latino. Sixty-seven percent of Latino students are English-learners and 96 percent are from low-income families. The opposite is the case for the White schools. The Latino school stands at the bottom 20th percentile in national test scores; the White school is at the top 10th percentile.[31] One Stanford education professor described the present situation across California as something approaching apartheid.[32] Obviously, immigration is at the root of the growing Mexican population.

The large Latino enrollment affects school districts' attendance figures during Christmas vacation, when an "exodus" of students returning to Mexico with family to celebrate the holidays reduces attendance significantly. Most cross over at San Diego, where in late December at least 180,000 cars stream into Mexico daily—an increase of 40,000 above the norm. Having learned their lessons well, the Santa Ana School District recently reorganized its school calendar to allow for an early start to the school year and a month off for Christmas break to accommodate the temporary homeland return. School districts throughout southern California (and probably wherever a large number of Mexican immigrants live) are now facing the same Christmas-season problem.[33]

Why Migration of Scale for Over a Century?

Although Huntington warns against the undermining of the cultural legacy of the United States, he offers no solutions for controlling Mexican and Latin American immigration, the source of the cultural "crisis." On the contrary, he seems besieged by doubts that anything can be done to stem the migrant tide. If anything, he appears to be more interested in calling attention to a perceived threat, and asking for a national discussion, than in proposing solutions. Nonetheless, one can extrapolate that lowering Mexican (and Latin American) immigration drastically over the next century would serve well to defuse the Hispanic Challenge. But why has a century of Mexican migration attracted so little attention from Huntington's adversaries? His critics seemingly accept this immigration as if it were nothing more than a matter of course, an immigration fitting a "one size fits all" paradigm, indistinguishable from European migrations. However, as previously argued, Mexican migration is far from identical to European migration, requiring that we distinguish it from previous migrations by examining its causes.

Huntington employs conventional immigration theory (used widely by politicians and immigration scholars), which contends that the main "push" propelling migration stems from the oppressive economic conditions indigenous to Mexico and that a "pull" is exerted by the promise of economic betterment north of the border. His critics would agree that "push-pull" explains Mexican immigration. However, this theory—and variations spinning from it having to do with social capital, social networks, human capital, and the like—is wide of the mark and, indeed, has been subjected elsewhere to critical examination.[34] A better method for explaining Mexican migration requires that we recognize that a century of U.S. economic domination over Mexico and a century of Mexican migration have occurred simultaneously—and that there is more than mere coincidence here. To truly understand Mexican migration, we must address the economic domination by U.S. large-scale capital in Mexico from the late nineteenth century to the present. Although Huntington celebrates imperialist Western civilization, like his critics he dismisses the imperialist expansion of American capital into Mexico beginning in the last decades of the nineteenth century and the consequent social and economic uprooting of vast sections of the Mexican population, resulting in mass migration to the United States. His detractors follow suit, celebrating immigration as a good thing—the realization of the "American Dream."

Convention has it that U.S.-Mexico economic relations constitute a normal relationship between neighboring countries—one of reciprocity, interdependence, and equality. However, this perspective has not always been borne by Americans, particularly investors who, in the late nineteenth century, deemed Mexico a colonial prize to be exploited for its natural resources as well as for its cheap and easily accessed labor. Well into the twentieth century a host of publications demonstrated not only a widespread imperial mindset in reference to Mexico but also a colonial strategy to systematically exploit Mexico's labor. Unfortunately, this aspect of U.S.-Mexico relations is rarely brought to light in studies of U.S.-Mexican history; at best, it has been excused as a short-lived imperialist foreign policy. Let's review the process that led to U.S. domination of the Mexican economy.

Shortly after the Civil War, American investors began a vigorous economic expansion into Mexico, described by William Rosecrans, an investor in railroads and minister to Mexico in the late 1860s, as the means to accomplish a "peaceful conquest" of Mexico. Within twenty years American railroads had constructed Mexico's rail lines, which were virtual extensions of the American network. Railroads then led to American investments in mining, oil, and agriculture. Foreign-financed and -controlled modernization amounting to a billion dollars by 1910 propelled the mass uprooting of hundreds of thousands of peasants from traditional farmlands, the largest mass relocation of the Mexican population in its history. Thousands of miles of U.S.-owned railroads crossed through peasant regions, displacing several hundred thousand people and forcing an internal migration. The same industrial operations financed by U.S. capital and administered by Americans recruited the migrating populations to work in mines, oil, and railroad maintenance, resulting in a massive redistribution of people northward. Over 130,000 worked in mining, 30,000 on railroads, and many thousands in oil exploration and extraction. During the internal migration northward that followed, more than 300,000 Mexicans uprooted from traditional farming communities were resettled in the northern tier of states bordering upon the United States. That same migration spilled into the United States as recruiting agencies working for railroads and mining operations moved labor north from the border. Agricultural enterprises then tapped into the migrating labor force to woo workers into their domain. From 1900 until 1930 a virtually open border allowed unlimited Mexican immigration; then the Great Depression struck and the welcoming mat was pulled up. With the hiatus caused by the economic crash, a drive to deport Mexicans and remove them from welfare benefits successfully removed nearly a half-million.

However, the war opened a window of opportunity to reintroduce Mexican labor to the American economy in the form of controlled guest workers—the braceros. The bracero program had the effect of spurring migration northward as men who would otherwise have returned to Mexico after their temporary stay often chose to remain in the United States; many settled along the border areas. With the end of the bracero program in 1964, illegal immigration supplanted bracero labor; but on the Mexican side a U.S.-owned system of assembly plants, or maquilas, was established to take advantage of the supply of cheap labor, particularly women, on the Mexican side. Maquila workers assembled components imported duty-free into finished products to be exported duty-free back to the United States. Initially, the plants were few in number, but as they multiplied, jobs opened and a northward migration of unemployed people in Mexico gradually boomed. This same migration spilled across the border, repeating a social process initiated in the first decade of the twentieth century.

Free Trade? Or the Imperialist Challenge?

Finally, with the passage of free-trade policies in the 1980s and the enactment of its quintessential formula, NAFTA, in 1994, the number of assembly plants expanded to over 3,000; the vast majority were located mainly along the northern border, causing further northward migration within Mexico. In 1975 maquilas employed only 67,214 workers, but by 1999 more than 1.3 million maquila workers were toiling for poverty wages that virtually guaranteed a life in the shack towns located within easy reach of the border. This description by a *Los Angeles Times* journalist of Tijuana maquila worker neighborhoods, little more than hovel outcroppings on hillsides, is difficult to believe unless one has witnessed them firsthand:

> The dwellings are made of sheets of scrap metal and prefabricated wooden walls—often discarded garage doors from across the border. Few homes have anything other than earthen floors. Fewer still have running water. Most bathrooms consist of a system of buckets and open rivulets, which wash the waste downhill.[35]

Down the borderline, in Coahuila, one finds the same scene.

In Ciudad Acuna, the fastest-growing city in northern Mexico, American corporations such as Alcoa, Allied Signal, and General Electric, among others, have set up shop. A *New York Times* journalist visiting the town described the conditions besetting the town's population:

> Mexican workers earn such miserable wages and American companies pay such minimal taxes that its schools are in shambles, its hospital crumbling, its trash collection slapdash, and its sewage lines collapsed. Half of Acuna's 150,000 residents now use backyard latrines.[36]

NAFTA brought even more distress to an already-depressed nation. The celebrated agreement lowered, and sometimes eliminated, Mexico's tariffs for American products, including nine basic foods: beans, corn, rice, sorghum, soya, wheat, barley, safflower, and sesame. Six years after the agreement was signed, imports of these agricultural products had more than doubled. In the case of meat products the figures are no less dramatic. Red meat imports rose by 442 percent, chicken imports by 100 percent, and egg imports by 55 percent. Imported milk now supplies 20 percent of Mexico's supply; imported beef, 60 percent; and imported corn from the United States, 70 percent.[37] The result: Mexico's small ranchers and farmers, whose small governmental subsidies were eliminated with Mexico's embrace of the "Washington Consensus," cannot compete with U.S. imports, particularly from a nation that subsidizes its farming corporations to the tune of $70 billion. Prices for basic food commodities are plummeting; the 3.5 million corn farmers cannot survive the 45 percent drop in corn prices recorded in 2000. Unable to compete with cheaper farming products, and denied price supports once accorded them but eliminated by NAFTA, ranchers are succumbing to bankruptcy across rural Mexico. As one small farmer sadly observed, "There is almost no place left in the country where a small farmer can make a good living." He later insightfully surmised: "[T]he problem for Mexico is that when farmers stop eating, everyone stops eating."[38] Studies have shown that 86 percent of rural inhabitants live in poverty (by Mexico's standards), while malnutrition has become a widespread critical problem affecting nearly half of the children under five; in indigenous rural areas, conditions parallel those of Africa.[39] As agriculturalists enter bankruptcy they close their operations and leave their farms, their inventories remaining unsold. Daily, 600 people exit the countryside and move northward; meanwhile, large swaths of the Mexican countryside are being deserted.

This mass departure from farming communities continues without respite, with the migration eventually reaching the United States. The words of one journalist, writing about the summer 2003 exodus from a village in Jalisco state, speak volumes: "Santa Maria de Arriba is a tiny village in Jalisco, Mexico. Like many other pueblitos in Mexico, it is disappearing due to massive migration. The migration rate is at an all-time high."[40] At one time Mexico's small rural towns and villages depended on migration and subsistence production for their livelihood;

now remittances are the principal means of survival, if they survive at all. As people leave their small farming communities, they move to cities and more often than not migrate north to seek work in a maquila plant. Small- to medium-sized retailers and manufacturers have also suffered the onslaught of foreign goods, as 28,000 shops disappeared and their workers were dismissed in favor of lesser-priced goods from abroad. As consequence, the northern border is overwhelmed by continual arrivals; in Tijuana, for example, an estimated 70,000 new residents arrive each year—three times the increase across Mexico.[41] Meanwhile, domestic production of foodstuffs falls precipitously while production of assembled goods for export grows.

Today, Mexico is a prime example of a nation that has lost its food independence, the foundation of modern nation-states. Human societies exist on the basis of reproduction and production; through reproduction they maintain themselves from generation to generation, and through the production of food they ensure the preservation of existing generations. When a nation loses its ability to produce the goods necessary to feed itself, it eventually declines as an independent state subject to the food supply and decisions of a foreign state.[42] So it is with Mexico, which, as agricultural production declines in the face of a flood of U.S. imports, loses its ability to feed itself and turns to those same imports for its basic food supply. In 2008 all limitations on the importation of a host of agricultural and animal products will be eliminated, ensuring that agricultural production will continue to decrease while migration intensifies.

For a century, U.S. economic policy in Mexico—economic imperialism—has led to widespread destruction of the social fabric of Mexico, massive internal migration northward, and, finally, migration to the United States. Pre-neoliberal migrations did not result in widespread desertion and disappearance of villages; but now, under "free trade," whole villages take flight to escape the onslaught of economic depression wrought by free trade. One journalist writing about these demographic alterations noted, "Tiny ranchitos are vanishing all over Mexico, where migration has surged to an all-time high.... [T]hey can't survive the exodus"; a resident of Casa Blanca in Zacatecas surmised, as he viewed his emptying village, "The question we always ask is, 'Will the community survive?'" From a population that at one time measured nearly 6,000, only 2,500 people remain; the majority of migrants live in the United States. The school population dropped from 500 in 1989 to 100 in 2000; once-active town plazas and parks are eerily silent. Casa Blanca is but one example of the mass removal of the states' citizens. Across Zacatecas at least 30,000 people leave their homesteads each year—and like those leaving their towns across Mexico, half end up in the United States. The remaining residents see themselves as living in virtual ghost towns, populated by the old and the young.[43] The example of the state of Guanajuato during the administration of the devoted free trader Vicente Fox (now president) is also telling: Shortly after the signing of the NAFTA 20 percent of this state's 250,000 rural families abandoned their communities and entered the migratory trail.

The mass removal recurs across Mexico as hundreds of thousands leave their towns and villages. According to studies by the Mexican Department of Labor, nearly 2 million people have left the country-side since the signing of the NAFTA.[44] A 2003 Carnegie Endowment study found that, roughly six years after NAFTA, rural employment fell by 1.3 million.[45] Unemployment and informal work (e.g., selling goods on a street corner or cleaning car windows at a stop light) has skyrocketed, reaching 47 percent in 2003; options other than maquila-dora employment are few. Not surprisingly, in the year 2000 refugees escaping neoliberal policies—that is, Mexican emigrants coming to the United States—comprised 8 percent of the total Mexican population. And according to recent studies by the National Population Council, an estimated 400,000 people migrated to the United States in 2004 alone.[46] Details like these find no place in Huntington's analysis; they are also ignored by his critics, who accept Mexican migration as a good thing, then embrace the "American Dream" and focus on the stereotypical aspects of the analysis.

A century of U.S. economic domination over Mexico, implemented under the rubric of "peaceful conquest" in the late nineteenth and early twentieth centuries and currently styled as "neoliberalism," "free trade," "Washington consensus," and "globalization" ("Western civilization" by Huntington), has indeed uprooted the Mexican people on a massive scale, sending them onto migratory path and eventual settlement into immigrant enclaves across the United States.[47] The United States promised that "globalization," and its quintessential manifestation NAFTA, would "lift of all boats"; but instead Mexico's economic independence has retreated while the country undergoes a process of recolonization. The connection between NAFTA and immigration is not lost on immigrants. As one accurately noted, "If it were true that NAFTA was good for Mexico we wouldn't be here.... [I]t just created more for those who already have more."[48] Should the Free Trade of the Americas agreement ever pass, the United States' economic hold will expand and deepen across Latin America and wholesale migration from across the continent will guarantee further "Latinization" of the United States. Meanwhile, the domestic version of neoliberalism (privatization, deregulation, budget cutbacks, welfare reform, etc.) exacerbates poverty and revives educational and residential segregation, promoting the very social conditions deplored by Huntington and a host of anti-immigrant politicians and activists who sanction border vigilantism, Operation Gatekeeper, and California's Proposition 187.[49]

We should keep in mind that low-wage workers, many of them Latinos, were deeply affected by NAFTA on the U.S. side. In El Paso County alone, once known as the "Blue Jean Capital," nearly 8,000 jobs were lost between 2001 and 2004 due to the displacement caused by NAFTA.[50] We should not be surprised that a former Latina textile worker living in El Paso would describe her situation as "an American dream ... turned into a nightmare."[51] (A job in a textile factory at minimal wages served as her "American Dream." Is this what the critics of Huntington had in mind?) The effects of NAFTA on the West Coast were similar; there, too, the loss of 117,000 jobs in California—many from the textile sector, which depends on Latino labor—can be traced to NAFTA.[52] In the Los Angeles County garment industry, a large employer of undocumented people, the number of employed people shrank from 104,000 in 1996 to 61,400 in 2003—a drop of 41 percent.[53]

Since immigrants now find fewer options for work, informal work—such as the employment of day workers and street vendors—has become a "growth area" (in Los Angeles day workers congregate at 125 sites). Owing to the presence of a largely undocumented workforce, many jobs settle underground; studies estimate that in Los Angeles between 10 and 29 percent of employment occurs in the informal off-the-books sector and is increasing.[54] Working for poverty wages has become the norm, and finding housing at these wages means living at the lowest end of the housing market. Housing quality is the first to fall.

The example of Texas is compelling. For many years colonias were a common feature along the Texas-Mexico border, but now they have moved northward. Shantytowns, largely populated by immigrants as well as by second- and third-generation Latinos, are now sprouting into the interior. One million people now live in unregulated "squalid developments" in Texas; without adequate improvements and marked by rutted roads, these can be found in and around Houston, Dallas, Corpus Christi, San Antonio, Beaumont, Austin, and Fort Worth. One local described the settlement in Corpus Christi as "just like Guatemala or Africa." Similarly, a Houston politician depicted living conditions in her district as markedly similar to the "Third World," where sick children abound and stray mangy dogs scurry about.[55]

Whole communities are affected by the neoliberal onslaught. One civil rights attorney compared some of the worst sections of Los Angeles to the favelas of Rio de Janiero, "feral" sectors where dysfunction is the norm.[56] In the case of Santa Ana, California, conditions are somewhat better, but they're still far below the standards for a city that deems itself an "All-American City" and for a nation that upholds the "American Dream." A recent study demonstrates that of all the cities in the United States, Santa Ana is the hardest "place to make ends meet" based on income, education, and housing. Insufficient incomes and lack of affordable housing contribute to living circumstances "where it's common to find apartments crammed with six, eight, ten people to a room and where sleeping on someone's living room floor can run you $150 a month."[57]

Those who insist that Mexican and, for that matter, all Latin American immigrants threaten English-language hegemony need to realize that it is the very economic policies being pursued by Washington that are at the root of the cultural divide. Economic imperialism and its social consequence, migration, are inseparable; moreover, guest worker programs will serve only to manage the flow in the interests of employers of Mexican labor. Huntington laments the very social conditions that are being propelled by an economic and political system operating under the rubric of "Western civilization," which he claims is imperiled. It is not Latino immigrants *per se* who imperil America. U.S. imperialist policies simultaneously destroy Mexico's sovereignty, undermine its social fabric, and uproot its people on a massive scale. U.S. imperial expansionism has created a vast reservoir of cheap labor that can be tapped into, when required, by U.S. capital.

Huntington, meanwhile, asserts that immigrants threaten the political culture of the United States. But like most of his compatriots, he has buried his head in the sand, oblivious to the fact that imperialism anchors U.S. foreign and domestic policy. Pockets of unassimilated immigrants are the social consequence of imperialism and the core of Huntington's celebrated Western civilization, which he defends as the foundation for the "American Dream"— the fabled Dream that his critics celebrate, indeed uphold. In so doing, they stand shoulder to shoulder with Huntington.

Conclusion

Huntington defends imperialism as falling under the mantel of Western civilization and all that it represents—including free trade, neoliberalism, and its agendas such as privatization, which undermines the cultural unity of the United States by pushing massive migration from Mexico. His critics celebrate that immigration as if it were nothing more than a chapter in the realization of the iconic "American Dream." But for Mexico that Dream is an imperialist nightmare. The victims of Mexican immigration are not "Anglo Protestant culture" and the political identity of the United States. Rather, unabated Mexican immigration in all of its varied forms (legal, undocumented, or "guest worker") is a measure of the destruction of Mexico's national sovereignty, the social face of the recolonization of Mexico. That fact, in itself, should be the focus of our attention.

Notes

1. Samuel P. Huntington, *Who We Are: Challenges to American National Identity,* New York: Simon and Schuster, 2004. Interestingly, one of the few critical responses to Huntington's book, written by Henry Cisneros, former secretary of Housing and Urban Development for the Clinton administration, appeared in the elite journal *Hispanic Business* (July–August 2004). In that publication, which caters to the small community of upscale Latino businesspeople, Cisneros repeated nearly verbatim the published responses to Huntington's article. Cisneros argued that Latinos are like all other immigrants and, therefore, that America is richer for having "youthful ... energetic ... young leaders ... due to Hispanic immigration" (Henry Cisneros, "Who Are We?" *Hispanic Business* [July–August 2004]. See also David Montejano, "Who Is Samuel P. Huntington?" *The Texas Observer,* August 13, 2004).

2. Samuel P. Huntington, "The Hispanic Challenge," *Foreign Policy* (May–June 2004): 91.

3. Online NewsHour: David Gergen Engages Samuel Huntington, January 9, 1997, available online at http://www.pbs.org/newshour/gergen/january97/order_1-10.html.

4. Stephen Peter Rosen, "The Future of War and the American Military," *Harvard Magazine* (May–June 2002).

5. Ben Wattenberg, "U.S. Should Look Out for No. 1," *Orange County Register,* June 28, 2001.

6. Interestingly, the work of Fresno State University classics professor Victor Davis Hanson—*Mexifornia: A State of Becoming* (San Francisco: Encounter Books, 2003)—anticipated much of Huntington's argument regarding an evolving cultural hybridism. Hanson focused his analysis within California's rural heartland and discussed the basic conditions leading to the cultural crisis that Huntington addressed. Hanson, however, was spared the same level of bellicose response.

7. See, for example, Seymour Martin Lipset and Aldo Solari, *Elites in Latin America,* New York: Oxford University Press, 1967. Following Weber's thesis, Lipset and Solari argue that "value systems" establish the parameters for economic development.

8. The theme of "Latino immigrants are like all others" has circulated for some time. For example, syndicated columnist Ruben Navarette, Jr., argued in a 2003 news article that "Latino immigrants in the 20th century matched and in some cases bettered their European counterparts," adding that "immigrants are the same the world over." Navarette used a Rand study authored by economist James Smith to buttress his contention. The latter remarked that the view that Latinos are different from the "European experience" is "just wrong" (Ruben Navarette, Jr., "Latino Immigrants Have Done Just Fine in Pursuing Dreams," *Los Angeles Times,* May 28, 2003). Others uphold the American Dream myth, including historian Camille Guerin-Gonzalez, who writes that the "American Dream" rests firmly within the psyche of Mexican immigrants: "Rather than a story of exclusion from access to economic security … the history of Mexican immigrants and Mexican Americans, as well as other immigrant groups in the United States, is one of violent conflict over the cultural, social, and political meanings of the American Dream" (Camille Guerin-Gonzalez, *Mexican Workers and American Dreams: Immigration, Repatriation and California Farm Labor, 1900–1939,* New Brunswick: Rutgers University Press, 1994, p. 138).

9. See "Huntington and Hispanics," *Foreign Policy* (May–June 2004): 4–13, 84–91. Gregory Rodriguez took a position similar to that of Cornelius, arguing that "Mexican Americans Are Building No Walls" (the title for his February 29, 2004, *Los Angeles Times* article). Linguistics professor Dennis Baron agreed that there is little evidence of language retention and, therefore, that the migrants pose no threat to the Anglo Protestant creed. Baron writes that "most native Spanish speakers in the U.S. are losing their Spanish by the second generation. That's considerably faster than the patterns for earlier groups" (Dennis Baron, "No Translation Needed: 'Door is Closed,'" *Los Angeles Times,* March 14, 2004).

10. Jorge Castenada, "Addition to the Melting Pot Requires a New Recipe Book," *Los Angeles Times,* April 2, 2004.

11. I found Huntington's use of the term "reconquista" most interesting inasmuch as Carey McWilliams, author of the first Mexican American history, *North From Mexico* (1950), employed a similar terminology to describe early-twentieth-century Mexican

migration. McWilliams also used the phrase "The Borderlands Are Invaded" as a descriptor of Mexican immigration, yet he never received the criticism that has been leveled at Huntington.

12. Demetrios G. Papademetriou, "The Shifting Expectations of Free Trade and Migration," in John Audley et al., *NAFTA's Promise and Reality Lessons from Mexico and the Hemisphere,* New York: Carnegie Endowment for International Peace, 2003, p. 49.

13. In six other cities, Latinos number over half the population: Pomona (65 percent), Salinas (64 percent), Norwalk (63 percent), Ontario (60 percent), Downey (58 percent), and Fontana (58 percent). See U.S. Census Bureau, *The Hispanic Population: Census 2000 Brief,* U.S. Department of Commerce, Economics and Statistics Administration (May 2001), p. 7.

14. J. Edward Taylor and Philip Martin, "Central Valley Evolving into Patchwork of Poverty and Prosperity," *California Agriculture,* vol. 54, no. 1 (January–February 2000): 27; see also Philip Martin and J. Edward Taylor, "For California Farmworkers, Future Holds Little Prospect for Change," *California Agriculture,* vol. 54, no. 1 (January–February 2000): 19.

15. Kathleen Reynolds and George Kouros, "Farmworkers: An Overview of Health, Safety and Wage Issues," *Borderlines,* vol. 6, no. 8 (October 1998): 2.

16. Robin Fields and Ray Herndon, "Segregation of a New Sort Takes Shape," *Los Angeles Times,* July 6, 2003. See also the work of Jorge Ramos, who finds conditions among Latinos much like those underscored by Huntington, including a growing bilingualism (Jorge Ramos, *The Other Face of America: Chronicles of Immigrants Shaping Our Future,* New York: Harper Collins, 2002).

17. See, for example, the work of Henry Gutierrez, "The Chicano Education Rights Movement and School Desegregation in Los Angles, 1962–1970," Ph.D. dissertation, University of California, Irvine, 1990.

18. "Remittances Reflect Latinos New Homes," *Orange County Register,* May 18, 2004.

19. Jennifer Mena, "Mexican Elections Heating Up—in U.S." *Los Angeles Times,* May 13, 2004.

20. Courtney Perkes, "State Governor from Mexico to Visit Friday," *Orange County Register,* April 15, 2004.

21. Jennifer Mena, "Michoacan Governor Welcomed in O. C.," *Los Angeles Times,* April 17, 2004. Two months after the Michoacan governor's visit, the governor of Guanajuato visited his expatriates in the same city. See Patricia Prieto, "Mexican Governor Visits Santa Ana," *Orange County Register,* May 31, 2004.

22. Jennifer B. McKim, "Mexican Governor Will Try to Match Funds," *Orange County Register,* July 7, 2002.

23. Mena, "Mexican Elections Heating Up—in U.S."

24. Jennifer Mena, "Expatriate Group Is Born of Like Minds and Hearts," *Los Angeles Times,* April 21, 2004.

25. Andrew Gumbel, "Pentagon Targets Latinos and Mexicans to Man the Front Lines in War on Terror," *The Independent* (London), September 10, 2003. See also Erika Hayasaki, "Campus Military Recruitment Roils Students," *Los Angeles Times,* February 8, 2004.

26. On California, see Jordan Rau, "Impasse Is Feared on License Bill," *Los Angeles Times,* May 26, 2004. On New York, see John J. Goldman, "Undocumented Workers Hit Roadblock in New York," *Los Angeles Times,* June 6, 2004. On the intelligence reform bill, see Dena Bunis, "Immigration Reformists Oppose Intelligence Bill," *Orange County Register,* December 7, 2004; and Mary Curtius, "Bush Scores Intelligence Bill Victory," *Los Angeles Times,* December 7, 2004.

27. Ricardo Alonso-Zaldivar, "Dueling Immigration Ideas Frame a Key Election Issue," *Los Angeles Times,* May 1, 2004.

28. Walter A. Ewing and Benjamin Johnson, "Immigrant Success or Stagnation? Confronting the Claim of Latino Non-Advancement," *Immigration Policy Brief* (October 2003): 2.

29. Darryl Fears, "Schools' Racial Isolation Growing," *Washington Post,* July 18, 2001. This reporter utilized the findings of Harvard University education professor Gary Orfield, whose research for the Civil Rights Project at Harvard uncovered the growing segregation across the nation.

30. Duke Helfand, Jean Merl, and Joel Rubin, "A New Approach to School Equality," *Los Angeles Times,* May 15, 2004.

31. Sarah Tully, "Next Door, Very Different," *Orange County Register,* May 18, 2004.

32. Helfand, Merland, and Rubin, "A New Approach to School Inequality."

33. Joel Rubin, "Latinos' Yule Trips Make Schools Wish for More 'Presents,'" *Los Angeles Times,* December 19, 2004. The *New York Times* reported that the U.S.-Mexico border was besieged by a "torrent of travel that began in mid-December ... [and] will peak just before Christmas. Then the travel will reverse back into the United States in mid-January after Dia de los Reyes, or Three Kings Day" (Charlie LeDuff, "Holidays Inspire a Rush to the Border," *New York Times,* December 23, 2004).

34. Gilbert G. Gonzalez and Raul Fernandez, *A Century of Chicano History: Empire, Nations and Migration,* New York: Routledge, 2003.

35. Abigail Goldman, "Sweat, Fear and Resignation Amid All the Toys," *Los Angeles Times,* November 26, 2004.

36. Sam Dillon, "Profits Raise Pressures on U.S.-Owned Factories in Mexican Border Zone," *New York Times,* February 15, 2001.

37. Victor Quintana, "Why the Mexican Rural Sector Can't Take It Anymore," in Gilbert G. Gonzalez, Raul Fernandez, David Smith, Vivian Price, and Linda Trinh Vo, eds., *Labor Versus Empire: Race, Gender and Migration,* New York: Routledge, 2004, p. 268; and Hugh Delios, "Altered Corn Ignites Furor in Mexico," *Chicago Tribune,* May 1, 2004. Ironically, it is the very people who have been pushed off their lands who migrate to the United States and then work in the production of goods, such as chicken processing, that are exported to Mexico, which in turn propels ranchers off the land and into the migrant stream—a vicious cycle constructed by U.S. capital.

38. Ginger Thompson, "Farm Unrest Roils Mexico, Challenging New President," *New York Times,* July 22, 2001.

39. Quintana, "Why the Mexican Rural Sector Can't Take It Anymore," p. 257. Quintana, a university professor and peasant rights leader in Mexico, writes: "Malnutrition affects approximately 44 percent of the native Indian children under five years of age—a rate equal to the rates in the poorest nations of Africa."

40. Valeria Godines, "Village Borders on Extinction," *Orange County Register,* August 3, 2003.

41. Chris Kraul, "Mexico's Schools Can't Keep Up," *Los Angeles Times,* September 21, 2004. Four years earlier the same journalist reported that uprooted people are "migrating to cities and inflating jobless rolls, creating political pressure, and a potential trade backlash. To be sure, others have found work at the booming maquiladoras, the foreign-owned manufacturing plants located mainly along the U.S.-Mexico border. But many have illegally entered the United States" (Chris Kraul, "Growing Troubles in Mexico," *Los Angeles Times,* January 17, 2000).

42. On this point see the work of Jared Diamond, who contends, and correctly so, that when societies lose their food supply, they perish. Diamond uses the example of the Vikings, who for unknown reasons failed to support their livestock-based system of production and eventually disappeared as a distinct society (Jared Diamond, *Guns, Germs, and Steel: The Fate of Human Societies,* New York: Norton, 1997; see also Scott Martelle, "The Risk of Being Civilized," *Los Angeles Times,* December 17, 2004).

43. Ginger Thompson, "Migrant Exodus Bleeds Mexico's Heartland," *New York Times,* June 17, 2001.

44. Quintana, "Why the Mexican Rural Sector Can't Take It Anymore," p. 270.

45. Sandra Polaski, "Jobs, Wages, and Household Income," in John Audley et al., *NAFTA's Promise and Reality Lessons from Mexico and the Hemisphere,* New York: Carnegie Endowment, 2003, p. 20. See also Michael Pollan, "A Flood of U.S. Corn Rips at Mexico," *Los Angeles Times,* April, 30, 2004; and Celia W. Dugger, "Study: NAFTA Bad for Rural Mexicans," *New York Times,* November 11, 2003.

46. "Mexico in 2004 Grew Population by Almost 1.1 Million," *Orange County Register,* December 29, 2004.

47. Huntington charges that globalization, which he never defines, constructs the need for establishing a firmer groundwork for national identity. He writes: "The United States' national identity, like that of other nation-states, is challenged by the forces of globalization as well as the needs that globalization produces among people for smaller and more meaningful 'blood and belief' identities" (p. 32). Thus, it is not globalization *per se* that is at the center of the struggle to preserve the Anglo Protestant identity; rather, the chief cause for grief comes from the Latino population.

48. Evelyn Iritani, "In U.S., Latino Discord Over Trade Accord," *Los Angeles Times,* August 23, 2004.

49. Along the U.S.-Mexico border, armed vigilantes can frequently be seen guarding pathways used by undocumented immigrants and accosting migrants. In 1995 the Clinton administration instituted Operation Gatekeeper, a militarized scheme to stem the tide of undocumented immigrants by intensifying border patrolling. This effort ultimately failed, however, as increasing numbers of border crossers used seldom-traveled paths to enter the United States. In California, voters passed by a 60 percent margin Proposition 187, a legal statute that denied public education and other social welfare programs to undocumented immigrants. This statute was declared unconstitutional, but similar legislation in several states is currently in the works to severely limit public programs for the undocumented. In Arizona, Proposition 200 passed by a wide margin in 2004; it requires proof of legal immigration status and, in cases where none is forthcoming, denies the individual "state and local welfare

benefits." Federally mandated programs are exempt from the proposition (David Kelly, "Illegal Immigrant Measure Upheld," *Los Angeles Times,* December 23, 2004). Judging from the serious economic conditions experienced by the majority of the Mexican, Central American, and Caribbean populations, none of these approaches to cut off public benefits for undocumented immigrants is likely to curtail illegal immigration.

50. Charlie LeDuff, "Mexican Americans Struggle for Jobs," *New York Times,* October 13, 2004.

51. Ibid.

52. Ibid.

53. Leslie Earnest, "Made in L.A. for Now," *Los Angeles Times,* January 16, 2005.

54. Nancy Cleeland, "Off-the-Books Jobs Growing in Region," *Los Angeles Times,* May 2, 2002.

55. Sylvia Moreno, "Shantytowns Migrate Far North of the Border in Texas," *Washington Post,* August 2, 2004.

56. Constance L. Rice, "L.A.'s Budding Mogadishus," *Los Angeles Times,* December 23, 2004.

57. Mike Anton and Jennifer Mena, "Hard Living, Santa Ana Style," *Orange County Register,* September 5, 2004.

Conclusion

Bᴇᴛᴡᴇᴇɴ ᴛʜᴇ 1960s ᴀɴᴅ 2000 Mᴇxɪᴄᴀɴ ᴍɪɢʀᴀᴛɪᴏɴ increased tenfold, and most of that increase was recorded during the era of "free trade." Practically all of the Mexican population has been affected; only 93 of Mexico's 2,443 municipalities currently have no migrants living and working in the United States.[1] As the countryside undergoes the ongoing crisis perpetrated by NAFTA and empties its surplus population, Mexico is following a path established 100 years ago. The main difference between the earlier era and the present is that the current conditions spurring migration are more destructive than any encountered previously. Within this context, the Bush and Fox administrations took the opportunity to design a "new" bracero program sugarcoated as a "guest worker" proposal. Nothing novel emanated from the negotiations; they merely followed a well-worn script that has existed for as long as the migratory pattern itself.

What is not generally discussed when guest worker agreements are negotiated is the transnational character of such agreements. For example, the bracero program exploited Mexican labor on a widespread scale in the United States, but the extreme difficulties besetting the braceros did not begin upon their crossing of the border. Indeed, they were affected by the agreement *within* Mexico as well, at the point when they acquired their initial papers and were recruited, processed, and transported to the United States and back to their villages in Mexico. As many of the men explained, their experience was a *via crucis* that entailed much suffering, but from which they also learned a great deal about the nation to the north.

This book has sought to elucidate the conditions propelled by a U.S.-inspired "peaceful conquest" that tore the Mexican countryside apart and stimulated migrations that started in Mexico and continued in the United States. The analysis has centered on state-managed bracero migration—a migration that serves the economic interests of employers habituated to using Mexican workers, both documented and undocumented. Note as well that in this study braceros are considered to be one segment of the total migration coming to the United States rather than a unique phenomenon disconnected from the traditional definition of Mexican immigrants who enter either legally or as undocumented workers.

As noted in earlier chapters, these immigrants have been incorporated into the deepest recesses of the largest enterprises in American economy—in railroads, agriculture, manufacturing, services, construction, and more. Whether the migrants are integrated into the economy for a lifetime, six weeks, or eighteen months is immaterial to the definition of "migration." Regardless of the legal parameters and the time frame in question, Mexican laborers perform many of the same functions, varying only on the basis of the demands placed upon them by employers—particularly the dominant corporations supported by federal policies designed to control the flow of labor. On the other hand, to allege that braceros constitute a unique case of Mexican migration would be to disregard the large numbers who currently reside in the United States. For example, as many as 600 braceros still reside in the Stockton, California, area where the first contingents of braceros landed. In the great San Joaquin Valley, 3,000 ex-braceros have made their homes; the Salinas Valley, California, counts 500; Orange county's ex-braceros number 400; in the Coachella Valley several hundred reside, and in the El Paso-New Mexico area some 3,000 dwell.[2] Although no census has ever been taken of braceros currently living in the United States, the numbers are substantial and organizations of former braceros are active in Chicago, El Paso, Los Angeles, Stockton, San Jose, Fresno, Santa Ana, San Diego, and in many more towns and cities.[3]

As we have also seen, bracero migration finds greater parallels with migrations of indentured labor from European colonies than with migrations arriving from Europe. In fact, the programs used for importing Mexican labor and those employed by the British and French for exporting labor from their colonial territories are strikingly similar. These parallels are more than coincidental; in all three instances, the conditions that created a surplus labor supply, the forced de-peasanting of the land, were identical. In the case of Mexico,

American investors applied a "peaceful conquest" approach recommended by the minister of Mexico, William Rosecrans, who assured them that they would reap all of the advantages of the full territorial acquisition of Mexico, without any of the disadvantages. Mexican elites represented by the dictator Porfirio Diaz, a firm ally of the United States, collaborated with that policy. And indeed, from the perspective of the investors of the day, who poured $1,000,000,000 into railroads, mining, oil, and agriculture, the "peaceful conquest" opened the door to great wealth. Of course, although these developments resulted in the modernization of Mexico's transportation system, oil production, and mining operations (while leaving its semifeudal land system intact), it also led to mass uprootings of peasants from the countryside and their placement on a migratory trail to the United States. Not even the 1910 Mexican Revolution altered the ongoing migration or the dominant presence of the United States in the Mexican economy. On the contrary, the United States gained greater economic power within Mexico in the postrevolutionary period. That dominating presence in the Mexican economy, I have argued, emanated from an imperialist agenda that remains in place to this day.

Throughout the era of the bracero program, a public relations endeavor by bracero users and federal officials was frequently distributed, designed to present a sanitized version of the program. Films, news reports, journal articles, and radio programs presented the public with the view that the bracero program benefited all: employers, braceros, and Mexico's economic development; all were said to be winners. But as we have seen, critics who challenged these public relations efforts with telling evidence that the bracero program was a virtual slave system were subject to federal, state, and private attempts to silence them. Government officials acting in the interests of agribusiness ruined the once-promising career of one such critic—UC Berkeley scholar Henry Anderson.

Every now and then someone in the United States or Mexico, usually a government official or a "specialist" in Mexican migration, proposes to initiate a new bracero program. An endeavor made by George W. Bush and Vicente Fox (which seemed clouded by international complications) followed the general template going back to the early twentieth century, except that this effort played within the context of free trade—namely, NAFTA and its political and economic consequences.

A century of migration, particularly the explosion of people from Mexico since the onset of free trade in the 1980s, has prompted the expression of concerns over the future of America. Perhaps no writing on the perils of migration from Mexico has gathered more criticism than the work of Samuel Huntington, author of what he termed "The Hispanic Challenge"—an article that focuses on the weakening of the Anglo Protestant ethic via a spreading bilingual Hispanic population. Unfortunately, his critics avoided some of the truths that Huntington catalogued and instead heaped praise on the fabled "American Dream," contending that Mexicans, among other Hispanics, were enjoying it. In so doing, the critics demonstrated that they had more in common with Huntington than they realized. Essentially, they dismissed the century of migration, insisted that migration is a good thing, and ignored the growing economic and social segregation of the immigrant community. In particular, critics representing mainline organizations like the League of United Latin American Citizens, the National Council of La Raza, and the Mexican American Legal Defense and Education Fund ignored the consequences of NAFTA—the most recent "peaceful conquest" of Mexico, which has spurred even greater migration.

The effects of free trade weigh heavily upon the Third World. Mexico is undergoing a NAFTA-propelled economic storm that is wreaking havoc on the working class and even the middle class. But, as noted, free trade has also caused severe problems for working people in the highly developed world. In the United States, although the situation is less dramatic, not just working people but the middle classes as well are faced with a deteriorating standard of living.

The conditions affecting many Americans today are not merely uninspiring; they are downright frightening. Poverty is on the rise, good-paying manufacturing jobs are relocating abroad, low-paying service jobs are absorbing those coming off the unemployed registers, public services such as higher education are becoming more and more privatized and expensive—the list goes on and on. Overall, the image is one of a society beset by increasing economic insecurity, a shrinking middle class, growing poverty, and an accelerating concentration of the nation's wealth in the hands of a few. Is this the result of free trade? The answer is yes. What we are observing here is the domestic face of imperialism. Let's review what is happening within the imperialist hegemon.

Free Trade and American Workers

A headline in an August 17, 2004, newspaper declared: "Haves Have It Even More Over the Have-Nots: The Rich Keep Getting Richer."[4] Another blared: "Largest Fortunes Resume Upward Path."[5] Both spoke to the widening gap—in fact, the doubling—between the rich and the rest of America from 1979 to 2000. Average wage workers, for example, "have been losing ground for 20 years," while the income share of the wealthiest 20 percent of the population "grew from 44 percent in 1973 to 50 percent in 2002"—that is, from an average of $81,883 in 1967 to $143,743 in 2002—a 76 percent increase (in 2002 dollars). A measure of the increasing concentration of wealth at the top is the ratio of CEO pay to worker pay, which went from 43 to 1 in 1973 to 531 to 1 in 2000 and receded to 301 to 1 in 2003 under the impetus of corporate corruption.[6] At the same time, the income share of those at the bottom 20 percent fell from 4.2 percent to a paltry 3.5 percent, and that of the middle classes fell from 17 percent to less than 15 percent. Meanwhile, the prices of basic consumer goods, health care, housing, tuition, gas, and food rose dramatically—and the tax burden shifted to the middle and working classes, rising by 2 percent while the tax paid by the top 20 percent fell by nearly a percentage point—making life more difficult for the majority.[7]

The foregoing leads to one conclusion: The fabled middle class, anchor of all that is good in the United States, is undergoing a process of retrenchment not of its own making. According to the Economic Policy Institute, income in the United States "is more unevenly distributed than at any time since 1941." The top 1 percent of Americans enjoy 38 percent of the nation's personal wealth while nearly 80 percent of the population can claim only 17 percent of the nation's assets.[8] In fact, the *U.S. News and World Report* notes that, of all the industrialized nations in the world, the United States exhibits the largest gap between rich and poor. Economists at the nonprofit National Bureau of Economic Research have found that the top 1 percent income earners hold the "largest share of before-tax income of any year since 1929."[9] Clearly, the rich have grown even richer in this era of free trade.

Median household incomes in the United States fell by 1.1 percent in 2001–2002 as the ranks of the poor increased by 1.3 million, reaching a total of 34.8 million people, or roughly 12.5 percent of the population—although Blacks and Latinos were affected to a far greater degree than Whites. However, since public welfare benefits are treated as income by the census bureau's analysis, the real poverty rate was closer to 15 percent across the board—and greater for minorities. The poverty rate for Blacks stands at 24.1 percent and for Latinos at 23 percent; these figures are much higher than the 7.8 percent for Whites. However, in the same period, the pace of impoverishment for Whites was greater, rising by .2 percent—a rate higher than that of Blacks and Latinos.[10] In addition, the median income of Whites slipped only three-fourths of a percent compared to 2.5 percent for Blacks and 3 percent for Latinos. Economic Policy Institute analyst Jared Bernstein said of the 2000–2001 recession: "It ... was tough on everybody, even white-collar, highly educated workers, but the recovery has been toughest on minorities."

Overall, the decline has been very clear at the middle-income levels, particularly during the seemingly imperturbable recession that followed the heady days of the 1990s. The decline has manifested in other ways as well. For example, double incomes are now necessary to ensure a middle-class standard of living. The number of two-income households increased from 37 percent of the total in 1970 to 69 percent in 2002. (Note, however, that incomes overall fluctuated up and down at rates double that in 1970.) What at one time were normal family events that at one time people could ride out without serious repercussions—illness, childbirth, work change, divorce, and so on—now brings in their wake perilous consequences; as a result, the number of families adversely affected by these events has risen significantly. For example, the percentage of families experiencing a 50 percent drop in annual income due to childbirth rose from 4.5 percent in the 1970s to 11.2 percent in the 1990s. Similar declines have been found in cases of divorce, the death of a spouse, retirement, illness, and others. The hazards associated with such events are reflected in the burgeoning number of personal bankruptcy filings over the past twenty years, rising from 288,000 to 1,625,200.[11]

Add to that decline in middle-class security the growth of low-wage service-sector employment, and we end up with a recipe for a permanently widening disparity between the rich and the rest of the population. Once California seemed the nation's economic star; more recently its gleam has been declining rapidly. Between 2002 and 2003 the number of people without health coverage increased by 200,000 to 6.5 million—nearly one person out of every five in the state.[12] One reason for this increase is the growth in the number of service jobs, which rose by 2.3 million since the advent of free trade; the average income earned in such jobs is only $30,000, while good-paying manufacturing jobs (which pay an average of $55,000) have decreased by 200,000.[13] The decline in good-paying jobs is largely due to free trade; over 879,000 jobs have been transferred overseas as a result of NAFTA. One thing is for sure: Income growth in mid-America is slowing and, in many instances, declining. Indeed, studies indicate that the nation's median income, adjusted for inflation, declined nearly 3.3 percent in 2002 alone.[14]

The Globalization of Poverty

Meanwhile, poverty strikes billions around the globe. The figures are grim. Since 1950 the difference in per capita income between rich and poor countries has doubled. Although millions of poor are employed in offshore production assembly lines mobilized by the neoliberal agenda, unemployment is endemic. Everyone talks about poverty, but no one does anything significant to end it. The United Nations invites representatives from around the world on a regular basis to discuss what to do about poverty, and headlines say things like "World Must Act to End Hunger, Summit Is Told." Yet, poverty pervades large sections of the globe—despite the "promises" of free trade (or, more accurately, because of it).

Between 1990 and 1999, the "golden age" of globalization, the World Bank proclaimed that the proportion of the world's population affected by absolute poverty had dropped from 29 percent to 23 percent. However, economist Sanjay Reddy has demonstrated that the World Bank's findings were based on very questionable analytic methods, leading him to conclude that the actual proportion is more than one-third of the world's population—a number that not only is increasing but also does not include those who live on the margins.[15] Indeed, income inequity is extreme across the globe. In Mexico, according to the conservative estimates of the World Bank, the top 10 percent of the population holds 43 percent of the national wealth (other sources suggest that this figure should be much higher), while the bottom tenth earns only 1.5 percent. After ten years of NAFTA, 63 to 73 percent of the people in Mexico are living in poverty and real income has fallen by over 40 percent.[16] Guatemala is another example. There the richest 10 percent control half of the nation's wealth whereas the poorest half have but 10 percent. Similar income gaps can be found in Brazil, Argentina, Chile, and Uruguay—gaps that clearly have not been closed by decades of free trade.

In Latin America approximately 221 million people—44 percent of the population—live in poverty; of this number 97 million (19 percent of the total population) cannot purchase food sufficient to meet their basic nutritional needs, and their health suffers.[17] The impact on children is alarming. Five percent of all Latin American children will die before their sixth birthday, and those who do survive will probably not finish elementary school.[18]

And yet the model for Mexico and all of Latin America proclaimed by the United States is *more* free trade and all that it encompasses. With the dramatic rise of poverty in Mexico, it has lost its ability to feed itself; farms and ranches are collapsing under the weight of U.S. imports. Meanwhile, a maquiladora boom is projected along the length of the border. In Mexicali, a huge industrial park covering 15 square miles has been designed to encompass the state-of-the-art "Silicon Valley" assembly factories that have been "envisioned." Meanwhile, guest worker agreements and forms of "regularization" are being debated.[19]

In nearby Tijuana, maquila plants hired an additional 15,000 workers in 2004–2005. Maquilas account for one-half of all of Mexico's exports, which in reality are not Mexico's at all. Mexico merely serves as the site for the production of goods consumed elsewhere. The plants' executives generally live in the United States, and profits accrue to the corporation; however, the labor supply is purely Mexican. Accompanying the buildup of maquila plants, the Bush administration has unveiled an "energy plan in Mexico" designed to open the "energy market," increase the energy flow to the United States, and supply the maquila expansion as well. What Bush has in mind is an increased supply of electricity to the United States and its investments along the border, ignoring the fact that Mexico is undergoing an energy crisis of its own and hasn't the financial resources to develop its own supply—the resolution of which Fox says is to come from foreign investors.[20] What is clear is that touting free trade drowns out interest in solving the problem of poverty; apparently, the connection between poverty and systems of production and uses of labor such as guest workers is rarely addressed at WTO and IMF roundtables organized to discuss poverty. In fact, these organizations, led by the United States, counsel nations to adopt free trade as the antidote to poverty![21] It is in this atmosphere that workers, peasants, and students have taken to the streets to demand an end to free trade and all that it entails—from legal, undocumented, and guest worker migration to maquila workers.

And then there is the seemingly endless war in Iraq; the cost of worldwide militarization; the determined opposition to U.S. economic domination by Japan, the European Union, Russia, and China; and, indeed, the popular opposition to free-trade agreements that is mounting around the world. While a "hot war" engages the United States in Iraq, Afghanistan, and the Middle East, an economic war is being waged by workers, students, peasants, and others against the spoils of free trade, of which guest worker proposals are but one part. The challenges come not only from the Third World but from the centers of free-trade dogma as well.

Confronting the Imperialist Challenge

Just as there are no "good" guest worker programs, there are no "good" free-trade agreements. Among the objectives of the former is to take advantage of cheap labor for the production of goods for consumption in the First World. All such agreements have one goal in mind; as Senator Phil Gramm put it, "You come, you work, you accrue the benefits of your work and you go home." Free trade provides a plentiful supply of maquila and immigrant labor in the form of legal, illegal, and guest workers. However, immigrant guest workers perform the lowest-wage work—a service category work that leads to poverty and the least security. Very possibly the same workers will at some time work on the Mexican side of the border, in maquila plants that will guarantee them poverty at the going rate for maquila workers. Meanwhile, the countryside is being destroyed, public services are undergoing privatization, and the people are responding in kind, "with keen skepticism of neoliberal policies in Mexico."[22] Some protests have been small, but others have encompassed tens of thousands of people at various places in Mexico.

As the effects of NAFTA have manifested throughout the nation, especially the countryside, small to medium farmers have actively entered into the national spotlight to oppose free-trade policies. In July 2001, 5,000 sugar cane farmers "converged on the capital and blocked access to government offices." One such farmer from rural Veracruz aptly described the situation created by seven years of NAFTA: "The entire Mexican countryside is a disaster." He went on to say that "[t]here is almost no place left in the country where a small farmer can make a good living." In the northwest state of Sinaloa, farmers protested by blocking access to gas stations to demand that the government increase tariffs on imports of U.S. corn. Apparently, the protests prompted the state governor to declare a state of emergency, hotels closed, and business services were reduced. Within a week, protests rang out in Campeche state as farmers took over two cereal plants to demand that the government renegotiate loans. And in the northern state of Chihuahua, farmers took over the customs station to halt shipments of agricultural goods imported from the United States. The leader of this last group contended that such protests would continue until the government agreed to implement legislation to help small farmers.

In February 2003 a small band of students gathered at the monument to Mexico's independence; climbing the 20-story monument, they attached a banner stating "No to NAFTA." At a mass protest in Mexico City later that year, tens of thousands of people, including students, secretaries, housewives, and peasants, marched against the economic policies of the Fox administration. The largest march in years, it brought 100,000 people to the capital's streets. An elderly peasant protester sadly noted the effects of NAFTA, saying, "It is the countryside that is dead, finished. It is not the countryside that we thought it was going to be. We feel cheated."[23] One banner rang out: "No to Privatization, VAT, and Imperialism." (VAT is a tax on food.) A year later another march brought thousands to protest President Fox's annual message to a joint session of congress, closing down the center of the capital once more. Men, women, and children protested against the farm policies operating under NAFTA guidelines as well as the privatization of many government workers' pensions.[24] Rather than addressing those concerns, however, Fox chose to reiterate that Mexico is "on the road to democracy." Of course, he did not dare to mention in his address that Mexico's economic sovereignty is rapidly disappearing.

Protests were heard across Latin America as a whole. In La Paz, Bolivia, thousands marched in October 2003 in protest of the president's plan to sell natural gas to the United States and Mexico. Miners marched with peasants, and in clashes with police the miners were described as having hurled dynamite, resulting in sixty-five deaths over three weeks of demonstrations. The president was forced to resign after the violence. Two years later, demonstrations again rocked the capital as protesters called for a rejection of the concession to privatize the city's water utility to a French concern. In the city of Santa Cruz, main highways were blocked as stores and offices closed. A radical labor movement and indigenous groups have expressed their direct opposition to free trade by demanding the nationalization of utilities and natural resources.[25]

Argentina was not spared the wave of protests. Thousands of unemployed workers there took to the streets in December 2002 to protest the economic crisis wrought by policies emanating from the neoliberal model; in that uprising, twenty-eight persons lost their lives. Several months later workers again took to the streets and turned Buenos Aires into a chaotic scene. Twenty percent of the labor force stood unemployed as Argentina entered into bankruptcy, unable to pay its loans.

The director of the Council on Hemispheric Affairs, Larry Birns, has studied neoliberal policies throughout the region; as he puts it, the "response from Latin America, the grass roots response, has been growing rage over the privatization thrust."[26] In Arequipa, Peru, citizens joined antigovernment demonstrations in June 2002 to protest the decision to auction off two state-owned power-generating enterprises to a Belgian concern connected to a giant French utility conglomeration. Observers noted that the Peruvian uprising is merely one example of the "deep frustration across Latin America" propelled by neoliberal policies devoted to the privatization of state-owned entities and state-provided services.[27] Despite a state of emergency called by the president, hundreds of protesters blocked roads and demonstrated openly in the town square.

Anti-American feeling is also percolating throughout the region. In Buenos Aires, for example, U.S. banks fortified their outlets with steel barriers and hired security guards. (It is said that the security guards are there to protect the bank's employees.) An Argentine nationalist member of congress, Elisa Carrio, summed up what many across Latin America are saying about free trade: the people of the United States "have already taken most of what we have—and now, they are coming for our lands."[28] In Colombia, Ecuador, and Peru the opposition to free trade is intensifying each day; in each case, large organizations are mobilizing the public to oppose free trade.[29] Colombian Senator Jorge Enrique Robledo has forcefully argued in parliament that the proposed Andean Free Trade Agreement promises a marked reduction in the protections for national food production and "an increase of foreign investment . . . that demands at least three unwanted conditions: the acquisition of low cost primary materials and businesses, low or no taxes, and cheap labor."[30] Robledo's and Carrio's words are well understood throughout Latin America, but especially in Mexico, which has experienced ten years of NAFTA and is suffering for it. A *New York Times* journalist on assignment described the huge migrations from the countryside under way as of mid-2001: "By the tens of thousands, peasants in Mexico are abandoning the small plots they considered their birthright."[31] The forces that engender the out-migration, declining crop prices, and lowered subsidies fall under the provisions demanded by "free trade under NAFTA." Meanwhile, Mexico's surplus labor grows daily, and the question of how to deliver it to the United States via guest worker programs is under discussion.

The future of Latin America hangs in the balance, and the inhabitants of the region are struggling to maintain their sovereignty. Around the world, people have become aware of the consequences of free trade and have taken an active role in opposition to it. From Seattle, Quebec, Miami, Genoa, Cancun, and beyond, these people have made the clear statement that free trade is not free at all; rather, it is an intensification of the exploitation of the Third World, its peoples, and its natural resources by imperialist policies.

While the United States continues "slog through" the deadly quagmire in Iraq and threatens to launch more imperialist misadventures, an economic war is being launched throughout Latin America. It must be a vital concern of the U.S. State Department that the people of Latin America are as determined to beat back that economic occupation as the nationalists of Iraq are determined to oust the United States. In Iraq a "hot war" against the American occupation rages on; in Latin America, a war against the imperialist economic occupation intensifies each day.

The people of Latin America have taken Ernesto Galarza's advice to heart and now focus upon the actions of U.S. capital for explaining the major social and economic issues facing their nations. As Galarza has said (and this is reiterated throughout the present book), Mexican migration—braceros, guest workers, legal or illegal—cannot be explained apart from the actions and consequences of U.S. capital across the social evolution of the Mexican nation. In the latest example of U.S. imperialist expansion, free trade—that is, guest workers—emerged as a matter of public policy discussion in Washington. That policy proposal does not stand alone; it cannot be explained or understood apart from the actions of U.S. imperial capital in Mexico and the destruction of that nation's economic independence. Explaining a hundred years of Mexican migration under its various guises requires that we begin with a thorough investigation of U.S. imperialist domination and its effects upon that nation. Using such an approach, we are bound to arrive at the conclusion that there is no such thing as a "good" guest worker program, inasmuch as all such programs depend upon the continual availability of uprooted people without options, refugees of an economic policy leading toward the recolonization of Latin America. This, indeed, is the imperialist challenge that the working people of Latin America and the United States have taken on.

Notes

1. John Rice, "Economic Opportunity Seen in Population Shift," *Orange County Register,* July 12, 2001.

2. One estimate placed the number in California at 20,000. See Garance Burke, "Labor's Lost Legacy: After Lifetimes in the Fields, Braceros Seek the Pensions They Were Promised," *Sacramento Bee,* August 22, 2004; Vanessa Colon, "Proposal Dissatisfies Braceros," *Fresno Bee,* April 30, 2005; Minerva Canto, "Braceros Suing for Back Pay Win Delay," *Orange County Register,* February 16, 2002; Lucero Amador, "Los Ex Braceros Tendran Seguro Medico del IMSS," *La Opinion,* November 11, 2003; Patricia Prieto, "Quieren Cuanto Antes Su Dinero," *Excelsior* (*Orange County Register*), January 28, 2005; Guadalupe Bellavance, "Ex-Braceros Mexicanos Desconocen Procedimiento Para Cobrar Retiro," *El Vistazo,* found at http://www.elvistazo.com. "The Alliance of Braceros of the Salinas Valley," The [Salinas] Citizenship Project, found at http://www.newcitizen.org/english/bracero-eng.htm; "Antiguos Braceros Se Openen Al Plan de Bush," *La Opinion,* January 14, 2004; Yvette Cabrera, "Braceros' Work Finally Pays Off," *Orange County Register,* January 16, 2005; and "Ex-Braceros Hopeful of Getting Money," *Kansas City Post,* May 2, 2005.

3. In my courses on Chicano history I discuss the bracero program, and the first time I lectured on the subject, at least eight students in the class said that they had

either a grandfather or a father who was a bracero at one time. Likewise, at least two administrators at the University of California, Irvine, where I teach, have grandfathers who served as braceros. In my most recent course, of a class of thirty, six students raised their hands in response to my question: "How many of you have a relative who once served as a bracero?"

4. Leigh Strope, "Haves Have It Even More Over the Have-Nots," *Orange County Register,* August 17, 2004.

5. Theresa Agovino, "Largest Fortunes Resume Upward Path," *Orange County Register,* September 19, 2003.

6. Derrick Z. Jackson, "A Steeper Ladder for the Have Nots," *Boston Globe,* May 18, 2005. Jackson points out that were the minimum wage to have kept up with CEO salaries it would "be $15.76 an hour instead of its current $5.15."

7. Strope, "Haves Have It Even More Over the Have-Nots,".

8. John Baltazar, "The Incredible Shrinking Middle Class," *Los Angeles Times,* May 19, 2002.

9. Lynnley Browning, "U.S. Income Gap Widening, Study Says," *New York Times,* September 25, 2003.

10. Robert Pear, "Poverty Rate in U.S. Rises as Median Income Falls," *New York Times,* September 25, 2002.

11. Peter Gosslin, "How Just a Handful of Setbacks Sent the Ryans Tumbling Off Our Prosperity," *Los Angeles Times,* December 30, 2004.

12. Scott Martelle, "Health Coverage Declines in California, U.S. Census Says," *Los Angeles Times,* August 27, 2004.

13. Lawrence Mischel, Jared Bernstein, and John Schmidt, *State of Working America 2000–1, An Economic Policy Book.* Ithaca, NY: ILR Press, an Imprint of Cornell University Press, 2001, p. 169; George Skelton, "Squeeze on Business Puts Strain on State's Declining Middle Class," *Los Angeles Times,* April 14, 2003; and Louis Uchitelle, "Blacks Lose Better Jobs Faster as Middle-Class Work Drops," *New York Times,* July 12, 2003.

14. Peter Gosselin, "Middle, Lower Classes Feel Pinch," *Los Angeles Times,* December 30, 2004; see also Kirk Semple, "Number of People Living in Poverty in U.S. Increases Again," *New York Times,* September 26, 2003.

15. Quoted in George Monbiot, "Poor, But Pedicured," *The Guardian,* May 6, 2003.

16. John Warnock, "Who Benefits from Free Trade Agreements?" Unpublished manuscript dated April 14, 2001. (Warnock is a political economist at a Canadian university.)

17. ECLAC, *Social Panorama of Latin America,* Briefing Paper 2004, New York: United Nations, 2004; Simon Romero, "Two Latin Americas, Two Diverging Outlooks," *New York Times,* May 5, 2002; Anthony DePalma, "Latin America's Poor Survive It All, Even Boom Times," *New York Times,* June 24, 2001; and Julio Boltvinik, "Poverty in Latin America: A Critical Analysis of Three Studies," *International Social Science Journal,* no. 148, June 1996, p. 16.

18. "Latin Summit Addresses Poverty Issues," *Orange County Register,* July 14, 2001.

19. Terril Yue Jones and Marla Dickerson, "Chip Factories Envisioned for South of the Border," *Los Angeles Times,* July 15, 2004. The authors point out that "American investors and Mexican officials unveiled an ambitious plan ... for an industrial park

in Mexico along the California border to entice computer chip companies to build multibillion-dollar factories there instead of exporting production to Asia." President Vicente Fox promised to "waive taxes for 10 years" for those companies setting up shop along the border. Backers of the project emphasized that the labor pool in nearby Mexicali, claimed to consist of at least 750,000 men, would supply the factories with endless supply of workers. See also Mary Jordan, "Mexican Officials Promote 'Silicon Border,'" *New York Times,* December 11, 2004.

20. Evelyn Iritani, "Bush Pushes Energy Plan in Mexico," *Los Angeles Times,* February 16, 2001.

21. Greg Palast, "The World Bank's Former Chief Economist's Accusations Are Eye-Popping," *The Observer* (London), October 10, 2002; Stephen Byers, "The IMF and World Bank Orthodoxy Is Increasing Global Poverty," *The Guardian,* May 19, 2003.

22. Warnock, "Who Benefits from the Free Trade Agreements?"

23. Elizabeth Fullerton, "Thousands March Against Mexico's Beleaguered Fox," *Washington Post,* November 27, 2003.

24. Kevin Sullivan, "As Mexicans Protest, Fox Pushes Democracy Vision," *Washington Post,* September 2, 2004.

25. Hector Tobar and Oscar Ordonez, "Bolivian Indian and Leftist Groups, Seeking Reforms, Seal Off 2 Cities," *Los Angeles Times,* January 12, 2005.

26. Juan Forero, "Peruvians Riot over Sale of 2 Regional Power Plants," *New York Times,* June 18, 2002.

27. Ibid.; Andres Oppenheimer, "Mexican Dislike for U.S. Growing," *Orange County Register,* November 15, 2003; Richard Boudreaux, "Bush Visits Neighbors No Longer So Friendly," *Los Angeles Times,* January 12, 2004. Boudreaux writes: "Bush is deeply unpopular in much of the region. Latin Americans view him as a distant neighbor at best—often at odds with them over security and trade policies."

28. Anthony Faiola, "Economic Crisis Spurs Anger," *Washington Post,* May 19, 2002.

29. During the final negotiations held in Cartagena, Colombia, in February 2005, thousands of anti-NAFTA demonstrators rallied to oppose the agreement, which stalled after negotiations failed to overcome disagreements. Among the groups demonstrating were Ecuador Decide, Campaña Peruana de Lucha Contra el TLC y el ALCA, Movimiento Boliviano de Lucha contra el TLC y el ALCA, Colombia's indigenous organization Mandato Indigena y Popular, and the more general group Red Colombiana de Acción frente al Libre Comercio y el ALCA (RECALCA).

30. Jorge Enrique Robledo, "Colombia and the Free Trade Agreement with the United States: A Statement by Senator Jorge Enrique Robledo," *Bulletin* of the Washington Office on Latin America (November 2004).

31. Ginger Thompson, "Farm Unrest Roils Mexico, Challenging New President," *New York Times,* July 22, 2001.

Bibliography

Books, Chapters, and Articles

Anderson, Henry. *The Bracero Program in California*. New York: Arno Press, 1976.

———. *Harvest of Loneliness: An Inquiry into a Social Problem*. Berkeley: Citizens for Farm Labor, 1964.

———. "Who Will Guard the Guardians?" Unpublished KRKW radio transcript (November 13, 1964).

———. *Fields of Bondage*. Privately published by Mr. Anderson (May 1, 1963).

———"Fields of Bondage: The Mexican Contract Labor System in Industrialized Agriculture," mimeographed typescript (1963).

———. "Social Justice and Foreign Contract Labor: A Statement of Opinion and Conscience." Typed manuscript (1958), Department of Special Collections, Stanford University Libraries.

———. "Chronology, 1958–1960." Typed manuscript (n.d.).

Anderson, Henry, and Joan London. *So Shall Ye Reap*. New York: Crowell, 1970.

Audley, John J., et al., *NAFTA's Promise and Reality: Lessons from Mexico for the Hemisphere*. New York: Carnegie Endowment for International Peace, 2004.

Baker, Verne A. "Braceros Farm for Mexico." *Americas,* vol. 5 (September 1953).

Bennoune, Mahfoud. "Impact of Colonialism and Migration on an Algerian Peasant Community: A Study in Socioeconomic Change." Ph.D. dissertation, University of Michigan, 1976.

Bernstein, Aaron. "Waking Up from the American Dream." *Business Week,* December 1, 2003.

Bolland, O. Neil. *The Politics of Labour in the British Caribbean: The Social Origins of Authoritarianism and Democracy in the Labour Movement*. Kingston, Jamaica: Ian Randle Publishers, 2001.

"Braceros, Mexico and Foreign Trade." *Farm Labor Developments.* Washington, D.C.: U.S. Department of Labor, Manpower Administration, Bureau of Employment Security (July 1966).

Burr, Clifford F., "South of the Border." *Employment Security Review,* vol. 28 (January 1961).

Clark, Victor. *Mexican Labor in the United States.* U.S. Department of Commerce and Labor, Bureau of Labor Bulletin no. 78 (Washington, D.C.: U.S. Government Printing Office, 1908).

Coalson, George E. "Mexican Contract Labor in American Agriculture." *Southwestern Social Science,* vol. 33 (September 1952).

Coombs, S. W. "Bracero's Journey." *Americas,* vol. 15 (December 1963).

Cornelius, Wayne. "Legalizing the Flow of Temporary Migrant Workers from Mexico: A Policy Proposal." Working Papers in U.S.–Mexican Studies 7, Program in United States–Mexican Studies, University of California, San Diego (1981).

Craig, Richard B. *The Bracero Program: Interest Groups and Foreign Policy.* Austin: University of Texas Press, 1971.

Cross, Harry E., and James A. Sandos. *Across the Border: Rural Development in Mexico and Recent Migration to the United States,* Berkeley: University of California Institute of Governmental Studies, 1981.

Daniels, Roger. "An Old New Immigration Policy, Flaws and All." *Chronicle of Higher Education,* February 6, 2004.

Davidson, Cecilia Razovsky. "Mexican Laborers Imported into the United States." *Interpreter Releases,* vol. 20, no. 38 (October 18, 1943).

Driscoll, Barbara. *The Tracks North: The Railroad Bracero Program of World War II.* Austin: University of Texas Press, 1999.

Eakin, Emily. 'It Takes an Empire' Say Several U.S. Thinkers." *New York Times,* April 2, 2003.

Ewing, Walter A., and Benjamin Johnson. "Immigrant Success or Stagnation? Confronting the Claim of Latino Non-Advancement." *Immigration Policy Brief* (October 2003).

Faux, Jeff. "NAFTA at Seven: Its Impact on Workers in All Three Nations." Economic Policy Institute *Briefing Paper* (Washington, D.C., 2001).

Flynn, John K. *A Century of Service to Agriculture.* Pasadena, Calif.: American Friends Service Committee (May 25, 1967).

Freeman, Alan P. *Immigrant Labor and Racial Conflict in Industrial Societies: The French and British Experience, 1945–1975.* Princeton: Princeton University Press, 1979.

Fuller, Varden, John W. Mamer, and George L. Viles. "Domestic and Imported Workers in the Harvest Labor Market." Berkeley: University of California Agricultural Experiment Station (January 1956).

Gamio Leon, Carlos. "Braceros Bring Home New Ways." *Mexican Life,* vol. 10, no. 37 (September 1961).

Galarza, Ernesto. *Farm Workers and Agri-business in California, 1947–1960.* Notre Dame: University of Notre Dame Press, 1977.

———. *Merchants of Labor: The Mexican Bracero Story.* Charlotte: McNally and Loftin, 1964.

———. *Strangers in Our Fields.* Washington, D.C.: Joint United States–Mexico Trade Union Committee, 1956.

———. "Program for Action." *Common Ground,* vol. 10, no. 4 (Summer 1949).

Gamboa, Erasmo. *Mexican Labor and World War II: Braceros in the Pacific Northwest, 1942–1947.* Austin: University of Texas Press, 1990.

Garcia, Mario T. *Mexican Americans: Leadership, Ideology, and Identity, 1930–1960.* New Haven: Yale University Press, 1989.

Gonzalez, Gilbert G., and Raul Fernandez. *A Century of Chicano History: Empire, Nations and Migration.* New York: Routledge, 2004.

Gonzalez, Juan. *The Harvest of Empire: A History of Latinos in America.* New York: Viking Press, 2000.

Gonzalez Navarro, Moises. *Historia Moderna de Mexico: El Porfiriato,* vol. 4. Mexico City: Editorial Hermes, 1957.

Grandin, Greg. "The Right Quagmire: Searching History for an Imperial Alibi." *Harper's Magazine* (December 2004).

Guerin-Gonzalez, Camille. *Mexican Workers and American Dreams: Immigration, Repatriation and California Farm Labor, 1900–1939.* New Brunswick: Rutgers University Press, 1994.

Hancock, Richard. *The Role of the Bracero in the Economic and Cultural Dynamics of Mexico.* Stanford, Calif.: Stanford University Hispanic American Society, 1959.

Hanson, Victor Davis. *Mexifornia: A State of Becoming.* San Francisco: Encounter Books, 2003.

Haraksingh, Kusha. "The Worker and the Wage in a Plantation Economy: Trinidad in the Nineteenth Century," in Mary Turner, ed., *From Chattel Slaves to Wage Slaves: The Dynamics of Labour Bargaining in the Americas.* Kingston, Jamaica: Ian Randle, 1995.

Hart, John Mason. *Empire and Revolution: The Americans in Mexico Since the Civil War.* Berkeley: University of California, 2002.

Huntington, Samuel P. "The Hispanic Challenge," *Foreign Affairs* (March–April 2004).

———. *Who We Are: Challenges to American National Identity.* Simon and Schuster, 2004.

Jacobson, David. *The Immigration Reader: America in Multidisciplinary Perspective.* Malden, Mass.: Blackwell Publishers, 1998.

Johns, Michael. *The City of Mexico in the Age of Diaz.* Austin: University of Texas Press, 1997.

Jones, Robert C., *Mexican War Workers in the United States,* Washington, D.C.: Pan American Union, 1945.

Kale, Madhavi. *Fragments of Empire: Capital, Slavery, and Indian Indentured Labor in the British Caribbean.* Philadelphia: University of Pennsylvania, 1998.

Kaplan, Amy. "'Left Alone with America': The Absence of Empire in the Study of American Culture," in Amy Kaplan and Donald Pease, eds., *Cultures of United States Imperialism.* Durham, N.C.: Duke University Press, 1993.

Kiser, George C., and Martha Woody Kiser, eds., *Mexican Workers in the United States: Historical and Political Perspectives.* Albuquerque: University of New Mexico Press, 1979.

Lai, Walton Look. *Indentured Labor, Caribbean Sugar: Chinese and Indian Migrants to the British West Indies, 1838–1918.* Baltimore: Johns Hopkins University Press, 1993.

Le Berthon, Ted. "At the Prevailing Rate," *Commonweal,* vol. 67 (November 1, 1957).

Lindsey, Robert B. "Texas," *Employment Security Review,* vol. 22 (March 1955).

Lipset, Seymour Martin, and Aldo Solari. *Elites in Latin America.* New York: Oxford University Press, 1967.

Mayer, Arnold. "The Grapes of Wrath, Vintage 1961." *The Reporter* (February 2, 1961).

MacMaster, Neil. *Colonial Migrants and Racism: Algerians in France, 1900–1962.* London: Macmillan Press, 1997.

Martin, Philip, and J. Edward Taylor. "For California Farmworkers, Future Holds Little Prospect for Change." *California Agriculture,* vol. 54, no. 1 (January–February 2000).

Massey, Douglas, et al. *Worlds in Motion: Understanding International Migration at the End of the Millennium.* Oxford: Clarendon Press, 1998.

Massey, Douglas, Jorge Durand, and Nolan J. Malone. *Beyond Smoke and Mirrors: Mexican Migration in an Era of Economic Integration.* New York: Russell Sage Foundation, 2002.

McWilliams, Carey. "They Saved the Crops." *The Inter-American,* vol. 2 (August 1943).

McWilliams, Carey. *North from Mexico: The Spanish Speaking of the United States.* New York: Greenwood Press, 1968. (Originally published 1949.)

"Mexican Labor and Foreign Capital," *The Independent,* vol. 112, no. 3869 (May 24, 1924).

Miller, Jr., Edward G. "Rewards of U.S.–Mexican Cooperation." U.S. Department of State *Bulletin,* vol. 36 (March 31, 1952).

Mohammed, Patricia. *Gender Negotiations Among Indians in Trinidad.* London: Palgrave, 2002.

Office of Agricultural Publications. "University-Farmer Cooperation in California: The Extent of Assistance Received by the Division of Agricultural Sciences from the Farmers." Berkeley: University of California Office of Agricultural Publications (1958).

Online NewsHour: David Gergen Engages Samuel Huntington, January 9, 1997. Available online at http://www.pbs.org/newshour/gergen/january97/order_1-10.html.

Papademetriou, Demetrios G. "The Shifting Expectations of Free Trade and Migration," in John Audley et al., eds., *NAFTA's Promise and Reality Lessons from Mexico and the Hemisphere.* New York: Carnegie Endowment for International Peace, 2003.

Pletcher, David. *Rails. Mines and Progress: Seven American Promoters in Mexico, 1867–1911.* Ithaca, N.Y.: Cornell University Press, 1958.

Pickett, John E. "Hired Man of 150,000 Farms." *California Magazine of the Pacific,* vol. 29, no. 4 (April 1939).

Polaski, Sandra. "Jobs, Wages, and Household Income," in John Audley et al., *NAFTA's Promise and Reality Lessons from Mexico and the Hemisphere.* New York: Carnegie Endowment, 2003.

Prochaska, David. *Making Algeria French: Colonialism in Bone 1870–1920.* Cambridge, U.K.: Cambridge University Press, 1990.

Quintana, Victor. "The Mexican Rural Sector Can't Take It Anymore," in Gilbert G. Gonzalez et al., eds., *Labor Versus Empire: Race, Gender and Migration.* New York: Routledge, 2004.

Ramos, Jorge. *The Other Face of the Americas: Chronicles of Immigrants Shaping Our Future.* New York: Harper Collins, 2002.

Randall, Laura. "Labour Migration and Mexican Economic Development." *Social and Economic Studies,* vol. 12, no. 1 (March 1962).

Reimers, David M. *Still the Open Door: The Third World Comes to America.* New York: Columbia University, 1985.

Reisler, Mark. *By the Sweat of Their Brow: Mexican Immigrant Labor in the United States, 1900–1940.* Westport, Conn.: Greenwood Press, 1976.

Reynolds, Kathleen, and George Kouros. "Farmworkers: An Overview of Health, Safety and Wage Issues." *Borderlines,* vol. 6, no. 8 (October 1998).

"Remittance Senders and Receivers: Tracking the Transnational Channels." Washington, D.C.: Pew Hispanic Center (November 24, 2003).

Rodney, Walter. *A History of the Guyanese Working People, 1881–1905.* Baltimore: University of Maryland Press, 1981.

Rosen, Stephen Peter. "The Future of War and the American Military." *Harvard Magazine* (May–June 2002).

Reubens, Edwin P. "Immigration Problems, Limited-Visa Programs, and Other Options," in Peter G. Brown and Henry Shue, eds., *The Border That Joins: Mexican Migrants and U.S. Responsibility.* Totowa, N.J.: Rowman and Littlefield, 1983.

Salas, Carlos. "The Impact of NAFTA on Wages and Incomes in Mexico." Economic Policy Institute *Briefing Paper* (Washington, D.C., 2001).

Santibanez, Enrique. *Ensayo Acerca de la Immigracion Mexicana en los Estados Unidos.* San Antonio, Texas: Clegg Co., 1930.

Smith, James P. "Assimilation Across the Latino Generations." *American Economic Review,* vol. 93, no. 2 (May 2003).

Smith, Robert Freeman. *The U.S. and Revolutionary Nationalism in Mexico, 1916–1932.* Chicago: University of Chicago Press, 1972.

State of California, Department of Employment. "Mexican Nationals in California Agriculture." Sacramento: California Department of Employment (November 2, 1959).

Stillwell, Hart. "The Wetback Tide." *Common Ground*, vol. 9, no. 4 (Summer 1949).

Spradlin, T. Richard. "Legislation Notes: The Mexican Farm Labor Importation Program—Review and Reform" (Part II, VI. Congressional Action), *The George Washington Law Review*, vol. 30 (December 1961).

Taylor, J. Edward, and Philip Martin. "Central Valley Evolving into Patchwork of Poverty and Prosperity." *California Agriculture*, vol. 54, no. 1 (January–February 2000).

Thompson, J. Eric S., ed. *Thomas Gage's Travels in the New World*. Norman: University of Oklahoma, 1958.

Thompson, Wallace. *Trading with Mexico*. New York: Dodd, Mead and Company, 1921.

Tinker, Hugh. *A New System of Slavery: The Export of Indian Labor Overseas, 1830–1920*. London: Oxford University Press, 1974.

Topete, Jesus. *Aventuras de un Bracero*. Mexico City: Editora Grafica Moderna, 1948.

"Unfair Advantage: Workers' Freedom of Association in the United States Under International Human Rights Standards." Human Rights Watch (August 2000). Available online at http://www.hrw.org/reports/2000/uslabor.

University of California, Division of Agricultural Sciences. "Seasonal Labor in California Agriculture." Berkeley: University of California Division of Agricultural Sciences (1963).

"University President Discusses Work of College of Agriculture and Its Value to the Farmers." *California Agriculture*, vol. 1, no. 1 (December, 1946).

U.S. Census Bureau, *The Hispanic Population. Census 2000 Brief*. U.S. Department of Commerce, Economics and Statistics Administration, U.S. Census Bureau (May 2001).

U.S. Department of Labor. James P. Mitchell, Secretary. *Farm Labor Fact Book*. Washington, D.C.: U.S. Government Printing Office, 1959.

Wolf, Eric. *Peasant Wars of the Twentieth Century*. New York: Harper and Row, 1969.

Interviews by the Author (with Assistance from Ms. Alicia Anaya)

Anderson, Henry. August 17, 2003, Berkeley, California.

Camacho Robledo, Erasmo. September 7, 2004, Stockton, California.

Cardenas, Conrado. September 4, 2004, Stockton, California.

Carrillo, Hilario. September 4, 2004, Stockton, California.

Cervantes, Sotero O. August 3, 2004, Stockton, California.
Diaz Lopez, Jesus. September 6, 2004, Stockton, California.
Espinosa Cortez, Luis. September 6, 2004, Stockton, California.
Espinosa, Heldefonso. September 8, 2004, Stockton, California.
Linares Ramirez, Bernabe. September 13, 2004, Stockton, California.
Luna Anaya, Rafael. September 5, 2004, Stockton, California.
Gonzalez, Jose Maria. September 4, 2004, French Camp, California.
Gutierrez, Sandoval. September 8, 2004, Jesus, Stockton, California.
Hernandez Diaz, Jose. September 4, 2004, Stockton, California.
Magaña Diaz, Luciano. September 13, 2004, Stockton, California.
Magaña Acevedo, Luis. September 15, 2004, Stockton, California.
Moreno Garcia, Arcangel. September 6, 2004, Stockton, California.
Naranjo Espinosa, Santiago. September 6, 2004, Stockton, California.
Perez Anaya, Rosendo. September 6, 2004, Stockton, California.
Perez Perez, Celedonio. September 7, 2004, French Camp, California.
Perez Serrato, Martin. August 5, 2004, Stockton, California.
Sanchez Martinez, Refugio. September 6, 2004, Stockton, California.
Solis Romero, Fidel. September 6, 2004, Stockton, California.

Interviews by Others

Garcia Perez, Rigoberto. April 6, 2002, interviewed by David Bacon.

Index

About the Author

Gilbert G. Gonzalez received his Ph.D. in history at the University of California at Los Angeles in 1974. His research on Chicano history has led to works on segregation and education, citrus workers and community, the entanglements of the Mexican government in Chicano political history, U.S. economic domination and Mexican labor migration, and writings by Americans on Mexico and its relation to Mexican immigrants. His work places U.S. imperialism at the center of Chicano history; or, put another way, imperialism matters.